IN THE CIRCUMSTANCES

In the Circumstances
About Poems and Poets

PETER ROBINSON

CLARENDON PRESS · OXFORD
1992

Oxford University Press, Walton Street, Oxford OX2 6DP

Oxford New York Toronto
Delhi Bombay Calcutta Madras Karachi
Petaling Jaya Singapore Hong Kong Tokyo
Nairobi Dar es Salaam Cape Town
Melbourne Auckland
and associated companies in
Berlin Ibadan

Oxford is a trade mark of Oxford University Press

Published in the United States
by Oxford University Press, New York

British Library Cataloguing in Publication Data
Data available

Library of Congress Cataloging in Publication Data
Robinson, Peter, 1953–
In the circumstances : about poems and poets / Peter Robinson.
Includes bibliographical references and index.
1. Poetry—History and criticism. 2. Authors and readers.
3. Reader-response criticism.   I. Title.
PN1042.R55 1992
809.1—dc20   91-24246
ISBN 0–19–811248–3

Typeset by Cambridge Composing (UK) Ltd
Printed and bound in
Great Britain by Bookcraft Ltd
Midsomer Norton, Bath

For Rosemary Laxton

Preface

The nine chapters which make up this book began as separate pieces of work. They nevertheless share concerns, and a purpose in writing them was to discover how these were connected. Each is differently engaged by the idea of other lives in poems, and poetry as a response to other lives and the otherness of those lives. Thus each considers the bearing in upon poems' textual context of contextual circumstance, of the world from which the poems arose and to which, in the first place, they returned. This world emerges in such things as allusions to political events of the day, the inclusion of proper names, and the individuation or absorption of others' words within the words of poems.

The term 'otherness' is often encountered in criticism and can be used to indicate ideas about the differentiation of perceiver and perceived, about the work of art as a free-standing object, and the incorporation into artworks of relations with a perceived world, with the opposite sex, and with foreign languages and cultures. The ideas of poems as 'other' and of various othernesses in poems are explored under the assumption that the differentiations involved—with their attendant, simultaneously aesthetic and moral values—are continuously at risk. The concept of reparation, explored in the first chapter and intermittently relevant throughout, is an impulse to achieve and restore otherness when, for whatever reason, damage has been inflicted upon the wholeness of other people so that their integrity and sincerity have been impaired. Many of the poems discussed constitute or are significantly shaped by acts of reparation, whether in the poet's own sphere or in the realm of public responsibilities.

In the course of life, and the life of writing, many occasions will arise in which the maintenance of a mutually supportive relation between integral figures proves impossible. Poems, like other works of art in different ways, may be situated within the fluctuating conditions of a benign respect for wholeness and a mutually hurtful interference. The attention given to processes of poetic revision and to translating from another language explores the behaviour of writers working within these fluctuating conditions.

The ordering of the chapters is not chronological. Nor is there a single thread of argument sustained throughout. The book attempts to understand better the creative activity of poets as it may be experienced in the behaviour of poems they have made. The first three chapters are each about the revision of a poem in the light of personal and public considerations. The fourth, fifth, and sixth examine poets' relations to regret and the attempt to make amends in art: with regard to a wife's death; in relation to decisions made in a writer's career and their consequences for his works and relations with other people; then in the contexts of religious, cultural, and political responsibilities. The final three chapters attempt to bring together othernesses by commenting on relations with a different culture. First, psychological and ethical impulses in translating are explored; then translation in the service of a theory of love and attempted political engagement; finally, a poet's treatment of love relations, his involvement in another country's political development, and his uses of documentary materials to present an imaginative evaluation of human relations in an earlier century and a foreign culture.

Though the chapters are not arranged chronologically, the discussion of poems includes some historical location, since the aim of the book is to understand more about how poets themselves worked in the circumstances. My hope is to provide pleasure and stimulus for those who, as readers and writers, are involved with poetry now.

P.R.

September 1990

Acknowledgements

Some of these chapters have been published in earlier versions. 'Lend-Lease and "The Dry Salvages"' was commissioned by BBC Radio 3 and first broadcast in 1982. 'In Another's Words: Hardy's Poetry' appeared in *English*, 31: 141 (Autumn, 1982). 'Geoffrey Hill's Position' is revised from a chapter in *Geoffrey Hill: Essays on his Work* (Open University Press, 1985). Some sentences have been added to it from 'Difficult Situations', a review of *The Lords of Limit*, in *English*, 33: 146 (Summer, 1984). 'Ezra Pound: Translation and Betrayal' adapts a few paragraphs from 'Ezra Pound and Italian Art', in Richard Humphries (ed.), *Pound's Artists* (Tate Gallery, 1985). It concludes with a section from 'Ezra Pound's Broad Analogies', which appeared in *PN Review* 46, 12 (1985).

This book has taken shape in my mind and on paper thanks to many people's promptings, example, help, criticism, and conversation. I want to acknowledge debts to John Alexander, Adam Clarke-Williams, Martin Dodsworth, Maura Dooley, Tim Dooley, Peter Edwards, Franco Fortini, Eric Griffiths, Judith Hawley, Philip Horne, Michael Hofmann, Kevin Jackson, Robert Jones, John Kerrigan, Warren Laxton, Tom Phillips, Ralph Pite, Adrian Poole, Jeremy Prynne, Alison Rimmer, David Roberts, Stephen Romer, Michael Schmidt, Vittorio Sereni, John Skelton, Tom Sutcliffe, Peter Swaab, Emmanuela Tandello, Ornella Trevisan, John Welch, and Clive Wilmer.

Time to complete the rewriting was given to me by the English Department in the College of Liberal Arts at Kyoto University, where I spent a year as a visiting lecturer in 1989–90, and also by the Japan Society for the Promotion of Science, which awarded me a research fellowship in 1990–1. I want to thank Shoichiro Sakurai for his help during these years.

Kim Scott Walwyn encouraged me in the work of writing and revision. I am grateful for the personal attention she was able to give to my book in its various stages.

I owe the rest to my family, to Marcus Perryman, and above all to Rosemary Laxton, my wife.

Contents

1 Reparation and 'The Sailor's Mother'   1

2 W. H. Auden Revises a Context   24

3 Lend-Lease and 'The Dry Salvages'   47

4 In Another's Words: Hardy's Poetry   58

5 Robert Lowell and 'Moral Luck'   83

6 Geoffrey Hill's Position   105

7 Envy, Gratitude, and Translation   142

8 Ezra Pound: Translation and Betrayal   173

9 Robert Browning's Grasp   198

Bibliography   241

Index   250

I

Reparation and 'The Sailor's Mother'

I

Bernard Williams, writing about regret and the desire to make amends, has observed that cases exist where

> there is no room for any appropriate action at all. Then only the desire to make reparation remains, with the painful consciousness that nothing can be done about it; some other action, perhaps less directed to the victims, may come to express this. What degree of such feeling is appropriate, and what attempts at reparative action or substitutes for it, are questions for particular cases, and that there is room in the area for irrational and self-punitive excess, no one is likely to deny.[1]

Poetry may arise from the many circumstances in which no appropriate action is possible, when the desire to make reparation which remains is expressed through the activity, less directed to the victims, of making poems. I think the 'other action' of writing a poem, since it is prompted by a sense of irreparability, of there being no 'appropriate action' of a direct kind, will have two interdependent aims: it will try to inhabit the circumstances of the irreparable, to describe its 'painful consciousness that nothing can be done'; and it will attempt, through the attributes of poems themselves, to perform a 'reparative action or substitute for it'. The precise interrelating of these two aims in particular poems will vary widely according to both the nature of the circumstances and the aesthetic dispositions of the poet. This chapter explores one such interrelation in a poem by William Wordsworth.

The *Oxford English Dictionary* gives meanings for 'reparation' under seven headings. Numbers 2 and 5 have particular bearing on this subject: '2. The action of restoring to a proper state; restoration or renewal (*of* a thing or part); upholding, maintenance.' The examples given include material and spiritual cases. Thus, in 1731

---

[1] Bernard Williams, *Moral Luck: Philosophical Papers 1973–1980* (Cambridge University Press, Cambridge, 1981), 29.

Arbuthnot wrote 'The fluids and solids of an Animal Body demand a constant Reparation.' In 1633, T. Adams had stated that 'The communication of the Divine nature to us, is by reparation of the Divine image in us.' Applications of the word to material objects and to states of mind, spirit, or value are central to a belief that the writing and revisions of a poem can stand as an emblem for acts of reparation to persons in their physical and spiritual lives.

Meaning 5 focuses on the word as used by Bernard Williams: '5. The action of making amends for a wrong done; amends; compensation.' Among many citations exemplifying the meaning is this from Farquhar's *Beaux' Strategem* (1706–7): 'You were very naughty last Night, and must make your Wife Reparation.' The word took on a new force in the aftermath of the First World War, and the *Supplement* gives further examples of meaning 5: '1919 *Treaty of Peace* VIII. Art. 234 The Reparations Commission shall after May 1, 1921, from time to time, consider the resources and capacity of Germany.' Contemporary difficulties in making reparations are illustrated too. The *Glasgow Herald* on 28 October 1921 noted: 'The mere purchase of foreign securities to meet reparations . . . simply means the transference of worthless papers from one body of financiers to another' while the *Times Literary Supplement* on 24 September 1931 noted the 'impossibility of real Reparation payments'. The word 'reparation' had gained by this date and was subsequently to develop meanings in the literature of psychoanalysis.[2]

The moral sentiment which prompts the desire to make reparation has had attributed to it a psychological hinterland which complicates the impulse and gives content to Williams's sense of 'irrational and self-punitive excess'. Richard Wollheim has written that 'There are, indeed, certain psychic forces, such as the reparative drive or the desire to establish whole objects, without which the general forms that art takes, as well as its value, would be barely comprehensible.'[3] These forces, 'the reparative drive' and 'the desire to establish whole objects', are adopted from the writings of Melanie Klein. They depend upon each other. Reparation in art strengthens by re-enactment processes through which a

---

[2] *OED*, 2nd edn., does not cite any examples of this usage.

[3] Richard Wollheim, 'Art as a Form of Life', T. Honderich and M. Burnyeat (eds.), *Philosophy As It Is* (Harmondsworth, 1979), 137, and see sections 46–9 of Wollheim, *Art and its Objects*, 2nd edn. (Cambridge, 1980), citing here p. 107.

feeling for the wholeness and integrity—physical, psychological, and moral—of other things and beings may come into existence.

Freud's view of artistic production may be summarized as a 'way back to reality'.[4] His interpretation of Jensen's *Gradiva* is the uncovering of a process by which a young man, Norbert Hanold, is won back from obsessional delusion to the love of his childhood sweetheart, Zoe Bertgang. The reparative process in Kleinian ideas of aesthetic work is, broadly, a development of this principle. For Freud, 'The artist, like the neurotic, has withdrawn from an unsatisfying reality into this world of imagination; but, unlike the neurotic, he knew how to find a way back from it and once more to get a firm foothold on reality.' Freud implies three processes for the return to reality through making art, and all three are beset with difficulties: 'The writer softens the character of his egoistic day-dreams by altering and disguising it, and he bribes us by the purely formal—that is, aesthetic,—yield of pleasure which he offers us in the presentation of his phantasies.' Thus the artist accommodates the images produced by phantasy to those accepted as representations of reality. Secondly, this accommodation involves coming into relation with other people, whom the artist bribes with pleasure. Furthermore, to achieve these returns, Freud notes thirdly that the artist 'possesses the mysterious power of shaping some particular material until it has become a faithful image of his phantasy'. The artist mediates what may be a flight from the communal back to social experience through a specialist concern for the reality of the creative medium. For the writer, where the medium is a communal property, attention to the particular material can itself be a return to social experience.

There are difficulties with Freud's ideas; these help to bring out the significance of a reparative urge in making art. First, the 'withdrawal from an unsatisfying reality' is too narrowly symptomatic an account of the pre-creative condition of the artist, which is likely to take more account of, if not to begin in actuality. Secondly, the bribery of 'purely formal—that is, aesthetic' pleasure does not account for the suitability of particular forms to specific works, either for a form-content amalgam, or for the contentual

[4] Five references to Sigmund Freud, *The Standard Edition of the Complete Psychological Works*, 24 vols., trans. and ed. J. Strachey (1953–66), xii. 224; xx. 64; ix. 153; xvi. 376; xiii. 188.

contributions to the artwork of forms as such. Thirdly, and crucially since this is the artist's sole means, the medium of art, the poet's language here, cannot 'become a faithful image of his phantasy', because the medium has a character of its own, to which the artist's 'phantasy' must submit, to which the artist must be responsible. If this were not so, it would not provide a way back to reality, but be a further instance of the withdrawal.

Freud, however, writes that 'art constitutes a region half-way between a reality which frustrates wishes and the wish-fulfilling world of the imagination—a region in which, as it were, primitive man's strivings for omnipotence are still in full force,' My argument is that 'strivings for omnipotence' are not 'still in full force', because the work of the artist is an overcoming of omnipotent fantasy through a developed moral concern for the reality of the world outside, of other people in it, and, as a means to these, of the artistic medium itself. Louis MacNeice observed that 'All poetry probably contains an element of wish-fulfilment and a certain recognition of hard facts, but they are obviously found in poets mixed in very different proportions.'[5] An attraction of reparation as a way, among others, of looking at the processes of making art is its capacity to sharpen MacNeice's terms 'wish-fulfilment' and 'hard facts'. It also combines legal, moral, psychological, and aesthetically technical concerns. Moreover, the processes of reparation are fluid enough to account for elements 'mixed in very different proportions'—for a human variety in artistic activity which none the less shares comparable qualities linking the intimate impulses of the self with larger cultural, political, religious, and social considerations.

Melanie Klein's 1929 paper 'Infantile Anxiety-Situations Reflected in a Work of Art and in the Creative Impulse' discusses the psychoanalytical content in Colette's libretto for Ravel's opera 'The Magic Word', and in the sudden emergence of Ruth Kjär's urge to paint. The former concerns the consequences of a child's aggressive feelings against its mother, and anxiety at the possibility of reprisal. In the latter, a sense of emptiness in Kjär's life, which Klein interprets as a loss of the mother destroyed in phantasy, is relieved by painting pictures:

[5] Louis MacNeice, *Modern Poetry: A Personal Essay* (Oxford, 1938), 7.

the desire to make reparation, to make good the injury psychologically done to the mother and also to restore herself was at the bottom of the compelling urge to paint these portraits of her relatives. That of the old woman, on the threshold of death, seems to be the expression of the primary, sadistic desire to destroy. The daughter's wish to destroy her mother, to see her old, worn out, marred, is the cause of the need to represent her in full possession of her strength and beauty. By so doing the daughter can allay her own anxiety and can endeavour to restore her mother and make her new through the portrait.[6]

Here the two aims of an art which embodies the irreparable and attempts to make reparative acts can be seen in the 'desire to destroy' and 'the endeavour to restore her mother'. In both cases the actions of destroying and restoring are projections of feelings, not literal acts of violence or appeasement. In the cases that Bernard Williams has in mind where something has happened in actuality, the possibilities of 'irrational and self-punitive excess' may derive from the congruence of events which occur in personal or public history with the early inner events of psychological growth that concerned Melanie Klein.

In a chapter from *The Thread of Life* on the growth of the moral sense, Wollheim, deploying Klein's ideas, makes a distinction involving a consciousness of the irreparable and the need to do something about it:

if we are to understand what reparative action is, we must borrow from the moral psychology of value. The psychology of obligation unaided will not help us. And that is because when, under the influence of depressive anxiety, the child, the person, is motivated to repair the damage that he has done, the operative desire is not, or is not generally, the desire literally to restore the world to the state it was in before the damage was done. The desire is rather to bring about a state of affairs that corresponds to, or matches, the undoing of what was done: reparative action is emblematic of repair.[7]

In cases where no appropriate reparative action in life is available, cases where a lateral shift into the emblematic activity of making art appears both natural and inevitable, a desire to 'restore the world to the state it was in before the damage was done' is categorically excluded, because the recognition that no appropriate

[6] Melanie Klein, *Love, Guilt and Reparation* (1975), 218.
[7] Richard Wollheim, *The Thread of Life* (Cambridge, 1984), 217.

means of reparation in life obtain depends upon a consciousness of irremediable wrong. A context for this lateral move into art would be one where a person felt that the formal social processes of reparation could not serve. Thus, bringing someone to trial, or exacting reparations from aggressors as in 1919, or paying insurance compensations can produce moral and emotional dissatisfaction. Wollheim nevertheless observes that the morality of reparation is best understood as intimate with social customs:

it has always seemed appropriate to the better class of moral philosophers to connect morality, at least initially, with the practices and beliefs of particular communities. For what the community does is fix, or pin down, the otherwise unregulated discernment of match or correspondence. The metaphors of reparation, which is what reparative action sets itself to satisfy, come to the moral agent, even before that is what he is, encoded in *sittlichkeit* or custom. Even if the agent remakes the correspondences, reinvents them, which is what he will want to do if he is in any way a critic of society and its ways, they provide him with the initial exemplars of match.[8]

The shape of Wordsworth's 'The Sailor's Mother' is one in which 'initial exemplars of match' are critically remade. The writing of this poem is one case where 'the agent remakes these correspondences, reinvents them', for the fact that art has needed to be made is itself a criticism of 'society and its ways', and there is the implication that nothing else could be done. This does not imply that Wordsworth is politically or socially aloof, quite the contrary. The work itself stands as an emblem of society's or humanity's failure. The feeling that no appropriate action of a direct kind is possible can stem from social conditions, from political, moral, or cultural stagnation, or because a limit in human possibility has been reached.

The reparative impulse in making art is driven by a correspondence between events in personal or public life, real occasions of damage done, and the growth of the moral sense through the damages and reparations in phantasy which contribute to psychological development. This helps explain why it is possible to feel a form of regret for the actions of one's own country when, strictly speaking, one was not personally responsible for those actions, nor

---

[8] Ibid.

in a position to prevent them. Thomas Nagel, in his essay 'Moral Luck', notes that

> it is nearly impossible to view the crimes of one's own country in the same way that one views the crimes of another country, no matter how equal one's lack of power to stop them in the two cases. One *is* a citizen of one of them, and has a connexion with its actions . . . This makes it possible to be ashamed of one's country, and to feel a victim of moral bad luck that one was an American in the 1960s.[9]

Nagel's logic makes historical guilt and patriotic shame structurally possible. The moral psychology of shame here requires that damage done by the state feels as if done by the individual. With its picture of destructive infantile phantasy, its description of a developing concomitant depression, and the additional feeling, in many cases, that reparative action directed towards the victims of the crimes is not available, Klein's theory helps account for Nagel's broadening of responsibilities. Furthermore, it is likely that reparative action simultaneously directed towards oneself as the victim of moral bad luck is not available either.

Donald Meltzer, discussing painting and psychology with Adrian Stokes, considers the impulse that gives rise to the lateral move into art, when conditions such as those suggested by Nagel occur. There is reparative work to be done, but no practical or direct means in everyday life by which to effect it. This presents the problem to psychoanalysts, that, however extreme the states of phantasy in infancy, they can be matched and outdone by the agencies of the external, adult world: 'as processes of reparation are more firmly established in psychical reality . . . its corresponding process in the external world is very partial, limited by the frailty of the human body'.[10] Nor is this the only limit to appropriate reparative action in the external world. As Meltzer notes: 'the laws of psychical reality differ considerably from the laws of external reality when non-human agencies, structuralized as "fate", play with human affairs'. This is to say that psychological health may make the anxieties of one's inner life and those of a life lived in the larger world easier to manage, but it does not in itself serve to criticize, work upon, or attempt to come into reparative relation with that outer world.

[9] Thomas Nagel, *Mortal Questions* (Cambridge, 1979), 34.
[10] Adrian Stokes, *The Critical Writings*, 3 vols., ed. L. Gowing (1978), iii. 213.

Meltzer affirms that 'this is the task from which the mature, exhibiting artist does not flee, but, to borrow Hanna Segal's words, with his "cautionary tales", he sets about "repairing the whole world".'[11] The breadth of Wordsworth's concerns, and the range of related issues drawn into the circumstances of his poem, depend upon a turning of attention out from the vicissitudes of the poet's inner life, to the complexity of life in nature, in a society, and in history:

the formal and emotive configuration of his works must be derived not only from the influence exerted upon him by his culture and fellow artists, but also by the force of his *concern* with the present and future of the whole world. In order to grasp the courage that this requires of such an artist, it is necessary to realize that every act of violence which he sees go unpunished and, above all, smugly unrepented, every cruel stroke of fate in the external world, threatens his internal harmony because of the pain and rage stirred.[12]

The pain and rage is nevertheless stirred because the artist, and in this he or she is not necessarily unlike other citizens except in having a particular means of emblematic reparation, feels responsibility for what has happened, as if he or she had performed the bad actions or contributed to the cruel stroke of fate, the moral bad luck.

An objection to Hanna Segal's picture of the artist setting about 'repairing the whole world' is that it has a component of omnipotent fantasy in it, and could be construed as megalomania at one remove:

> Pity the planet, all joy gone
> from this sweet volcanic cone;
> peace to our children when they fall
> in small war on the heels of small
> war—until the end of time
> to police the earth, a ghost
> orbiting forever lost
> in our monotonous sublime.[13]

---

[11] Ibid. 231–2.   [12] Ibid. 232.

[13] Robert Lowell, *Selected Poems*, rev. edn. (Farrar, Straus & Giroux, Inc., New York, 1977 and Faber & Faber Ltd.), 144; see, for Lowell's letters to Presidents Roosevelt and Johnson, *Collected Prose*, ed. R. Giroux (1987), 367–71; Christopher Ricks's essay 'Robert Lowell: "The War of Words"', *The Force of Poetry* (Oxford, 1984), 256–73, is illuminating on a doubleness in Lowell's relations with state

When Robert Lowell writes 'Pity the planet, all joy gone' in 'Waking Early Sunday', is his concern for America and its world in the 1960s the denunciatory and lamenting face of his own intermittent manic identifications with tyrants?[14] A crucial element in Wordsworth's poem is its chastening the poet figure's lofty thoughts. In art, to avoid wishful thinking it is necessary for the poet, in W. B. Yeats's phrase of 1907, to enter 'upon a submissive, sorrowful contemplation of the great irremediable things'.[15] The work of art has to contain and express a sense of the irreparable at one and the same time as seeking to repair 'the whole world'. The desire to repair the whole world, unless significantly qualified by recognitions of the nature of experience and its consequences, would be a fantasy in the everyday meaning of the word. It would not exemplify the responsibility of art towards the world, but be an evasion of the world's conditions through art.

II

'For Wordsworth, adult wisdom is a profound recognition of the existences of other beings. That is the power the mother's feelings impart to the infant, and the element upon which Wordsworth bases his recognition of the infant's human nature'. Alice Goodman, in her essay 'Wordsworth and the Sucking Babe', finds the poet's moral and imaginative sources in the earliest reciprocal experiences of feeding and being fed: 'When the poet's imagination moves from the child's mind to the mother's to the spectator's, it pays tribute to the knowledge first gained at the breast; the baby's

---

power and violence. See also Alan Williamson, 'The Reshaping of "Waking Early Sunday Morning"', *Agenda*, 18 (Autumn 1980), 47–62, where he notes 'The equation of Lowell's worst vision of himself with Johnson acts like a chemical catalyst . . . But the real marvel is that, within the space of one page, Lowell's identification with Johnson has deepened to include not only the deliquescent over-extension of themselves but also the most primordially human and valuable level of their explosive energies' (p. 55). The connection made appears accurate. I do not myself agree with the evaluation. Seamus Heaney seems, however, to have only praise for the stanza quoted here, in his lecture 'Lowell's Command', *The Government of the Tongue* (1988), 140.

[14] See e.g. Ian Hamilton, *Robert Lowell: A Biography* (1983), 209–12.
[15] W. B. Yeats, 'Poetry and Tradition', *Selected Criticism and Prose*, ed. N. Jeffares (1980), 163.

pleasure at the breast is correspondingly seen as the source of the poetic imagination.'[16] Decently concerned with the benign, Goodman did not have space to be troubled by the scope of the knowledge received, the imagination fed, its infliction with anxieties as well as its relief from them. The ideas of reparation and the irreparable sketched above may then variously contribute to understanding Wordsworth's poem of maternal loss and endurance.

A desire to make high claims for what a poem can do, however virtuous in intention, miscarries if art is freed from correlating its independent powers with the circumscribed conditions of experience. Poems will not be 'a profound recognition of the existences of other beings' if so freed. When Wallace Stevens narrates ideas of Leo Stein's in his essay 'The Relations between Poetry and Painting', the other term in the reciprocal relation is weakened:

Composition was his passion. He considered that a formally complete picture is one in which all the parts are so related to one another that they all imply each other. Finally he said, 'an excellent illustration is the line from Wordsworth's Michael . . . "And never lifted up a single stone."' One might say of a lazy workman, 'He's been out there, just loafing, for an hour and never lifted up a single stone,' and no one would think this great poetry. . . . These lines would have no existential value; they would simply call attention to the lazy workman. But the compositional use by Wordsworth of his line makes it something entirely different. These simple words become weighted with the tragedy of the old shepherd, and are saturated with poetry. Their referential importance is slight, for the importance of the action to which they refer is not in the action itself, but in the meaning; and that meaning is borne by the words. Therefore this is a line of great poetry.[17]

Wordsworth's art does not consist of works where 'all the parts are so related to one another that they all imply each other', or if they do, it is only within sharp discontinuities. Of 'The Sailor's Mother', Coleridge wrote: 'I would ask the poet whether he would not have felt an abrupt down-fall in these verses from the preceding stanza?'[18] There is a down-fall, and the brokenness of the poem, at that point and elsewhere, is part of its remaking what Wollheim

---

[16] Alice Goodman, 'Wordsworth and the Sucking Babe', *Essays in Criticism*, 33 (April 1983), 122.
[17] Wallace Stevens, *The Necessary Angel* (1960), 162–3.
[18] S. T. Coleridge, *Biographia Literaria*, ed. J. Engell and W. Jackson Bate (Princeton, NJ, 1983), 71.

called the 'initial exemplars of match'. Nor, when Wordsworth composes, does his literary power make the words 'something entirely different' from their uses in life. Nor, similarly, can it be said that 'Their referential importance is slight, for the importance of the action to which they refer is not in the action itself, but in the meaning', because the meaning would not be intelligible without its simultaneous connection with and separation from the action. Just as the words must refer so as to be understood in and as poetry, so too for those acts of reparation which occur in and through poetry when no appropriate action is available: the metaphor, the emblem of reparation, complexly depends, for the recognition of 'match', on its correlation with the irreparable in life.

Wordsworth revised 'The Sailor's Mother' on numerous occasions between its first drafting on 11 and 12 March 1802 and 1850, the year of his death. He did so most considerably between 3 and 12 November 1806, when it was first prepared for the press, and then in small but significant details for texts of 1815, 1820, 1827, 1832, 1836, 1840, and then minimally in 1845, 1847, 1849, and 1850. Two initial observations about the revisions[19] can be made: no one version is in all parts better than another; and Wordsworth's work on this poem is barely intelligible if action and meaning are held to be entirely distinct, for 'The Sailor's Mother' was altered to adjust the relationship between the poem understood as a report on an event (an encounter between two real people in the North of England) and the poem understood as an independent literary artefact acting metaphorically upon that event.

When Wordsworth dictated a note to Isabella Fenwick about the poem in 1843, he said:

Town-End, 1800. I met this woman near the Wishing-Gate, on the high-road that then led from Grasmere to Ambleside. Her appearance was exactly as here described, and such was her account, nearly to the letter.[20]

Wordsworth simplifies the poem, and is misleading about the nature of the encounter as it is rendered: 'exactly as here described' doesn't take account of the poet's own perplexities about the

---

[19] My citations of Wordsworth's 'The Sailor's Mother' in its various versions are all from *Poems, in Two Volumes*, and Other Poems, 1800–1807, ed. J. Curtis (Ithaca, NY, 1983), 77–9.

[20] Ibid. 404.

woman's appearance in the poem; 'nearly to the letter' equivocates about whether they are her words or not. He is right to equivocate for his 'nearly' is the space in which the relations and separations between the world of irreparable circumstances and acts of reparation in art can move. In defence of his theory of diction, Wordsworth is being ingenuous, for he had altered the woman's words variously on various occasions.

Here is what she said when Wordsworth wrote 'The Singing Bird' on two successive days in March 1802:

> She answer'd soon as she the question heard,
> "A simple Burthen, Sir, a little singing Bird!"
>
> "My eldest Son, a Sailor, sail'd
> "With God's good blessing many a day,
> "But at the last, his fortune fail'd—
> "—In Denmark he was cast away:
> "At Hull he liv'd where I have been to see
> "What Clothes he might have left, or other property.
>
> "The room in which he lodg'd was small;
> "And few effects were in it, when
> "I reach'd the place; I sold them all,
> "And now am travelling home again.
> "I live at Mary-port, a weary way!
> "And scarcely what I have will for my journey pay.
>
> "The Bird and Cage they both were his,
> "'Twas my Son's Bird;—and neat and trim
> "He kept it—many voyages
> "This singing-bird hath gone with him;
> "And I, God help me! for my little wit,
> "Trail't with me, Sir! he took so much delight in it!"

The main features of what she says remain. Wordsworth, however, alters most of her phrasing in 1806, then changes numerous details over the next thirty-odd years. To begin with a small example, 'Trail't', the first word of the poem's final line, is freed from some of its provincialism when it becomes 'I trail it' for the first published version of 1807. Twenty years later Wordsworth had further thought and made her utter a word he, as the poet in the poem, had introduced at line 16 in the 1806 revisions: 'What's that which on your arm you bear?' says Wordsworth, and, in 1827, she concludes: 'I bear it with me, Sir!' 'Trail't' sounds like what she might have said; 'I trail it' seems appropriate to her but increases a note of self-deprecation, because appearing chosen, not uttered as an unconsidered provincialism for 'carry'. 'I bear it' is much more 'saturated with poetry' for it puns resonantly on carrying a burden, giving birth to a child, and enduring a loss—meanings relevant to the woman's circumstances.

A second alteration between the draft and first published text involves the place names. In 1802 there were three: '—In Denmark he was cast away', 'At Hull he liv'd', and 'I live at Mary-port'; by 1850 only one remains. It is Denmark, and there is something to say about this survival. Mary-port is the first to go; in November 1806 the penultimate stanza was entirely reshaped by adopting the first four tetrameter lines of the 1802 final stanza and adding to it a new pentameter and alexandrine couplet:

> When last he sail'd he left the Bird behind;
> As it might be, perhaps, from bodings of his mind.

The reference to Hull alters for the first published text, becoming—

> And I have been as far as Hull, to see
> What clothes he might have left, or other property.

When Coleridge cited the stanza in the *Biographia Literaria* it had become 'And I have travelled far as Hull, to see' in 1815, but, five years later, and after Coleridge had doubted 'the appropriateness of the thoughts and expressions to which the metrical form is superadded', the line became 'And I have travelled many miles to see'. This is how it stayed for seven years, until one of the woman's words from 1802 returns: 'many miles' becomes 'weary miles'. Distinct differences of tone may be felt here. In 'I live at Mary-port, a weary way!' the word 'weary' is part of an exclamation about how far it is from Hull to Mary-port, across the Pennines, the breadth of England, in winter, and it is part of her explanation for why '—She begg'd an alms, like one of low estate'; she tells the poet: 'And scarcely what I have will for my journey pay.' When the line has finally become 'And I have travelled weary miles to see' the adjective has become a solicitation of general sympathy, for by now both Hull and Mary-port have gone, and there is no external context for the literal weariness of her journey.

Wordsworth, some forty years after the event, said to Isabella Fenwick that he had met the woman in 1800. By the time he wrote

'The Singing Bird' in March 1802, an event had occurred to which the poem makes a topical allusion, and of which the woman could not have spoken in 1800. The allusion is in the place-name 'Denmark':

This woman says that her son was 'cast away' 'in Denmark', a mysterious way of putting it, but no less weightily allusive than the 'sea-fight' in 'Old Man Travelling'. Denmark had on December 16 1800 joined in a league with Russia, Prussia and Sweden, backed by France, to resist Britain's claim to the right to search at sea. When Denmark refused to comply with an ultimatum demanding its withdrawal from this league, a British fleet was sent into the Baltic, and victoriously fought the Battle of Copenhagen on April 1–2 1801. The mention of Denmark prompts us to infer that this woman's son has died in similar circumstances.[21]

The idea that the sailor was in the Royal Navy is supported by the revised penultimate stanza of November 1806:

> many voyages
> This Singing-bird hath gone with him;
> When last he sail'd he left the Bird behind;
> As it might be, perhaps, from bodings of his mind.

The alexandrine here was altered in 1827 to 'From bodings as might be that hung upon his mind.' It is not inconceivable that a superstitious merchant seaman might take his pet on 'many voyages', but leave it behind, inexplicably, because of 'bodings'; however, it makes more sense of his mother's speculation if he is in the Royal Navy, for then different voyages in altering conditions of peace and war would understandably produce rational bodings.

The question is relevant to the poem as a whole because of issues raised by the first two stanzas. This is how they began in 1802:

> The day was cold and rain and wet;
> A foggy day in winter time,
> —A Woman in the road I met,
> Not old, though something past her prime;
> —Majestic seem'd she as a mountain storm;
> A Roman Matron's gait—like feature and like form.

---

[21] Peter Alexander Swaab, 'Wordsworth and Patriotism', Ph. D. thesis (Cambridge, 1989), 132. I am indebted to the author for numerous conversations about 'The Sailor's Mother' in which my sense of the poem and convictions about an allusion to the Battle of Copenhagen were formed.

The ancient Spirit is not dead;
Old times thought I, are breathing there;
Proud was I that my Country bred
Such strength, a dignity so fair.
—She begg'd an alms, like one of low estate;
I look'd at her again, nor did my pride abate.

Wordsworth made significant changes for the first published version. He adjusted the first line to 'One morning (raw it was and wet'; he recast the pentameter and alexandrine of the first stanza to read: 'Majestic in her person, tall and straight; | And like a Roman matron's was her mien and gait.' This is much more decisive, with the ballad-like tetrameters of the first four lines coinciding with the meteorological context of the meeting, then the vision of the woman swelling grandly with the increasingly heroic and epic character of the metre. The tread of her 'gait' fits the motion of the metrical feet. But why a Roman matron? And why is Wordsworth proud 'that my Country bred | Such strength, a dignity so fair'? The patriotic feeling implied here recalls the stoicism of Roman women facing domestic losses in the interests of the state. This coincides, as if unintentionally, with the woman's condition, later revealed, for she may be one who has lost her son on active service.

Peter Swaab sees the issues involved as part of Wordsworth's concern to curb an imaginative tendency to rash judgement, and observes:

When the narrator sees the woman, he swells into patriotic pride: 'Proud was I that my country bred | Such strength'. As I have suggested, the poem reveals this response to be partial and obtuse. Nonetheless, it is not entirely repudiated. For it belongs with the imaginative tendency to see in this figure an incarnation of the ancient republican virtues. She looks and moves 'like a Roman matron', and seems to show the survival of the 'ancient Spirit'. The plot of the poem acts as a complex caution against the imaginative exorbitance of these first assumptions.

I will return to the relation between the 'complex caution' and the 'narrator' with an eye on the theme of reparation. Meanwhile, Swaab makes a further point about the lines:

The early stanzas of the poem had offered two similes; the woman's bearing was 'like a Roman matron's' (line 6) and she begged an alms 'like one in poor estate' (line 11). Eventually these two ideas move into compatibility, and the second is confirmed as truth, not fancy (she *was* in poor estate). Conceiving a simile is shown to be a dangerous business . . .[22]

Wordsworth is sensitive to the simultaneous senses that the 'like' of a simile performs. The woman reminds him of a Roman matron, but is not one; she seems to be 'in poor estate' but may not be. My disagreement involves the meaning of 'in poor estate': does it imply that she is 'one of *the poor*', one about whom the analogy with a Roman matron seems suddenly inapt? Roman matrons aren't, after all, beggars. Or does it suggest that she seemed to be one of a class of mendicants at first, but, when she'd told her story, it became clear that she was temporarily short of money? She may be poor without being one of the poor. The poem doesn't clear this question up, and there is a good reason. Wordsworth's request for information which invites her tale needs to be motivated; he must be in a real confusion about her status and need to beg. Equally, even if she were one of the poor, undeserving from another point of view, would Wordsworth want to say that then it wouldn't be right to give alms? The poem raises the issue of means-testing, but it doesn't align itself with any operative distinction between deserving and undeserving poor.

In November 1806, Wordsworth altered 'like one of low estate' to 'like one in poor estate'. The 'like' in both cases allows him to imply that the woman may not be what she appears from the fact that she has 'begg'd an alms'. The alteration changes the social presumptions engaged. Is she 'low' or 'poor'? The second is far better because not merely a condition of external labelling. A context of social responsibility is introduced by 'poor'. Something can be done about it. This is hardly the case with 'low'. She may be poor, but she seems honest, for Wordsworth writes 'I look'd at her again, nor did my pride abate', a line which remains virtually unchanged throughout. It says that Wordsworth is not wrong to see her as a Roman matron, or, at least, as honest in appearance and, as he discovers, a woman of stoical temperament. His initial 'match', his tone of imaginative recognition, though, leaves something to be desired.

When Coleridge quotes the second stanza of 1815, it has gained exclamation marks at 'Old times, thought I, are breathing there!'

---

[22] Two citations from Swaab, ibid. 130–1, 132.

and 'Such strength, a dignity so fair!'[23] This increases the poet's
patriotic enthusiasm, and raises the pitch of the stanza's tone. It is
then in the transition from this to the third stanza that Coleridge
pointedly 'would ask the poet whether he would not have felt an
abrupt down-fall in these verses from the preceding stanza?' Here
is the 1802 version:

> When from my lofty thoughts I woke,
> With the first word I had to spare
> I said to her, "Beneath your Cloak
> What is it you are carrying there?"
> She answer'd soon as she the question heard,
> "A simple Burthen, Sir, a little singing Bird!"

The first four lines of this stanza went through many vicissitudes,
suggesting that Wordsworth also reported his own words 'nearly
to the letter'. For the 1807 printed text, the poet simply altered 'are
carrying there' to 'on your arm you bear'; but in 1820, again after
Coleridge's comments, a radical recasting produced:

> When from these lofty thoughts I woke,
> "What treasure," said I, "do you bear,
> Beneath the covert of your Cloak
> Protected from the cold damp air?"

Wordsworth was unsure about 'treasure'; it disappeared in 1827
with the new line: ' "What is it," said I, "that you bear,["]' but
returned for the 1840 text only with 'What treasure is it that you
bear'. Throughout, it should be noted, Wordsworth retains his
'lofty thoughts' from which he wakes to ask the woman a question
which sounds as though it is indirectly designed to relieve the poet
of his confusions about what kind of person has accosted him for
alms. The 'abrupt down-fall' that Coleridge notes is part of the
poem's original shape, a fault in the structure which is at the heart
of Wordsworth's feelings about the occasion.

The qualm about 'treasure' lies in a question of tact with regard
to the woman and the reader: how overtly should Wordsworth
insist on his means-testing question? Is he implying deviousness in
the woman's begging by adopting the word 'covert'? The word
'lofty' is part of his self-criticism in the poem, for his own patriotic
pride is just such an association of an individual's moral and

---

[23] Coleridge, *Biographia*, 71; and see Curtis, *Poems*, 77–9.

emotional life with the conduct of the state that Nagel identifies when he says, 'it is nearly impossible to view the crimes of one's own country in the same way that one views the crimes of another'. This means that the exorbitant imaginative appropriation of the woman to Roman matron status in the first stanza is implicated with the behaviour of the country. Swaab has pointed out the continuity of this aspect of the poem with similar work of the same time:

His sonnets of 1802, for instance, are patriotic chiefly in their excoriation of his country rather than pride in its virtue. Moreover, it would be possible, certainly, to detect political intention in Wordsworth's dramatis- ation of the bereavement of these needy and unsupported parental figures—an implicit condemnation of an ungrateful economic system. His letter to Sara Hutchinson about 'The Leech-Gatherer' cites 'the necessities which an unjust state of society has entailed upon him'.[24]

Yet Wordsworth's imaginative action is itself implicated in the 'implicit condemnation' of the conditions in which the sailor and his mother lived, made more pungent by the bad luck that 'his fortune fail'd', that he may have died in the service of his country. In the 1802 version the woman tells the poet,

> "The room in which he lodg'd was small;
> "And few effects were in it, when
> "I reach'd the place; I sold them all . . ."

Selling the things might seem callous, but it increases the implied value to her of the bird, and she doesn't make a great profit on her son's possessions: 'And scarcely what I have will for my journey pay.'

Wordsworth[25] in the poem, and as a representative figure for

---

[24] Swaab, 'Wordsworth and Patriotism', 131, and for Wordsworth's letter, see *The Letters of William and Dorothy Wordsworth, The Early Years 1787–1805*, ed. E. de Selincourt, 2nd edn., rev. C. L. Shaver (Oxford, 1967), 366–7.

[25] A further hinterland to the irreparability of personal and political contexts in 'The Sailor's Mother' is suggested by the fact noted in Dorothy Wordsworth's diary that, between 21 December 1801 and 24 March 1802, with the easing of relations between France and England leading up to the Peace of Amiens, a continuous correspondence between Annette Vallon and Wordsworth was reassumed. See Émile Legouis, *William Wordsworth and Annette Vallon* (London and Toronto, 1922), 46, and Dorothy Wordsworth, *Journals of Dorothy Wordsworth*, 2 vols., ed. E. de Selincourt (1941), i. 127–8, where, 10 days after Wordsworth finished 'The Singing Bird', Dorothy writes, 'Mr Luff came after dinner and brought us 2 letters from Sara H. and one from poor Annette. I read Sara's letters while he was

our cautionary instruction, is doubly at fault: he begins by abstract-
ing the 'Spirit' of patriotic stoicism from its real circumstances, and
he imputes dubious motives to the woman, suspecting her of
deceiving him about her financial state so as to extract money. One
of these moral failures in the poet is a fault of loftiness, the other
of lowness. This is the ethical trajectory of Coleridge's 'abrupt
down-fall', and it is cast into the shade by the woman's narrative
which silences the poet. The different versions of what Wordsworth
asks the woman, with their varyingly overt degrees of self-inculpation, are all responded to by the woman in substantially the same
way:

> She answer'd soon as she the question heard,
> "A simple Burthen, Sir, a little singing Bird!"

The woman's reply is entirely disarming as it cuts through the
poet's divided perplexity. That phrase 'soon as she the question
heard' means that she has nothing to hide, and that she understands
his implied request to be told about her financial means. That
Wordsworth was uncannily right to sense a patriotic stoicism in
her way of bearing her loss does not remove the damaging
abstraction in his manner of formulating this intuition to himself:
the congruence of his 'lofty thoughts' with the prompting of his
heroic metres: the pentameter and alexandrine which elevate the
diction and tone of the tetrameters in the opening stanza. Wordsworth too readily fits an abstract version of her qualities into his
poetic form. Thus, a third fault may be imputed: there is at the
beginning of the poem an over-readiness to latch on to others'
lives, to find a 'match', one conveniently emptied of contingent
individuality, for the consolatory contemplations of the poet's art.

The reparation for these three faults, and for the irreparable loss
of her son in war, is performed in the act of rendering a form of
her words into the stanza that he had created for *his* thoughts. This
emblem of reparation involves the misfitting of diction and metre
about which Coleridge, sensing it fully, complained:

Metre in itself is simply a stimulant of the attention, and therefore excites
the question: Why is the attention to be thus stimulated? Now the question

---

here, I finished my letters to M. and S. and wrote to my brother Richard. We talked
a good deal about C. and other interesting things. We resolved to see Annette, and
that Wm. should go to Mary.'

cannot be answered by the pleasure of the metre itself: for this we have shown to be *conditional,* and dependent on the appropriateness of the thoughts and expressions, to which the metrical form is superadded.[26]

Coleridge feels the 'down-fall' because his expectations and tastes tell him that there should be an elevated and elevating consistency of diction and metre. Yet the human, political, and aesthetic complexity of Wordsworth's poem lies in the range and density of feelings that can be started by the discrepancies between these features of the poem. Wordsworth suggests as much in a passage on metre in his Preface; Coleridge is alluding to Wordsworth's ideas with the word 'superadded'.[27] Wordsworth thought that

from the tendency of meter to divest language, in a certain degree, of its reality, and thus to throw a sort of half-consciousness of unsubstantial existence over the whole composition, there can be little doubt but that more pathetic situations and sentiments, that is, those which have a greater proportion of pain connected with them, may be endured in metrical composition, especially in rhyme, than in prose.[28]

The interrelated issues of reparation and the irreparable are informing Wordsworth's observation. The irreparable lies in those 'more pathetic situations and sentiments' which have 'a greater proportion of pain connected with them'. They have to be 'endured' because they cannot be undone; metre may, however, 'throw a sort of half-consciousness of unsubstantial existence over the whole composition'. It is analogous to the sailor's mother being abstracted into the unsubstantial Roman matron and her alexandrine's 'gait'. Yet it is only a 'half-consciousness', and here Wordsworth's equivocation, as in 'nearly to the letter', speaks volumes: the other half-consciousness remains firmly in the circumstances, the 'situations' with their 'greater proportion of pain'.

The double consciousness implied by a discrepancy between metre and diction shows in the alexandrines that the sailor's mother speaks. None of them have the smooth confidence of 'And like a Roman matron's was her mien and gait.' Two are extended to

---

[26] Coleridge, *Biographia,* 69.

[27] See Wordsworth, 'Preface to *Lyrical Ballads*', *The Poems,* 2 vols., ed. J. O. Hayden (Harmondsworth, 1977), i. 876.

[28] Ibid. i. 885. There is an illuminating passage on Wordsworth's poem and metre which relates to these concerns in Eric Griffiths, *The Printed Voice of Victorian Poetry* (Oxford, 1989), 71–7.

alexandrine length only by the insertion of a 'Sir!' at the caesura: ' "A simple Burthen, Sir, a little singing Bird!" ' and ' "Trail't with me, Sir! he took so much delight in it!" ' Wordsworth's revision of the final line for the 1807 text lengthens the metre further, so that a fourteener is detectable: 'I trail it with me, Sir! he took so much delight in it.' The 'Sir!' in each case indicates a social barrier between speaker and poet. The woman finds herself almost apologizing to the stranger for not having also sold the bird and cage: 'God help me! for my little wit'. Yet she also speaks with dignity, forthrightly across the divide between them. She lives up to the alexandrine but its music is not hers. The music is that of Wollheim's initial match, a series of lengthening metrical forms adopted from the customs of poetry to confer dignity, which also frames her economic necessity, giving it voice and distorting it. The world of custom and poetry is calling the tune, expecting her to face its music. She maintains her stature by recognizing that expectation, exacting the word 'Sir!' from her, and still pressing candidly her case. Even if near the breadline, the sailor's mother too maintains her resolution and independence.

Here is the reparative emblem of Wordsworth's poem, the necessary powerlessness of art, to which is complexly superadded its power, a reparative act which does not so much make the event more endurable, as render the sailor's mother her due, shape her endurance of loss into an example of value. T. S. Eliot quotes a sentence of a letter from Wordsworth to Charles James Fox in 1801:

But recently by the spreading of manufactures through every part of the country, by the heavy taxes upon postage, by workhouses, Houses of Industry, and the invention of Soup shops, &c. &c. superadded to the encreasing disproportion between the price of labour and that of the necessaries of life, the bonds of domestic feeling among the poor, as far as the influence of these things has extended, have been weakened, and in innumerable instances entirely destroyed.[29]

The words 'superadded' and 'disproportion' here indicate a secondary association of the metre of a poem. Not only may it serve like an incantation to bring ease for suffering, and like a drug to bring 'unsubstantial existence' to pains hard to bear, but it may serve as an analogy for the restrictions and conditions within which people

---

[29] Wordsworth, *The Letters of William and Dorothy Wordsworth*, 313–14.

must continue to endure. It can be a sign of the tune that the country is singing. Wordsworth's composition of the woman's words into his metres seeks to change that tune. T. S. Eliot goes on to note: 'Wordsworth was not merely taking advantage of an opportunity to lecture a rather disreputable statesman and rouse him to useful activity; he was seriously explaining the content and purpose of his poems: without this preamble Mr. Fox could hardly be expected to make head or tail of the Idiot Boy or the sailor's parrot.'[30] Eliot is being relaxed here: in 1801 the 'sailor's parrot' did not exist, nor does the poem ever tell us what kind of bird it was, probably not a parrot, though, for it is important that it sings.

Two revisions of the final stanza in 1827 introduce into the poem's conclusion an overt sense of what the 'singing-bird' means to the mother and to Wordsworth:

> ["] He to a Fellow-lodger's care
> Had left it, to be watch'd and fed,
> And pipe its song in safety;—there
> I found it when my Son was dead;
> And now, God help me for my little wit!
> I bear it with me, Sir! he took so much delight in it."

As noted, the late revision of 'trail' to 'bear' increases the literariness of the final line: it binds together in a pun the actions of bearing a burden, of bearing a child, and of bearing a loss. What is more, these meanings are structurally linked in the woman's story: she bears the bird because she bore a son. This meaning is prepared in stanza 4, 'I had a Son'—itself a pun, meaning both 'I gave birth to a son' and 'I have lost a son'. There is in Wordsworth's final stanza a suggestion implied in all versions, but made more overt later, that her bearing the bird, which eventually sings in safety like the poet and his poem, helps her to bear her loss. The reparative action of the poem is to side, technically, with her, at the same moment as framing her in the irreparable predicament. The super-addition of the metre does both these things, and it is correlated with a diction both appropriate to her, if not exactly hers, and uneasily accommodated to the poem's frame. A complex relation of the uneasy and the appropriate gives form to the irreparable circumstances and the reparative action.

---

[30] T. S. Eliot, *The Use of Poetry and the Use of Criticism* (1933), 73.

This is Wordsworth's greatness here, and Geoffrey Hill expresses something similar when he cites four lines from 'The Female Vagrant':

> She ceased, and weeping turned away,
> As if because her tale was at an end
> She wept;—because she had no more to say
> Of that perpetual weight which on her spirit lay . . .

Hill then states,

In 'as if' and 'because', pedantically isolating her, we glimpse the remoteness of words from suffering and yet are made to recognize that these words are totally committed to her existence. They are her existence. Language here is not 'the outward sign' of a moral action; it is the moral action.[31]

'They are her existence' goes too far, takes the imaginative wish for the deed in experience, momentarily forgets 'the remoteness of words from suffering'. Wordsworth's 'The Sailor's Mother' is, as Hill affirms for the lines he singles out, 'the moral action'. The truth and value of its morality live in the commitment to, and simultaneous separation from the woman, for it restores her stoicism to its context in her life and words, while composing them into its form. It is to be hoped that Charles James Fox was roused to useful activity. Perhaps the poet found the sailor's mother some money. Wordsworth gave his readers the silence which follows her having his poem's final word.

---

[31] Geoffrey Hill, *The Lords of Limit: Essays on Literature and Ideas* (André Deutsch Ltd., 1984 and Random House, Inc., 1984), 116–17.

2

W. H. Auden Revises a Context

I

In an essay on the poetry of D. H. Lawrence, W. H. Auden wrote:

The difference between formal and free verse may be likened to the difference between carving and modeling; the formal poet, that is to say, thinks of the poem he is writing as something already latent in the language which he has to reveal, while the free verse poet thinks of language as a plastic passive medium upon which he imposes his artistic conception.[1]

Just as an initial response to this remark might be T. S. Eliot's *'vers libre* does not exist, for there is only good verse, bad verse, and chaos',[2] so reasons exist for wishing to value the interdependence of carving and modelling.[3] Auden recalls Adrian Stokes's contrasting conceptions to praise carvers, whom he unjustly aligns with formal poets, for their awareness of responsibilities. The responsibilities derive from obligations to the demands of form, which in turn are analogies for 'those involuntary relationships created by

---

[1] W. H. Auden, *The Dyer's Hand* (1963), 287.

[2] T. S. Eliot, 'Reflections on *Vers Libre*', *To Criticize the Critic* (1965), 189.

[3] Adrian Stokes began by preferring carving to modelling, but in later volumes such as *The Invitation in Art* and *Reflections on the Nude* he formulated a theory founded upon the interdependence of these two concepts. Stokes's books relevant to these concerns can be found in vol. iii of *The Critical Writings*, ed. L. Gowing (1978). A helpful discussion of Stokes's work is the Introduction to Richard Wollheim's selection from his writings *The Image in Form* (Harmondsworth, 1972). Donald Davie has written extensively on his earlier work in 'Adrian Stokes and Pound's "Cantos" ', *The Twentieth Century*, 160 (Nov. 1956), 418–36; in *Ezra Pound: Poet as Sculptor* (1965) 127–32, 154–8; and in 'Two Analogies for Poetry', *The Poet in the Imaginary Museum*, ed. B. Alpert (Manchester, 1977), 108–12. For Davie's later views on Stokes, see 'From the Manifest to the Therapeutic', *TLS* 4126 (30 Apr. 1982), 483, and 'Adrian Stokes Revisited', *Paideuma*, 12 (Autumn, Winter 1983), 189–97. For Stokes's application of his later conceptions to the art of poetry, see my 'On an Unpublished Poem by Adrian Stokes', *Adrian Stokes 1902–1972: A Supplement*, ed. S. Bann, *PN Review 15*, 7 (1980), and the Introduction to *With All the Views: Collected Poems of Adrian Stokes*, ed. P. Robinson (Manchester, 1981).

social, economic and political necessity'. Because Lawrence did not have 'firsthand knowledge' of these involuntary relationships, he was not in a position to write effectively about social ills. 'Very few artists can be *engagé* because life does not engage them: for better or worse, they do not quite belong to the City.'[4] Auden's 'for better or worse' and his 'not quite' hint at a disbelief in the divorce which proposed to separate those who have been lawfully joined together. Even if they want to, the poets can't quite leave the city, though they may 'not quite belong'.

Are the decisions made by poets in writing and revising analogous to the decisions of politicians? Ezra Pound implied that they were when he wrote,

I don't believe any estimate of Mussolini will be valid unless it *starts* from his passion for construction. Treat him as *artifex* and all the details fall into place. Take him as anything save the artist and you will get muddled with contradictions.[5]

Auden also accepted that such analogies were conceivable, so much so that he argued, in 'The Poet & The City', for the separation of the two. Because a state might be like a work of art, and a ruler like an artist, he thought it better not to imagine that anything could be properly understood by the comparison. To make the analogy frightening and repulsive, Auden gives a parodic and misleading account of what is involved in revision and in the poet's relation to the poetic medium. Auden's picture of composition and revision needs to be contested before I look at his work on 'A Summer Night'.

Here is the passage from 'The Poet & The City':

All political theories which, like Plato's, are based on analogies drawn from artistic fabrication are bound, if put into practice, to turn into tyrannies. The whole aim of a poet, or any other kind of artist, is to produce something which is complete and will endure without change. A poetic city would always contain exactly the same number of inhabitants doing exactly the same jobs for ever.

Moreover, in the process of arriving at the finished work, the artist has continually to employ violence. A poet writes:

The mast-high anchor dives through a cleft

[4] Auden, *The Dyer's Hand*, 293.
[5] Ezra Pound, *Jefferson and/or Mussolini* (1935), 34.

changes it to

The anchor dives through closing paths

and changes it again to

The anchor dives among hayricks

and finally to

The anchor dives through the floors of a church.

A *cleft* and *closing paths* have been liquidated, and hayricks deported to another stanza.

A society which was really like a good poem, embodying the aesthetic virtues of beauty, order, economy and subordination of detail to the whole, would be a nightmare of horror for, given the historical reality of actual men, such a society could only come into being through selective breeding, extermination of the physically and mentally unfit, absolute obedience to its Director, and a large slave class kept out of sight in cellars.

Vice versa, a poem which was really like a political democracy— examples, unfortunately, exist—would be formless, windy, banal and utterly boring.[6]

This simplifies revising, making it analogous to omnipotent fantasy. A poet, it suggests, can change any word to any other word he or she fancies. The only thing specified by implication is that the changes have to follow grammar rules: a noun phrase for a noun phrase, a verb for a verb. A moment's reflection should allow that the words in a poem do not show 'absolute obedience to a Director', and, for that matter, neither are they 'liquidated' or 'deported'.

The senses of words in poems depend upon their places in a language and a society in which those words are spoken and have meanings. The poet is dependent upon that dependence. Auden writes about revising as if the author invented the language as he went along. Thus, to remove a word from a poem is to 'liquidate' it. Once out of the poem the word ceases to exist. This is not so; at the very worst, the word could be said to be 'exiled' from the poem. Yet this too is misleading, for the words in a poem derive their meanings from continuing relations with other words which are not in the poem, and never were. The word 'black' in a poem donates its meanings and connotations to the poem in the given understanding of a relation to its absent opposite. This is one example of the vast range of such meanings in relations.

[6] Auden, *The Dyer's Hand*, 85.

Because a poet's language is shared to a large extent with other people whose language it also is, the degree of violence which can be deployed successfully in revising and finishing a poem is restricted by the nature of the language. This, the poet did not invent. It is restricted too by the implied natures of those who speak the language and have spoken it, who, once again, did not invent it. Auden's *reductio ad absurdum* is misleading not because tyrants never behave as he describes them, but because poets do not. Analogies are only partially helpful in illuminating one aspect of a relationship and distort understanding when offered as illustrations of identity in all aspects.

What is involved in revising a poem can best be shown by examples since it is thus, and not by prescription, that poets work. However, it may be noted in passing that revision of lines to shape or improve rhythm will depend upon the rhythms of other parts of the work, and will involve a respect for what has already been given or achieved; that changing a line to make a rhyme means acknowledging the constraints of form as well as its imposition; and that the revision of single words ('replace' to 'repair' or 'restore', for example) seeks to improve the significance of a passage not by the violent liquidation of meaning, but by an encouragement of implications which suggests a fraternity of senses between the words remaining as well as those supplanted. These counter-examples to Auden's picture of the tyrannical poet do not exclude an element of violence from the processes of making art. They are simply to indicate that without an untyrannical feeling for the interdependence of elements in the medium of poetry, no poet could produce those works of 'beauty, order, economy and subordination of detail to the whole' which Auden sees as analogous in politics to 'a nightmare of horror'.

What Auden's analogy does show is that the poet's will, considered in isolation from the medium, may well be tyrannical and dangerous; but it is because the medium of art is a material with its own nature and which can resist imperiousness or executive confidence that poems do demonstrate qualities of human attention which, far from being tyrannical, can show respect for others, concern about injustices, feelings of love and affection. Auden's account of making poems cannot be right because the emotional impulses engaged in the production of art will leave their mark on the work. If the quality of attention that a writer focuses on the text undergoing revision is the equivalent of 'a nightmare of horror', then the text will not show 'subordination of detail to the whole', rather, it will display the domination by one or more details of the others.

In 'The Public v. the Late Mr William Butler Yeats', Auden has the Counsel for the Defence say, as if conclusively,

The case for the prosecution rests on the fallacious belief that art ever makes anything happen, whereas the honest truth, gentlemen, is that, if not a poem had been written, not a picture painted, not a bar of music composed, the history of man would be materially unchanged. (p. 393)[7]

No end of evidence (Shakespeare's contribution to the English language, for example) could be cited to indicate that this statement, understood literally, is untrue. Yet it is a slippery sentence, and might wriggle out of the counter-instances, for 'materially' could mean 'in relation to material life', food and houses; or mean 'substantially', whereby the history of man would be more or less unchanged. The first implication allows the retort: 'Ah yes, but would it be spiritually unchanged?' The second would let art make something happen, but only marginally and insignificantly, receiving to the retort a counter, 'Who cares about spiritual changes anyway?' Furthermore, 'makes anything happen' is another argument *ad absurdum*. If cases could be isolated where art appeared to be a sufficient cause for a historical occurrence, to claim it as such would be to mistake the instrument for the agent. It would be like calling the knife the cause of the 'necessary murder'.[8] This indicates that what concerned Auden in 1939 when he wrote the sentences above was not 'Can poetry make anything happen?' but 'Can poets make anything happen?' or even 'Can I . . . ?' Art is not usually a sufficient cause, but it may be a significant precondition, or a contributory factor. By suggesting that to be judged on its contribution to the material history of man, art must be taken as a

---

[7] Page references from Auden, *The English Auden*, ed. E. Mendelson (1977), are given in parentheses.

[8] 'To-day the deliberate increase in the chances of death, | The conscious acceptance of guilt in the necessary murder', W. H. Auden, *Spain* (1937), 11; Mendelson's text has the revised 'guilt in the fact of murder' (p. 212), and see George Orwell, *The Collected Essays, Journalism and Letters*, 4 vols., ed. S. Orwell and I. Angus (1968), i. 516: 'All very edifying. But notice the phrase "Necessary murder". It could only be written by a person to whom murder is at most a *word*.' Frank Kermode discusses these issues in *History and Value* (Oxford, 1988), 77–9.

sufficient cause, or what the Defence calls an 'effective agent', is to release it from possible prosecution by eliciting the reply: of course it can't, and it therefore must be granted immunity.

MacNeice commented, 'The fallacy lies in thinking that it is the *function* of art to make things happen and that the effect of art upon actions is something either direct or calculable.'[9] Because art is not usually a sufficient cause, we are left free to consider its value as a less direct, not literally calculable, contribution to the development of human society and culture. Art's being a reparative emblem might be one such contribution. This is what the Defence does in Auden's essay when saying of Yeats: 'However false or undemocratic his ideas, his diction shows a continuous evolution towards what one might call the true democratic style.' (p. 393) Thus the defence counsellor compounds slippery argument with undemonstrated and unlikely assertion. Auden wrote these sentences to affirm that Yeats's work would be cherished by many who had little use for his stated values—a true observation Auden also made in the second part of 'In Memory of W. B. Yeats':

> You were silly like us: your gift survived it all;
> The parish of rich women, physical decay,
> Yourself; mad Ireland hurt you into poetry.
> Now Ireland has her madness and her weather still,
> For poetry makes nothing happen . . .   (p. 242)

'You were silly *like us*': the lines are also a self-defence, an argument for the continuing value of poets from the 1930s, that 'low dishonest decade' (p. 245). The importance of these two issues, poetic revision and the instrumentality of art, is that the composition of 'Out on the lawn I lie in bed', and its revision into 'A Summer Night', straddle Auden's writing these defences of W. B. Yeats.

II

For clarity, the version of the poem printed in *Look, Stranger!* (1936) will be called 'Out on the lawn I lie in bed', and the version in Auden's *Collected Poems*, 'A Summer Night'. Both can now be

---

[9] Louis MacNeice, *The Poetry of W. B. Yeats* (Oxford, 1941), 225.

read in texts which carry the date June 1933.[10] Dates at the foot of poems are inherently ambiguous in being understandable as refer-ring either to the occasion from which the poem derives, or the time at which it was written. The third line of both versions refers to 'the windless nights of June', suggesting that the event of the poem took place in June 1933. The weather was unusually warm that year, and Humphrey Carpenter in his biography of Auden explains that the poet

manhandled his iron bedstead with its mountain of blankets down the stairs into the garden of the Lodge, the bachelor masters' house. Here he slept for several weeks, putting up an umbrella if it rained. Sometimes a group of geese came to share the shelter of the umbrella.[11]

Auden had become a teacher at the Downs School in Worcester-shire in 1932. He was to stay there until 1935. A large portion of the school slept outdoors during that June. Carpenter's information about the weather comes from the school magazine. Geoffrey Hoyland, the poem's dedicatee, was Auden's headmaster. Auden wrote to Iris Snodgrass: 'The headmaster I believe to be a great man, in spite of religion. (We are quakers here.)'[12] I will come back to religion.

So 'June 1933' refers to when the occasion of 'Out on the lawn I lie in bed' was experienced. If it were also to refer to the date of composition, a reader could locate the process of its writing within a political and historical context. Here is where a first difficulty appears. Auden left England in 1939 and spent the years of the Second World War in America. During late 1941, he suggested to his American publishers, Random House, that they issue his earlier poetry in a collected edition. They eventually agreed, and Auden began compiling the book in spring 1942. He wrote to Louise Bogan:

Now and then I look through my books and is my face red. One of the troubles of our time is that we are all, I think, precocious as personalities

---

[10] For 'Out on the lawn I lie in bed' see Auden, *The English Auden*, 136–8, and for 'A Summer Night', *Collected Poems*, ed. Mendelson (Faber & Faber Ltd., 1976 and Random House, Inc., copyright 1937 by Random House, Inc., and renewed 1965 by W. H. Auden), 103–4. I refer extensively to both texts throughout this essay; it will be clear which version is being cited, but to avoid excessive clutter I will not give the page nos. in each case.

[11] Humphrey Carpenter, *W. H. Auden: A Biography* (1981), 160.

[12] Ibid. 142.

and backward as characters. Looking at old work I keep finding ideas which one has no business to see already at that age, and a style of treatment which one ought to have outgrown years before.[13]

Carpenter reports that Auden did not have copies of all his books, and had to borrow them from the library of Swarthmore College. By 'A Communist to Others', a poem in the same 1936 volume as 'Out on the lawn I lie in bed', Auden wrote 'O God what rubbish'. He cut the poem completely. He had, by 1942, become a convert to Christianity. The librarian, we read, was enraged at finding that the author had used the College's editions to mark up his texts for the Random House printers. This is when 'A Summer Night' was compiled and rephrased. 'Out on the lawn I lie in bed' first appeared in *The Listener* on 7 March 1934, under the title 'Summer Night'.[14] While the date at the bottom of 'Out on the lawn I lie in bed' accurately reports the time of its occasion, and reasonably accurately indicates the time of its composition, the date on 'A Summer Night' reports the former, but makes no allusion to its substantial revision in America nearly ten years later.

So small a detail can make a large difference to how the poem is read, to what can be heard in it, and to what it may be thought to refer. Consider these lines which remain the same in both texts:

> And, gentle, do not care to know,
> Where Poland draws her Eastern bow,
> What violence is done

Auden, however, altered the original semi-colon after 'done' to a comma. Joseph Warren Beach, whose 1957 volume, *The Making of the Auden Canon*, is the pioneering work on Auden revising, thought that perhaps the lines were an allusion to Tennyson's *Maud*, 'Shall I weep if a Poland fall? shall I shriek if a Hungary fail?'[15] The speaker of *Maud* is a young man disturbed by the suicide of his father and his love for a girl of a higher social

---

[13] Two references to ibid. 330.

[14] It lost its title in other printings until the 1942–3 revisions. 'Out on the lawn I lie in bed' was the second poem in *Look, Stranger!* and was numbered: II. It appears as XIV in Mendelson's volume of Auden's works in their 1930s texts, *The English Auden*. The poem is called 'A Summer Night 1933' in *Collected Shorter Poems 1930–1944* (1950), 110.

[15] Joseph Warren Beach, *The Making of the Auden Canon* (Minneapolis, 1957), 46–7, and Alfred, Lord Tennyson, *The Poems of Tennyson*, 3 vols., ed. C. Ricks (1987), ii. 532.

standing. He oscillates early in the poem between rabid political denunciation and the shrill quietism of the line above. Its attitude of the moment is defined in the last line of the same stanza: '*I have not made the world, and He that made it will guide.*' Beach's suggestion may be part of the poetic hinterland to Auden's lines, but the wording is not near enough to support an allusion. However, I also come back to Tennyson.

A different context is offered by Stan Smith:

> What the poem does not care to know is the whole historic hinterland of its timeless privileged moment. The poem was written in June 1933. On 28 May the Nazis had won the elections in Danzig, setting the seal on a half-year of triumph. In January Hitler had come to power; in February he suspended civil liberties and the freedom of the press; in March an election confirmed his majority, and an enabling law allowed him to assume dictatorial powers until 1937; in April the persecution of the Jews began, with a national boycott of all Jewish business; in May the trade unions were suppressed.[16]

This is important for 'Out on the lawn I lie in bed', but it is neither fair nor correct to say that the poem 'does not care to know'. For a poet to tell his reader that someone doesn't care to know something, he has to give an idea of what that thing is. Thus, the poem informs by saying it would be preferable not to be informed. Poland is mentioned, implying perhaps the Danzig elections, and 'What violence is done'—not in detail, but this is a poem, not a newspaper report, a history book, or piece of literary criticism. Auden's poem is implying that happiness at particular moments would be lost if we were to dwell exclusively on the world's bad news, and happiness is a part of the world's events; at the same time, it is not the be-all and end-all of the world's events, so we should not be unaware of what else is happening. The poem emphasizes the former idea, and shadows in the latter—not least by the trace of benign mockery in the vocative 'gentle', which refers to the 'we' of the previous stanza. The poet too is one of those who 'do not care to know'. It cannot be true that Auden did not care to know. He had been living in Germany in 1929 during political unrest, and in 1935 he arranged a marriage of convenience between himself and Erika Mann to help her leave Germany.[17] Yet, the poet

---

[16] See Stan Smith, *W. H. Auden* (Oxford, 1985), 81–2.
[17] See Carpenter, *Biography*, 175–7.

is also a man divided between wanting to be personally happy, and caring for the future of the wider world. By telling us something of what we 'do not care to know', he works that division into his poem as part of its subject.

The full significance of Danzig for the history of the inter-war years was not, of course, clear in June 1933. However, in the spring of 1942 it certainly will have been to Auden. Less than three years earlier, he had written a poem called 'September 1, 1939'. It was the day that Hitler invaded Poland and thus precipitated the Second World War by provoking the British Government either to break a treaty of support for Poland, or to declare war on Germany. They did the latter on 3 September. The pretext for the invasion of Poland was Danzig and the problem of the 'Polish Corridor'. Danzig, after the Treaty of Versailles, was a free city on the Baltic coast, surrounded by land which had become part of Poland. The band of territory separating Danzig from the rest of Germany was the Polish Corridor. This explains why 'Poland draws her Eastern bow': Auden is voicing German propaganda against the isolation of Danzig. The Poles are threatening German territory in an eastward direction. Jósef Korbel reminds us that 'A real crisis developed over Danzig in February [1933] when Poland sent reinforcements to Westerplatte, the harbour of the free city, to reinforce her rights, which were being endangered by its administration, now under full Nazi control.'[18] When Auden wrote the line sometime in or soon after June 1933, he was alluding to a problem in inter-war politics. When it appears in 'A Summer Night', despite the fact that Poland still seems the aggressor, the lines, and the emblematic word 'Poland', are enough to signal the threat of a war which had, by the time of the revision, become the reality.

This supposition about what the line in 'A Summer Night' might refer to is strengthened by the largest revision—the cutting of stanzas 10, 11, and 12 in 'Out on the lawn I lie in bed':

---

[18] Jósef Korbel, *Poland Between East and West: Soviet and German Diplomacy towards Poland, 1919–1933* (Princeton, NJ, 1963), 280. This crisis was resolved for the time being by the Declaration of Non-Aggression and Understanding between Germany and Poland, signed and published on 26 Jan. 1934. See also Antony Polonsky, *Politics in Independent Poland 1921–1939* (Oxford, 1972), 383, where the crisis is indicated as taking place in March, and for details of the accommodation with Germany, Jozef Lipski, *Diplomat in Berlin 1933–1939*, ed. W. Jędrzejewicz (New York and London, 1968), 70–127.

The creepered wall stands up to hide
The gathering multitudes outside
    Whose glances hunger worsens;
Concealing from their wretchedness
Our metaphysical distress,
    Our kindness to ten persons.

And now no path on which we move
But shows already traces of
    Intentions not our own,
Thoroughly able to achieve
What our excitement could conceive,
    But our hands left alone.

For what by nature and by training
We loved, has little strength remaining:
    Though we would gladly give
The Oxford colleges, Big Ben,
And all the birds in Wicken Fen,
    It has no wish to live.

These stanzas give a context in domestic politics for the world
outside the school garden. The first of the three cut stanzas picks
up an idea from two verses earlier ('we | Whom hunger cannot
move') and fixes the contrast between 'Our picnics in the sun' and
'The gathering multitudes outside | Whose glances hunger wors-
ens'. The Wall Street Crash had occurred less than four years
before, and the British economy was in depression. The poem's
concern at this point is less focused on events in Eastern Europe,
more on class unrest at home. In the next stanza, Auden aligns the
good intentions of people like himself and his class, the talk and
ideals of social transformation, with others' intentions to act, those
others outside the garden wall, more purposeful and capable,
driven by hunger, by need.

The third of these stanzas says that 'what by nature and by
training | We loved' has 'no wish to live'. The list of symbolic
institutions—Oxford colleges, Big Ben, Wicken Fen—implies that
'what' we love is the educational system, parliamentary democracy,
and the National Trust (which owns the bird sanctuary of Wicken
Fen in East Anglia). Each of the stanzas shapes a division: between
their 'wretchedness' and our 'metaphysical distress'; between their
ability to 'achieve', ours only to 'conceive'; between what we loved,
would gladly give, but which is bent on self-destruction and 'has

no wish to live'. Auden indicates divided loyalties by a mixed tone in the stanzas. It is urgent and self-mocking. There's comedy in the rhyme of 'worsens' and 'ten persons', and in the sing-song list of stalwart institutions. There's urgency in the tightly inexorable structure of the stanza itself where the second half answers the pattern of the first. Ambiguous tones indicating divided loyalties can be infectiously unstable. The stanzas are significant because they make the anguish of 'Our metaphysical distress' appear silly, but also do the same to the urgent political changes invoked. The sing-song list makes the stanzas sound glib, the gestures betrayed by their facility.

Auden could have found reasons for feeling he had lost control of his poem's tone here, for feeling that it would be better without the three stanzas. When they are removed, the poem moves straight from Poland's 'Eastern bow' and 'Our picnics in the sun' to 'Soon through the dykes', only now with an extra 'Soon': 'Soon, soon, through the dykes of our content | The crumpling flood will force a rent'. The additional 'Soon' turns the description of an inevitability into a prophetic warning. 'Soon through the dykes' says that it will happen, as if a force of nature; 'Soon, soon' includes that, but implies there is not much time, we are about to lose something, and we will have to act in response to it. This small change alters the orientation of the people in the garden regarding the 'flood' that will break through its wall. In 'Out on the lawn I lie in bed', this flood is the revolutionary zeal of the 'gathering multitudes', their force a desired value as conceived by the fellow-travellers inside the garden. In 'A Summer Night', it is violence and war that will break down the garden wall, signalled by 'Poland' and reinforced by an earlier revision whereby 'blankly as an orphan' becomes 'blankly as a butcher'. Stan Smith is sharp about that change:

'Orphan' recalls Auden's characterization of the middle class. But it also points to a people disenfranchised and a Europe soon to be overflowing with orphans. In post-war versions of the poem Auden changed 'orphan' to 'butcher', and while this is appropriately subversive of an arcadia where hunger and carnivores are like allayed, its main effect is to turn the moon simply into a philistine shopkeeper, insensitive to the great art treasures which we more 'gentle' souls appreciate.[19]

---

[19] Smith, *W. H. Auden*, 82.

An orphan blank with awe and wonder is turned into a tradesman blank with incomprehension; but just as orphans can retrospectively signal a political sense, so too 'butcher' may indicate barbarian atrocities (the butcher of Lyons, for example), and this retrospective association, whereby indifference is threatening, Auden may have considered when revising. He will have known the Nazis' attitude to modern art.[20]

Auden changes the meaning of the flood and subtly alters the way the people in the garden are to be aware of it. This change is carried through in more detailed revision of the closing stanzas. The crucial change here is in the penultimate where 'May this for which we dread to lose | Our privacy' becomes 'May these delights we dread to lose, | This privacy'. Then, to maintain the grammatical agreement, 'may it calm' in the last becomes 'let them calm'. But what is 'this' and 'it' in 'Out on the lawn I lie in bed'? It isn't clear, and could be mistaken for the flood itself, the revolutionary tide. However, the flood is synonymous with 'that strength' in 'Out on the lawn I lie in bed', so then 'this' and 'it' are the comradeship and equality described in the first five stanzas. Auden makes the link clearer by revising the impersonal pronoun to 'these delights'— but in doing so alters the tenor of the comradeship to an epicurean relaxation. They become leisure. It is easier to understand how a concept of equality and comradeship might help to 'calm | The pulse of nervous nations'; it is harder to see how leisure activities could. In 'Out on the lawn I lie in bed', the privileged comradeship (inextricably connected with education, teaching literature, preparation for service) will be joined to the strength of the revolutionary tide. In 'A Summer Night', where the crumpling flood means the coming war and fascist barbarism, the delights and privacy are to be joined to 'that strength'; but now, without the 'gathering multitudes', this strength is the 'sounds of riveting' which follow the 'crumpling flood'. Without the theme of a revolutionary upheaval succeeded by a phase of socialist industrial revival, the 'sounds of riveting' become foreshadowings of post-war reconstruction; they become, in 1942–3, thoughts for the rebuilding of Europe, to which leisure activities may be joined in making a peaceful future.

---

[20] The exhibition of 'degenerate art' was held in Munich and Vienna in 1937; see for instance, Oskar Kokoschka, *My Life* (1974), 152.

Here too, the 'orphan' is relevant. In 'Out on the lawn I lie in bed', the penultimate stanza concludes:

> As through a child's rash happy cries
> The drowned voices of his parents rise
> In unlamenting song.

'A Summer Night' has 'The drowned parental voices'. By removing the 'orphan' and detaching the parents from the child, making them an adjective for the older generation, Auden removes an allegorical strand. In 'Out on the lawn I lie in bed', the child is not necessarily Stan Smith's middle class as orphan, but the wondrous and awestruck new era, an image of the gathering multitudes who will compose the new socialist world. The drowned parents are the ruling middle class and aristocracy. There is a Freudian Oedipal struggle grafted on to the Marxist class struggle by this analogy, whereby the burgeoning new must destroy its progenitors. In 'Out on the lawn I lie in bed', the parents, or those *in loco parentis*, want this to happen; what they represent 'has no wish to live', so they will join the child's cries with their 'unlamenting song'. What does the song represent? The orphaned child will stare blankly at the 'marvellous pictures'; he lacks cultural knowledge to understand works of art, but stares at them with wonder. Thus a role emerges for the comradely schoolteachers of the opening verses, because their 'unlamenting song', poetry for instance, will need reorientating to celebrate the new order, and with the 'marvellous pictures' will help to 'calm | The pulse of nervous nations' and to 'surpass | The tigress her swift motions'. Edward Mendelson pointed out in *Early Auden* that the poem's final line is an allusion to 'Strange Meeting'. The dead man encountered in Wilfred Owen's poem had also had poetic ambitions. He regrets the non-existence of works of art he might have made which could have helped save the world from further barbarism:

> And of my weeping something had been left,
> Which must die now. I mean the truth untold,
> The pity of war, the pity war distilled.
> Now men will go content with what we spoiled,
> Or, discontent, boil bloody, and be spilled.
> They will be swift with swiftness of the tigress.[21]

---

[21] Wilfred Owen, *The Complete Poems and Fragments*, 2 vols., ed. J. Stallworthy (1983), i. 148.

Auden is taking up the responsibility required of poets and artists in Owen's famous poem. This is true of both Auden's versions. The difference lies in the nature and desirability of the 'crumpling flood', and so in the idea of reconstruction afterwards, to which art will lend its calming influence.

III

Carpenter writes that the poem 'tries to provide an answer, declaring that soon will come a major upheaval in the form of war or revolution', and he concludes that the answer, the appeasing power of love, 'proved to be too glib for Auden's own satisfaction'.[22] But it makes a difference whether the cataclysm foreseen is 'war or revolution', and 'unlamenting song' is what will do the calming. Carpenter is not wrong to mention love, as a look at the first five stanzas of the poem shows. Revising, Auden cut one of them:

> Moreover, eyes in which I learn
> That I am glad to look, return
>   My glances every day;
> And when the birds and rising sun
> Waken me, I shall speak with one
>   Who has not gone away.

Auden found reasons for cutting the three stanzas already discussed. Their mixture of tones had begun to infect the poem, and made it sound, in Carpenter's word, 'glib'. The stanza above, though, demonstrates how beautifully apt the choice of verse-form was for the experience Auden wished to narrate and explore. 'Equal with colleagues in a ring', the third verse begins, and the stanza form mimics the situation, composed of two equal parts like matching semi-circles. The rhyme of 'learn' and 'return' performs the meeting of eyes in the answering sounds. This is also true of the trimeter lines 3 and 6, where in the returning rhyme-sound we hear that someone 'has not gone away'.

Why did Auden cut it? He had been examining the importance of love in his critical writing. In the *Criterion* for October 1933,

---

[22] Carpenter, *Biography*, 162, 163.

Auden reviewed *The Book of Talbot* by Violet Clifton. It is an enraptured religious memoir of a husband by his widow. Auden observed that it 'shows more clearly than anything I have read for a long time that the first criterion of success in any human activity, the necessary preliminary, whether to scientific discovery or to artistic vision, is intensity of attention or, less pompously, love' (p. 319). Ending with an uneasy recognition of conflicting allegiances similar to the mention of his headmaster in the letter to Iris Snodgrass, Auden writes:

One may be repelled by Roman Catholicism; one may regard the system of society which made Talbot's life and character possible as grossly unjust, but I cannot imagine that anyone who is fortunate enough to read this book, will not experience that sense of glory which it is the privilege of great art to give.   (p. 320)

Love as the 'first criterion of success', as the 'necessary preliminary', is what the first five stanzas of 'Out on the lawn I lie in bed' seek to establish. Auden described the experience which lies behind the poem in 1964 under the heading 'The Vision of Agape':

One fine summer night in June 1933 I was sitting on a lawn after dinner with three colleagues, two women and one man. We liked each other well enough but we were certainly not intimate friends, nor had any one of us a sexual interest in another.

Later he writes: 'For the first time in my life I knew exactly— because, thanks to the power, I was doing it—what it meant to love one's neighbor as oneself.' Auden concludes by observing that 'among the various factors which several years later brought me back to the Christian faith in which I had been brought up, the memory of this experience and asking myself what it could mean was one of the most crucial, though, at the time it occurred, I thought I had done with Christianity for good'.

Mendelson observes that it 'is the work of Auden the middle-aged churchgoer writing about Auden the young atheist, but there is no reason to doubt any of it'. There is, though, something to examine in the separation Auden effects between 'sexual interest' and 'what it means to love one's neighbour', a distinction which does not tally with 'Out on the lawn I lie in bed'. In 1964, Auden insists on a division between Eros, sexual love, and Agape, spiritual or neighbour love. It is hard to define Agape in English. Auden notes: 'My personal feelings towards them were unchanged—they were still my colleagues, not intimate friends—but I felt their existence as themselves to be of infinite value and rejoiced in it.'[23] 'Out on the lawn I lie in bed' describes a different scene:

> Lucky, this point in time and space
> Is chosen as my working place;
>   Where the sexy airs of summer,
> The bathing hours and the bare arms,
> The leisured drives through a land of farms,
>   Are good to the newcomer.

The 'sexy airs of summer' is a memorable instance of Auden's chattily relaxed style. It suggests a vague but unmistakable erotic atmosphere. The presence of a benign sexual well-being does have a contribution to make in Auden's feeling of equality among colleagues. There is in stanza 5, expunged from 'A Summer Night', a hint of attachments both personal and dependent:

> And when the birds and rising sun
> Waken me, I shall speak with one
>   Who has not gone away.

The 'one' introduces a private note into the more public ring of fellow-teachers. Those who do not know might ask if the 'one' is the poem's dedicatee. To avoid this unwished-for suspicion might be reason enough to cut the stanza.

Auden may have intended the idea that, unlike in some sexual relationships, this spending nights outdoors with colleagues in a ring means that the person near you when you went to sleep is still there in the morning. However the stanza is understood, its presence or absence asks whether the versions conceive of Eros and Agape as involved with each other, or as separate categories of experience.[24] A difficulty that the vision of Agape introduces is that Auden's earlier version had come to focus on a politicized comradeship, a mild confusing in the poem of the erotic, the neighbourly, and the altruistic. Auden would like the later version to be

---

[23] See Mendelson, *Early Auden* (1981), 159–76.

[24] For a recent study of the relations between sexual and political interest in an 'other' during the 1930s, see Kermode, *History and Value*. Particularly relevant is 'Eros, Builder of Cities', the chapter devoted to Auden.

understood as a spiritual awakening to the absolute equality of people seen as if in the eyes of God.

A stanza in 'September 1, 1939' shapes a sharp distinction:

> The windiest militant trash
> Important Persons shout
> Is not so crude as our wish:
> What mad Nijinsky wrote
> About Diaghilev
> Is true of the normal heart;
> For the error bred in the bone
> Of each woman and each man
> Craves what it cannot have,
> Not universal love
> But to be loved alone.   (p. 246)[25]

Not only does sexual love not foster brotherly or neighbourly love, it actively precludes them. If you came to believe this, and wanted to strengthen your vision of Agape, cutting the fifth stanza is a good idea, because it reduces the possibility of confusion. However, although there is an advantage in having different words to differentiate separate characters of love, the English word 'love', while it lumps them together, also serves to relate them. As a native English speaker, it would be hard for me to imagine what loving everyone was, or what God's love might be like, if I had never loved or been loved by one person alone. There are strengths in holding Eros and Agape apart; yet there are benefits too in seeing sexual love, and the love where our own interests are engaged, as a ground from which wider, more generally benevolent experiences of love may arise. This is what 'Out on the lawn I lie in bed', confusing its categories, assumes—sliding, for instance, from 'sexy airs' to 'dove-like pleading' in the space of two stanzas. What's more, Auden did not delete the 'bare arms' or the 'sexy airs' or the 'bathing hours' when compiling 'A Summer Night'.

A final reason why Auden may have cut stanza 5 in 1942–3 at Swarthmore College, USA, is that he could no longer 'speak with

---

[25] Homosexual erotic love in a society hostile to its acknowledgement might be felt as set apart from universal love, whereas heterosexual feeling, more widely sanctioned, may appear to sponsor a greater confidence in linking the erotic with the altruistic. For detailed comments about this poem's technique, see Joseph Brodsky, 'On "September 1, 1939" by W. H. Auden', Less Than One (Harmondsworth, 1986), 304–41.

one I Who had not gone away'. He himself had gone away from the Downs School seven years before. This raises a question about the truth a poem tells, or tries to tell, and about the poet's relationship to his own composing past in verse. Should the truth of a poem be related only to its particular circumstances? Or should the poet feel responsible for the truth of what a poem states at any time after the event? This is particularly pressing when poets write about contemporary political events, for they, like anyone else, can misread the direction history is taking. Auden's stated reasons for dropping two poems with dates in their titles, 'September 1, 1939' and 'Spain 1937', involve this problem and conceal it by assuming that poems cannot contain statements which are literalistically untrue, bad, or in which the poet no longer believes.[26]

In love poetry too the alliance that brought about the work may not survive its celebration in cold, enduring print. Auden's 'Foreword' to his *Collected Shorter Poems 1927–1957*, published in 1966, says of revising:

A good many of the poems have been revised. Critics, I have observed, are apt to find revisions ideologically significant. One, even, made a great to-do about what was in fact a typographical error. I can only say that I have never, consciously at any rate, attempted to revise my former thoughts or feelings, only the language in which they were first expressed when, on further consideration, it seemed to me inaccurate, lifeless, prolix or painful to the ear.[27]

There are many revisions Auden could have pointed to, in which, no doubt, he thought he was doing what he says. One might be the change in stanza 2 of 'good to the newcomer' to 'good to a newcomer'. Auden came to believe he had used the definitive article excessively. There are four others in the same stanza. Another might be the revision of the poem's fourth line to remove the clumsy 'done complete'. Yet if you believe that the thoughts or feelings are in the words, not expressed through them, any change, however minute, will alter a poem's thought or feeling. Stan Smith notes of a composite 'A Summer Night' in which the two versions are taken as meaning much the same: 'Encouraged by Auden's

---

[26] Carpenter, *Biography*, 416, gives Auden's reasons for omitting from the *Collected Shorter Poems 1927–1957* (1966) both 'Spain 1937', on account of the lines 'History to the defeated I May say Alas but cannot help or pardon' (p. 212), and 'September 1, 1939', because of 'We must love one another or die' (p. 246).

[27] *Collected Shorter Poems 1927–1957*, 13.

later alterations to the poem, and by his retrospective anecdote . . .
critics have stressed the extent to which it prefigures his later
Christian commitment.'[28]

The poet's remarks at the time about the headmaster's Quaker-
ism and about Talbot Clifton's Roman Catholicism, not to say his
commenting in 1964 that he thought he 'had done with Christianity
for good' should discourage such a view. Most of the revisions to
'Out on the lawn I lie in bed' could not be regarded as mere
adjustments to expression. The most significant of these are the
alteration in the meaning and historical context of the 'crumpling
flood' and the shift in how sexuality is felt to relate to altruistic
love. It is mistaken to believe that a writer can improve the
language of his work without altering what its thoughts and
feelings are and mean. Changing 'May this' to 'May these delights'
in the penultimate stanza, Auden makes the antecedent of 'this'
clear by substituting an apparently synonymous noun phrase 'these
delights'; but there are no exact synonyms. A synonym acts by
redefining what has gone before, and this is what 'delights' serves
to do. It refocuses what the comradeship of the opening is, what it
signifies, and to what purpose it may lend itself.

Auden also wrote in 1966, 'On revisions as a matter of principle,
I agree with Valéry: "A poem is never finished; it is only abandoned." '[29] This remark could be taken in a number of ways. It
may be a testimony to the poet's perfectionism, his tireless efforts
at removing impurity and defective phrasing, which can never
reach the ideal poem the artist projects as a goal. It could also
appear a licence issued by the poet allowing him to return to
anything published and treat it as if still locked in his desk, a
perpetual entitlement to tinker till you die. No one is in a position
to suspend or confiscate this licence; but readers are entitled to
object to the tinkerings.

Why did Auden remove the capital letters on the points of the
compass in the lines 'Now North and South and East and West |
Those I love lie down to rest'?[30] Perhaps he, or a copy editor, did
not like the look of the typography. His using capitals in the first

---

[28] Smith, W. H. Auden, 79.

[29] Collected Shorter Poems 1927–1957, 13.

[30] Auden was fond of the line, and redeployed a variation on it in 'Stop all the
clocks, cut off the telephone' of April 1936: 'He was my North, my South, my East
and West', The English Auden, 163.

place may have been prompted by a memory of Tennyson's 'Palace of Art':[31]

> Four courts I made, East, West and South and North,
>   In each a squarèd lawn, wherefrom
> The golden gorge of dragons spouted forth
>   A flood of fountain-foam.
>
> And round the cool green courts there ran a row
>   Of cloisters, branched like mighty woods,
> Echoing all night to that sonorous flow
>   Of spouted fountain-floods.

Here the points of the compass are also capitalized, and the lines share with Auden's stanzas the lawn, the woods, the night, and, what his poem does not mention, buildings which have educational or religious associations: the courts, the cloisters. Tennyson's poem is about a sense of guilt derived from committing oneself to art at the expense of social usefulness and moral engagement. The palace is a place from which to view the world, like the moon in Auden's stanzas, with a dubious equanimity:

> Then of the moral instinct would she prate
>   And of the rising from the dead,
> As hers by right of full-accomplished Fate;
>   And at the last she said:
>
> 'I take possession of man's mind and deed.
>   I care not what the sects may bawl.
> I sit as God holding no form of creed,
>   But contemplating all.'

One problem with having a vision of Agape, or of becoming happy and equal with colleagues is that you might grow complacently enlightened, and lose your inner reasons for struggling against injustices. These inner reasons may also be what make you personally unhappy, and you want to be rid of them, so that your motives for being a social reformer are impure. Nevertheless, you may be a more morally good being with your compelling weaknesses and unhappinesses than you become when free of them. Auden, in 'Out on the lawn I lie in bed', wants to extend the possibility of his vision of comradeship in the teaching profession

---

[31] *The Poems of Tennyson*, i. 439, 452, 456.

to the gathering multitudes outside. You may think him silly for desiring it, but he feels guilty about his privilege.

The last stanza of 'The Palace of Art', like 'Out on the lawn I lie in bed' and 'A Summer Night', holds out a hope for the role of art:

> 'Yet pull not down my palace towers, that are
> So lightly, beautifully built:
> Perchance I may return with others there
> When I have purged my guilt.'

'A Summer Night' expunges the focus of the original guilt. The revised poem does not show any good reason for needing to beg that 'these delights' have a role to play in post-war reconstruction, for, in the light of Nazi barbarism, would any sympathetic reader wish to doubt it? The case appears differently if it is a socialist criticism of middle-class culture and privacy. By revising, the poet cleared and secured his ground, but also weakened his poem. Barbara Everett has pointed to a strength in its initial weakness; she may be referring to 'A Summer Night', but the case is more apt for 'Out on the lawn I lie in bed': 'Even its peculiar limitations have value: the insularity of the "possible dream" of the close, the fairy-tale new life that will arrive with oceanic force and splendour, bearing the seeds of the "shy green stalks" of promise, is a necessary part of the reverie that forms the subject of the whole.'[32] This fine point suggests that the truth of a poem may lie in its being subject to powerful illusions, to reverie. Retrospectively, the poet may feel inclined to write 'O God what rubbish', but would be wrong to cut. The 'rubbish' carries the significance of a moment in history, the particular circumstances, the truth of the poem as a specific human act. By trying to strengthen his poem with revisions, Auden made a weaker, more defended piece. The precarious balance between inside and out, between Eros and Agape, real hopes and wishful thinking, is what makes 'Out on the lawn I lie in bed' so significant a poem.

Introducing a selection of Tennyson, Auden wrote that he 'had the finest ear, perhaps, of any English poet; he was also undoubtedly the stupidest'. A footnote informs us that 'T. S. Eliot pointed

---

[32] Barbara Everett, *Auden* (1964), 40; and see *Poets in Their Time* (1986), 229, where she sums up Auden's weaknesses thus: 'His career has no real pattern as his life has no real form: there are only the enormous number of good poems which he wrote, all of them highly vulnerable to criticism for one thing or another. Why not?'

out to me that he could think of two or three English poets who were stupider, and I had to agree.'[33] It is a dangerous game. Poets might be wary of the criticism they make of their fellows; their words may easily rebound upon themselves. Tennyson is a great poet partly because he has the strength of his own weakness, the auditory intelligence to articulate illusions and foolishnesses. Auden might have been better advised to keep faith with his own past in print, to see the poetic wisdom even in his precocious personality's mistakes.

[33] Auden, *Forewords and Afterwords* (1973), 222.

3
Lend-Lease and 'The Dry Salvages'

On 15 February 1941, T. S. Eliot wrote a letter to the editor of the *New English Weekly*, the paper in which 'The Dry Salvages' first appeared twelve days later. He was concerned about some final revisions to the poem:

I am particularly [anxious] to get the last six lines right . . . It is important, because, however I have tried it, it turns out to be something to which people will give a topical allusion—not part of the fundamental intention—and if so, then it must not be a wrong twist which will put the rest of the poem out of joint . . .

Helen Gardner has commented that 'Presumably it was the word "undefeated" that Eliot feared might in 1941 give a "topical allusion"'; yet, despite a number of recastings, he allowed 'unde-feated' to remain in the final text.[1] Eliot was not saying that the last lines must avoid a topical allusion. The possibility of finding one which will be taken for the fundamental intention has caused him to think again. Rather, since people would find a topical allusion there, that allusion must not give the poem a wrong twist. If the letter warns against too readily assuming the poem's wartime context, it also reminds us that it had one, and prompts the question of what the wrong twist could have been.

In writing *Four Quartets*, Eliot was conscious of the way a word's various meanings introduce allusions and associations: the poet's task was then to try and ensure that these meanings are composed in the poem, not discordantly producing wrong twists. He regarded the multiplicity of meaning in words as one source of a poem's music. Introducing a selection of Kipling's verse made after completing 'The Dry Salvages', Eliot warned: 'the use of the word "musical" and of musical analogies, in discussing poetry, has its dangers if we do not constantly check its limitations: for the music of verse is inseparable from the meanings and associations

---

[1] Letter and quotation from Helen Gardner, *The Composition of Four Quartets* (1978), 147.

of words'.[2] In a lecture not long after, he enlarged on this inseparability:

The music of a word is, so to speak, at a point of intersection: it arises from its relation first to the words immediately preceding and following it, and indefinitely to the rest of its context; and from another relation, that of its immediate meaning in that context to all the other meanings which it has had in other contexts, to its greater or less wealth of association.[3]

Such a music of contexts can be heard in 'East Coker' when the writing of poetry is described as a 'raid on the inarticulate | With shabby equipment' or when Eliot confronts 'Undisciplined squads of emotion' (p. 203).[4] These phrases align the writing of poetry with drilling the Home Guard.

'The Dry Salvages' does not appear to intertwine so tightly the composition of poetry and the experience of war, but, nevertheless, the sea 'tosses up our losses', losses which include 'the gear of foreign dead men'. Amongst the sea's voices is 'The menace and caress of wave that breaks on water', while the tolling bell is heard 'under the oppression of the silent fog' (pp. 205–6). These foreign dead men, this menace and oppression, while not exclusively war experiences, do suggest peril on the sea, the peril of a naval and convoy war during 1940 and 1941, when Eliot was composing the poem. Other more overt associations of sense and context can be heard in:

> our own past is covered by the currents of action,
> But the torment of others remains an experience
> Unqualified, unworn by subsequent attrition.   (p. 209)

Here, 'currents of action' and 'attrition' touch on conflict at sea, acute suffering, and the daily grind that wears us out. More clearly still, voyagers and seamen are called 'you whose bodies | Will suffer the trial and judgement of the sea' and their predicament is related to conduct 'On the field of battle'. (p. 211)

There is also the secondary evidence of a word Eliot revised out of section 4. The lines remember Psalm 107:23, 'They that go down to the sea in ships, that do business in great waters':

---

[2] 'Rudyard Kipling', in T. S. Eliot, *On Poetry and Poets* (1957), 238.
[3] 'The Music of Poetry', ibid. 32–3.
[4] Citations of T. S. Eliot's poems are from *Collected Poems 1909–1962* (Faber & Faber Ltd., 1963 and Harcourt Brace Jovanovich, Inc.), to which the page nos. in parentheses refer.

> Lady, whose shrine stands on the promontory,
> Pray for all those who are in ships, those
> Whose business has to do with fish, and
> Those concerned with every lawful traffic
> And those who conduct them.   (p. 211)

The final line had read: 'And those who defend them',[5] a phrase in which 'defend' makes a direct allusion to the then topical subject of convoy escorts, and might be thought to exclude merchant seamen (the usual conductors of traffic on the sea) from its prayer—by seeming to concentrate on the Royal Navy. The word 'conduct' does not exclude either merchant or military seamen, nor does it presume engagement with some enemy, which 'defend' would do. Direct reference to naval combat is a note the printed poem hardly sounds.

Donald Davie has referred to 'The Dry Salvages' as 'the most American' of the *Four Quartets*;[6] this point is usually supported by referring to Eliot's biography, to a strain in the poem of qualified nostalgia for his roots. The first section opens with evocations of places important to Eliot since childhood: the Mississippi river of his birthplace, St Louis, and the small group of rocks, the Dry Salvages, off the north-east coast of Cape Ann, Massachusetts, where he went sailing in his holidays. The scope of these allusions to the southern states and to New England is wider than can be indicated by referring to the poet's biography alone. At the beginning of his poem, Eliot remembers 'the rank ailanthus of the April dooryard' from St Louis, and 'The tolling bell' which 'clangs' (pp. 205–6) from the New England coast; both these memories further recollect Walt Whitman's elegy for Abraham Lincoln, 'When Lilacs Last in the Dooryard Bloom'd' with its memorialization of 'the tolling tolling bells' perpetual clang'[7] and also the scent

---

[5] See Gardner, *Four Quartets*, 140.

[6] Donald Davie, 'Eliot in One Poet's Life', *The Waste Land in Different Voices*, ed. A. D. Moody (1974), 226. On the same page Davie notes 'I have reached the *Four Quartets*, poems of a nation at war; and poems which I, myself at war (I remember reading them in Arctic Russia), discovered for myself'. It was through reflecting on Davie's account of first reading 'The Dry Salvages'—and he sees a war context in the 'juxtaposition of Asia with the Edgware Road' in the poem's final section—that I began to think about its relations to the moment of its composition.

[7] Walt Whitman, *Leaves of Grass*, ed. H. W. Blodgett and S. Bradley (1965), 331.

of lilacs—blossoms which crop up more than once in Eliot's poetry.[8] Lincoln was assassinated in April 1865 and that may be one reason why, in *The Waste Land*, 'April is the cruellest month, breeding ǀ Lilacs out of the dead land' (p. 63). By recalling Whitman and Lincoln, Eliot is remembering the American Civil War: he found that war between North and South embodied in his own family history, and in himself—a child of New England stock living in the South, then a young man from the South educated in New England. Here is how Eliot considers Rudyard Kipling's outwardly different life and attachments:

What life would have made of such a man, had his birth, growth, maturity and age all taken place in one set of surroundings, is beyond speculation: as life directed, the result was to give him a peculiar detachment and remoteness from all environment, a universal foreignness which is the reverse side of his strong feeling for India, for the Empire, for England and for Sussex, a remoteness as of an alarmingly intelligent visitor from another planet. He remains somehow alien and aloof from all with which he identifies himself.[9]

However detached from the places and countries with which they identified, these uprooted figures could both register intensely the discomforts of finding their countries divided or at odds with each other. *Four Quartets* as a whole seeks the reconciliation of opposed parties, of the factions of old wars. At this point early in 'The Dry Salvages' that general desire for reconciliation finds an occasion in American ground.

During the winter of 1940–1 when he was writing 'The Dry Salvages', Eliot had reason for being concerned about America and the unity of the United States, a unity he is pondering in the allusion to Whitman and the American Civil War. As early as 10 December 1939, I. A. Richards, writing to Eliot in London from Cambridge, Massachusetts, commented on the issue:

Opinion about the War here puzzles me greatly. No public man— apparently—dares say anything but *Keep America Out*! But I can't believe there aren't those who *think* going in is inevitable and that therefore *the sooner* the less bloody! Yet I haven't met *one* such even among those whose sympathies are most pro-Ally. I wish I knew why the intervention

---

[8] See Eliot, *Collected Poems 1909–1962*, 19, 63, 104.
[9] Eliot, 'Rudyard Kipling', *On Poetry and Poets*, 241–2.

view can't be voiced (elections apart) and if this strange unanimity won't cause an equally united reaction later.[10]

The question of America's neutrality in the Second World War assumed urgent proportions after the fall of France in June 1940. On the 28th of that month, Winston Churchill wrote to Lord Lothian that Britain had 'really not had any help worth speaking of from the United States so far'.[11] Roosevelt, who was intent on winning the presidential election of 1940, moved only tentatively towards American entanglement in the European conflict. He believed the United States should side with Britain but was reluctant to lose the support of the isolationist lobby.

The first indications that he was prepared to assist Britain came with talk of the 'destroyer deal' in September 1940, a deal by which the United States received bases in Canada and the Caribbean from Britain in exchange for naval and military aid, including some destroyers left over from the First World War. A *St Louis Post-Dispatch* headline following the announcement of this deal read: 'Dictator Roosevelt Commits an Act of War'.[12] The second agreement which confirmed Roosevelt's move towards involving America in the European war was the 'lend-lease' legislation, much discussed in early 1941, as Eliot was making final revisions to 'The Dry Salvages' for its first publication. Under this agreement, the United States provided Britain with military equipment and war materials on credit, an arrangement of which many Americans

[10] I. A. Richards, *Selected Letters of I. A. Richards*, ed. J. Constable (Oxford, 1990), 104–5, and see, for Richards's comments on *Four Quartets* and the Kipling essay, 112–13.

[11] For the entire letter, see Winston S. Churchill, *The Second World War*, 6 vols., new, rev., and reset edn. (1949), ii. 201. Churchill's version of the 'Destroyer Deal' and Lend-Lease can be followed in chs. 20 and 28. Roosevelt's position, once the presidential election of that autumn had been won, can be read in his radio broadcast to the nation of 30 Dec. 1940, when he stated that 'If Britain should go down, all of us in all the Americas would be living at the point of a gun, a gun loaded with explosive bullets, economic as well as military. We must produce arms and ships with every energy and resource we can command. . . . *We must be the great arsenal of Democracy*' (cited by Churchill, ibid. 506–7). Not everyone was in sympathy with this view. Ezra Pound wrote to the Japanese poet Katue Kitasono on the same day as Roosevelt's broadcast: 'Anyhow, Happy New Year/ damn Churchill and lets hope that Frankie Roosevelt will lie down now he has a third term to play with', *Ezra Pound and Japan: Letters and Essays*, ed. S. Kodama (Redding Ridge, Conn., 1987), 107.

[12] Charles Callan Tansill, *Back Door to War: The Roosevelt Foreign Policy 1933–1941* (Chicago, 1952), 599.

were suspicious. Four days after John Hayward received the first draft of the poem from Eliot, the *New York Times* for 5 January 1941 quoted Senator Wheeler:

If it is our war, how can we justify lending them stuff and asking them to pay us back? If it is our war, we ought to have the courage to go over and fight it, but it is not our war.[13]

Eliot's letter to Mairet, in which he speaks of a topical allusion, is dated 15 February 1941. Roosevelt signed the Lend-Lease Bill confirming the agreement on 11 March, less than two weeks after 'The Dry Salvages' first appeared in print on 27 February 1941.

Eliot's reticence and concern about the 'wrong twist' of topical allusions in the poem may be understood as an appropriate caution; he did not want his lines to sound polemically for, or equally against, the debated issue of American neutrality; and he recalled the American Civil War because he was also engaged by the divisions in the United States during 1940 over the issue of involvement in the European conflict. It wasn't that he didn't believe in the justness of the war against the Axis powers. On the significance of two characters in Kipling's *They*, he wrote: 'One is the defender of a civilization ... against barbarism; the other represents the essential contact of the civilization with the soil.'[14] That word 'soil' is the final note in 'The Dry Salvages', ending the six lines about which he had expressed anxiety:

> Who are only undefeated
> Because we have gone on trying;
> We, content at last
> If our temporal reversion nourish
> (Not too far from the yew-tree)
> The life of significant soil.   (p. 213)

As a native American who had taken British citizenship, he did not want his poem to adopt sides in a debate which threatened to divide the American people and, at the same time, threatened to isolate the country of his birth from the country of his adoption. *Four Quartets* is a sequence of reconciliation, and, in any such reparative endeavour, although it may be necessary to take sides, it

---

[13] Ibid. 605.
[14] Eliot, 'Rudyard Kipling', *On Poetry and Poets*, 245.

will also be necessary, between those who oppose and those who are opposed, not to forget what is held in common.

Eliot was well aware of the limited force of polemic in poetry, and also of the potential ephemerality—in the life of a poem that endures—even of the most momentous of political events:

People are often inclined to disparage poetry which appears to have no bearing on the situation of today; but they are always inclined to ignore that which appears to bear only on the situation of yesterday. A political association may help to give poetry immediate attention: it is in spite of this association that the poetry will be read, if it is read, to-morrow.[15]

If Eliot exaggerates here, it is because he wants to help his poem survive beyond its immediate time; but this does not mean he was unwilling to incorporate responses to the immediate time into his work. 'The Dry Salvages' invites a belief that

> to apprehend
> The point of intersection of the timeless
> With time, is an occupation for the saint—
> No occupation either, but something given
> And taken . . .   (p. 212)

The lines advance and withdraw their own insight with a characteristic motion of consideration, of brooding through time over what you have said and can say. 'Occupation' is a difficult word to use in 1940, and the desire to withdraw it—'No occupation either'—is understandable; but to seem to deport such a word because of its military meaning would be to undervalue its peaceful senses, and poetry is also one of the arts of peace. Readers of 'The Dry Salvages', though not saints either, need to comprehend the work's relation to its time if hinting or guessing at its intersection with the timeless.

Both the 'destroyer deal' and the lend-lease legislation relied for their effectiveness on the sea lanes between Britain and North America being kept open. The occupation of the Lowlands of Holland in June 1940 allowed the German Navy to launch U-boat attacks from its new bases against the approaches to Britain's western coasts; and from May 1940 to the end of the year, the German Navy sunk 745 ships, 471 of them British, a total of

---

[15] Ibid. 229.

3,239,190 tons.[16] Such peril may have lent to passages of 'The Dry Salvages' their quietly endangered tone. The message of preparation for death at every moment is appropriate for those unaggressively waiting and enduring moments not of 'action or inaction' undergone by seamen in a submarine war:

> Here between the hither and the farther shore
> While time is withdrawn, consider the future
> And the past with an equal mind.
> At the moment which is not of action or inaction
> You can receive this: 'on whatever sphere of being
> The mind of a man may be intent
> At the time of death'—that is the one action
> (And the time of death is every moment)
> Which shall fructify in the lives of others:
> And do not think of the fruit of action.   (pp. 210–11)

Suffering through time and the suffering that time preserves, two kinds of endurance, are contained in the poem's second section:

> the torment of others remains an experience
> Unqualified, unworn by subsequent attrition.
> People change, and smile: but the agony abides.   (p. 209)

Revising these lines, Eliot made 'is an experience' read 'remains an experience' and 'agony remains' read 'agony abides'. Here he is pondering the meanings of *endurance*. Related senses connect the duration of the poem with the suffering of those who are in the services for the war's duration; the poem approaches the 'torment of others' with a non-combatant's reserve. Equally, the lines are not restricted to the contexts of action and attrition in the Second World War, but can include such experiences as a close relation's agony, a husband's or a wife's, the experience of being obliged to stand and wait while another is suffering close by. Eliot's poem affirms that 'the moments of agony'

> are likewise permanent
> With such permanence as time has. We appreciate this better
> In the agony of others, nearly experienced,
> Involving ourselves, than in our own.   (p. 209)

Eliot places 'nearly' in 'the agony of others, nearly experienced' with a care which is at once technical and ethical; 'nearly experi-

---

[16] Figures from Churchill, *Second World War*, ii. 639.

enced' involves us in the agony of others because what the others experienced nearly happened to us too. And this is right, especially for a poem which includes associations with the experience of military action, when, for example, the person standing next to you is killed and you survive, for in war it is luck or accident which will largely determine precisely who suffers and who, outwardly, does not. Also, 'nearly experienced' may mean 'intimately experienced', or 'experienced close to home': to be helplessly at hand is itself an agony. Those who are present at the torment of others do not escape entirely unscathed, though their suffering may seem like nothing in the face of the other's pain.

Eliot's care with words as he thought through the suffering of others also shows in a care with rhythms. The sestina which begins the second section of 'The Dry Salvages' has been criticized for artificiality and awkwardness—especially in its repetitive rhyme-scheme. Davie asked, 'Should we not be justified in seeing here a case of sheer incompetence?'[17] Yet the passage, whose subject is the unending attrition of rote, of habituation, achieves its intimacy with the conditions it describes by grinding out a formal arrangement of words which does indeed get the poet into what Davie calls 'patent difficulties' though these are not 'dishonesties', as he asserts in a parenthesis, but difficulties consciously taken on:

> There is no end, but addition: the trailing
> Consequence of further days and hours,
> While emotion takes to itself the emotionless
> Years of living among the breakage
> Of what was believed in as the most reliable—
> And therefore the fittest for renunciation.   (p. 207)

'There is no end, but addition': in finding difficult end-rhymes for each of the stanza's six lines, for each of the six stanzas, Eliot's phrasing endures the imposed stanza form. Within a poem which

[17] Davie, 'T. S. Eliot: The End of an Era', *The Poet in the Imaginary Museum*, ed. B. Alpert (Manchester, 1977), 34. His discussion continues: 'Is it not plain that the trouvaille at the head of the page, "Dropping their petals and remaining motionless", gets the poet into more and more patent difficulties (and dishonesties) once the rhyme on it has been taken up as a determining feature of the stanza-form? "Emotionless"—how? "Oceanless"—grotesque! "Erosionless"—does he mean "uneroded"? And "Movement . . . pain . . . painless . . . motionless"—our confidence in the poet has by this time been so undermined that we cannot, in justice to ourselves, take this as anything but incantatory gibberish.'

acknowledges that there are long passages of time where others must endure the wastage of routine in the service of larger goals, his sestina respects those actions by representing them through the toils of verse writing.

Eliot considered the composition of regular verse as something which could faithfully undergo the experience of attrition. Of Kipling's technique he wrote: 'Nor is the versification too regular: there is the monotonous beat only when the monotonous is what is required'. Eliot adds, in a footnote: 'Kipling could manage even so difficult a form as the sestina.' His own recent experience of verse writing is informing the passage; he observed of 'Danny Deever':

The regular recurrence of the same end-words ... gives the feeling of marching feet and the movement of men in disciplined formation—in a unity of movement which enhances the horror of the occasion and the sickness which seizes the men as individuals ...[18]

The sestina in 'The Dry Salvages' is verse of this kind, whose rhythmic purpose similarly attends to a state of being ground down that we, as readers, are asked to experience—nearly.

'Now, we come to discover that the moments of agony I ... are likewise permanent I With such permanence as time has.' (p. 209) This, the third quartet, embraces those two senses of the word 'endurance' by embodying the torment and agony of others in its lines, and by preserving that suffering in its own poetic time, in a shape of verse which has survived and will survive, for 'you are the music I While the music lasts.' (p. 213) Eliot means by 'lasts' here both 'the duration of the music' and 'as long as the music is still played'. In the lines which follow, that musical and aesthetic 'intersection of the timeless I With time' reaches towards Christ's exemplary endurance of suffering:

> These are only hints and guesses,
> Hints followed by guesses; and the rest
> Is prayer, observance, discipline, thought and action.
> The hint half guessed, the gift half understood, is Incarnation.   (p. 213)

The words 'discipline' and 'action' are to be felt now in spiritual and military senses here.

Eliot, whose fundamental intention may have been to write a

---

[18] Eliot, 'Rudyard Kipling', *On Poetry and Poets*, 232–3.

poem about his homeland, found that events had made it more difficult, requiring a reticence about the actualities of war which surrounded Britain so as to prevent his poem being opportunistically misunderstood when it appeared. That reticence may seem to some wrong and twisted. 'The Dry Salvages' is oblique. It hints at contexts and experiences it does not address. It bears these difficulties because it wishes to resist appropriating the experience of others, to resist sounding a jingoistic or militaristic note. All the same, it finds a place for the experience of others and the dimension of the war, for to write what would appear private poetry in the early 1940s would have seemed in itself a polemical statement.

'It will be enough if I can help to keep him out of the wrong pigeon-holes',[19] Eliot wrote of Kipling, and that 'wrong twist' which he feared would 'put the rest of the poem out of joint' is, likewise, one of the ready attitudes to these matters which the poem asks readers to survive without. 'The Dry Salvages' is the poem of someone who, as a non-combatant, does not think it his place to make a stand on the sufferings of others; yet the poem is neither discouraged nor uncommitted. As poetry by a Christian, published in wartime, it acknowledges the Christian virtues of selflessness and sacrifice in those who did fight, who felt it their duty to endure a war which they did not wish upon the world, out of which they would make no capital. In that context of actual torments, the poem resists the weaknesses which would be wrong twists of meaning, suffers 'the failing | Pride or resentment at failing powers' (p. 207) and undergoes at one remove 'the agony of others, nearly experienced' (p. 209). Nor does 'The Dry Salvages' draw overmuch attention to its own virtues. This it cannot do if it is to keep faith with the agony others endured, an agony which endures for each reader while the poem lasts.

[19] Ibid. 239.

4

In Another's Words: Hardy's Poetry

In her short memoir, *Some Recollections* (a manuscript completed on 4 January 1911), Emma Lavinia Gifford, Thomas Hardy's first wife, recalled the time of their courtship in the early 1870s: 'We grew much interested in each other and I found him a perfectly new subject of study and delight, and he found a "mine" in me, he said'.[1] Mrs Hardy had attempted to rival her husband as a writer, which may explain the curious air of people taking notes on each other in 'a perfectly new subject of study and delight', an air which runs on beyond the comma to inform the reciprocating 'and he found a "mine" in me', followed by the faintest note of possible recrimination in the halting, comma'd-off 'he said'. Hardy introduced details of their courtship into *A Pair of Blue Eyes* (1873), as Mrs Hardy knew; he adopted phrases and incidents from *Some Recollections* when composing the poems that followed upon her death in the autumn of 1912. To account for the hold another's words can have on the imagination of a writer conceiving and composing poems, I want to examine related qualities in Hardy's work: regular and irregular rhythms and stanza forms; the unforeseen in human experience, and the predestined or fated; then, quoted or spoken words within inverted commas and the stanza forms they fit. James Joyce, referring to the final chapter of *Ulysses* in a letter to Frank Budgen of 28 February 1921, wrote: 'The last word (human, all too human) is left to Penelope. This is the indispensable countersign to Bloom's passport to eternity.'[2] An 'indispensable countersign' in Hardy's 'self-excelling'[3] poems is what I hope to depict.

---

[1] Emma Hardy, *Some Recollections*, ed. E. Hardy and R. Gittings (1961), 58. It is a disappointment to me that the 2nd edn. (1979) has been revised so that the quotation reads, in accord with Hardy's version in *The Later Years of Thomas Hardy*: 'We grew much interested in each other. I found him . . .' (p. 35).

[2] James Joyce, *Selected Letters*, ed. R. Ellmann (1975), 278.

[3] See Donald Davie, *Thomas Hardy and British Poetry* (1973), 41–62.

I

The poet defends his versification in *The Later Years of Thomas Hardy*:

He knew that in architecture cunning irregularity is of enormous worth, and it is obvious that he carried on into his verse, perhaps in part unconsciously, the Gothic art-principle in which he had been trained—the principle of spontaneity, found in mouldings, tracery, and such like—resulting in the 'unforeseen' (as it has been called) character of his metres and stanzas . . .[4]

The phrases 'cunning irregularity' and 'the principle of spontaneity' both indicate an equivocation. Hardy has adopted a quality observed in Gothic architecture as an aesthetic theory. Through this conscious formulating, the 'unforeseen' becomes the precon-ceived. Donald Davie thought that poems by Hardy are, in this sense, regularly irregular. He suggests that 'sometimes this is what offends us in Hardy's poetry—its form mirrors a cruel self-driving, a shape *imposed* on the material, as if it were with gritted teeth'. Or again, 'the heavy-handedness drives any lived experience out of sight beneath the verbal surface'. In contrast to these 'heavy-handed' works, Davie set pieces such as 'After a Journey', poems which have an achieved irregularity that embodies the 'unforeseen':

The 'cunning irregularity', achieved by 'metrical pauses, and reversed beats,' permeates this poem from first to last; it is not to be located in this 'touch' or in that, and accordingly—so far is it from *appliqué* or deftly engineered—we experience it no longer as technical expertise, but as human and as it were manual skill, as 'fingering'.[5]

I come back to those words 'touch' and 'fingering' later.

In the light of Hardy's self-defence, Davie is reinterpreting a Victorian quandary in Hardy's aesthetic, one informing his entire sensibility. Here is the defence again:

stress rather than syllable, poetic texture rather than poetic veneer; the latter kind of thing, under the name of 'constructed ornament', being what

---

[4] F. E. Hardy, *The Later Years of Thomas Hardy* (1930), 78–9.
[5] Four citations from Davie, *Thomas Hardy and British Poetry*, 22–3, 16, 17, 56.

he, in common with every Gothic student, had been taught to avoid like the plague.[6]

Trained in the Gothic Revivalist style of architecture, Hardy was employed to help restore a number of churches. It was through this work that he came to meet his first wife. For Ruskin in 'The Nature of Gothic' the unforeseen irregularities in Gothic stone-carving were proper confessions of human imperfection, rewarded and rewarding in so far as the mason strives honourably but falls short:

And it is, perhaps, the principal admirableness of the Gothic schools of architecture, that they thus receive the results of the labour of inferior minds; and out of fragments full of imperfection, and betraying that imperfection in every touch, indulgently raise up a stately and unaccusable whole.[7]

A Victorian church-restorer, from admiration of this moral aesthetic in imperfections, would replace the gargoyles and tracery in old churches. The Gothic Revival produced a style which did not thus betray 'imperfection in every touch', but successfully imitated imperfection, touched it up. Hardy's defence equivocates between the true 'Nature of Gothic', and self-conscious Gothic Revivalism, the mock-Gothic. Hardy was capable of the 'filling-in' that the mock-Gothic requires when writing poems:

Among his papers were quantities of notes on rhythm and metre: with outlines and experiments in innumerable original measures, some of which he adopted from time to time. These verse skeletons were mostly blank, and only designated by the usual marks for long and short syllables . . .[8]

Over and above Hardy's words about the mock-Gothic (his writing of '*cunning* irregularity', and not of 'spontaneity' but 'the principle of spontaneity') there is the evidence of his biography itself. Although written in the third person and published under the name of his second wife, Florence Emily Hardy, it was composed almost entirely by Hardy himself: 'He knew that in architecture cunning irregularity is of enormous worth, and it is obvious that he carried on into his verse, perhaps in part unconsciously, the gothic art-

---

[6] F. E. Hardy, *The Later Years*, 79.

[7] John Ruskin, *Works*, library edn., 39 vols., ed. E. T. Cook and A. Wedderburn (1903–12), x. 190.

[8] F. E. Hardy, *The Later Years*, 79–80.

principle in which he had been trained.' Protesting too much, the passage betrays a touch of the bad poet T. S. Eliot describes in 'Tradition and the Individual Talent', being 'unconscious where he ought to be conscious, and conscious where he ought to be unconscious'.[9] The 'it is obvious' displays an author's all-too-wounded tone of scornful self-justification, where a partisan biographer need only be reasonably certain, and the 'perhaps in part unconsciously' strikes a falsely speculative note. A poet can distinguish principles of style from accidentally or subliminally arrived-at felicities. Hardy's secret composition of his own biography exemplifies resistance to the unforeseen—what shape, for example, someone else might find in his life. He cunningly imposes the form he prefers.

II

The preformed, the cunningly irregular, in contrast to the unforeseen, the spontaneous, also indicate a quandary in Hardy's feelings about how human experience is ordered. As the 'ghost' writer of his own biography, the cunning artificer of irregularities, and the constructor of fiercely complex, regular stanzas, Hardy was an all-too-self-conscious writer. Self-consciousness was sustained by two of his character traits. He betrayed a physical reserve, a shrinking away from touch, and he tended to be wrapped up in himself. As a boy, Hardy 'tried also to avoid being touched by his playmates . . . This peculiarity never left him, and to the end of his life he disliked even the most friendly hand being laid on his arm or his shoulder'.[10] 'A Thunderstorm in Town', subtitled 'A Reminiscence: 1893', relates an incident in one of Hardy's platonic associations with literary ladies. They are waiting 'snug and warm' in a hansom cab:

> Then the downpour ceased, to my sharp sad pain,
> And the glass that had screened our forms before
> Flew up, and out she sprang to her door:
> I should have kissed her if the rain
> Had lasted a minute more.[11]   (p. 313)

[9] T. S. Eliot, *The Sacred Wood* (1920), 58.
[10] F. E. Hardy, *The Early Life of Thomas Hardy* (1928), 32.
[11] My citations of Hardy's poetry are taken from *The Variorum Edition of the Collected Poems*, ed. J. Gibson (1979), to which the page nos. in parentheses refer.

The poem's incident dates from the decade in which the Hardys' marriage was at a low ebb; in a notebook from the 1890s Hardy wrote 'Love lives on propinquity, but dies of contact.'[12] A physical reserve stiffens the poems that Davie dislikes, the poems he calls 'heavy-handed', though he also describes them too as machine-made—untouched by human hand.

Hardy tended to be self-absorbed as well as physically self-conscious. He could be aware of a proneness to letting his self-communing become a consuming self-interest that endangered himself and others. Concluding a piece of correspondence with Edmund Gosse on the latter's review of *Jude the Obscure*, Hardy exclaims: 'What a self-occupied letter!'[13] Davie draws attention to Hardy's rigid insistence of technique; he doesn't see this insistence as the over-insistence that 'Overlooking the River Stour' acknowledges:

> And never I turned my head, alack,
>   While these things met my gaze
>   Through the pane's drop-drenched glaze,
> To see the more behind my back . . .
> O never I turned, but let, alack,
>   These less things hold my gaze!   (p. 482)

Tom Paulin affirms that the poem is a self-conscious criticism of the poet's own self-communing with these 'less things'. He writes, 'The poem is set during what he [Hardy] termed "the Sturminster Newton idyll"—the early years of his marriage—and is another backward look at lost happiness.'[14] 'Missed' instead of 'lost' happiness might have been closer to the poem's import. The 'more behind my back' is Emma, and the 'Overlooking' of the title is ambiguous in a deliberately self-critical manner: in looking over the river he 'overlooks' his wife. Hardy appears, not as he says he would have himself remembered in 'Afterwards' as 'a man who used to notice such things' (p. 553), but as one who 'missed' (overlooked), or 'missed' (felt the lack of) such things.

'The Self-Unseeing' reinforces this sense of lack. It faces the

---

[12] Cited in Carl J. Weber, *'Dearest Emmie'* (1963), 25, and see F. E. Hardy, *The Early Life*, 288.

[13] Thomas Hardy, *The Collected Letters*, 7 vols., ed. R. L. Purdy and M. Millgate (Oxford, 1978–87), ii. 89.

[14] Tom Paulin, *Thomas Hardy: The Poetry of Perception* (1975), 170.

technical problem of presenting the insensibility of the moment recalled, and expressing—retrospectively—qualities not then noticed:

> She sat here in her chair,
> Smiling into the fire;
> He who played stood there,
> Bowing it higher and higher.
>
> Childlike, I danced in a dream;
> Blessings emblazoned that day;
> Everything glowed with a gleam;
> Yet we were looking away!   (pp. 166–7)

In its regular rhythms the final stanza embodies the insensible pleasure, the happiness unperceived: four lines with full alternated rhymes, seven syllables in each line. It is possible to scan all four with the same pattern, but this would be to maul the final line where both 'Yet', because of the regular expectation, and 'we', because of the sentence's intonational tune, should be stressed. This unostentatious irregularity spots what had gone unnoticed, makes sensible what had been lullingly, unseeingly blessed. Another poem, 'Self-Unconscious', shows the participant self-consumed in 'specious plans that came to his call'. He is too wrapped up in himself to recognize the 'immortal' meaning of the scene:

> O it would have been good
> Could he then have stood
> At a clear-eyed distance, and conned the whole ... (p. 332)

The retrospective awareness is now 'mere derision', is itself a taunt. 'Self-Unconscious' testifies to the importance in Hardy's poetry, and his life, of unforeseen occurrences that prove to be the occasions of what is best, and by the same token, worst, in life, but which also—in being unforeseen—have an irregularity that draws attention to them, pressing on the experiences a consciousness of fortune, good or bad. To see the unforeseen might, then, be one further benefit of human imperfection.

III

Two momentously unforeseen occurrences in Hardy's life were his
meeting with Emma Gifford on 7 March 1870 and her death on
27 November 1912.[15] At least three poems concern themselves
with Hardy's journey to St Juliot Vicarage, Cornwall, which ended
in their first encounter. The second stanza of 'When I Set Out for
Lyonnesse' emphasizes the event's accidentality in a form whose
refrain-like repetitions have an echoing predictability:

> What would bechance at Lyonnesse
>   While I should sojourn there
>   No prophet durst declare,
>   Nor did the wisest wizard guess
> What would bechance at Lyonnesse
>   While I should sojourn there.   (p. 312)

The poem is eloquent in not saying what did bechance, and though
prophet and wizard cannot say, the stanza retrospectively incorporates a formal inevitability in the unexpected meeting. A second
poem, 'The Wind's Prophecy', is more complex:

> I travel on by barren farms,
> And gulls glint out like silver flecks
> Against a cloud that speaks of wrecks,
> And bellies down with black alarms.
> I say: 'Thus from my lady's arms
> I go; those arms I love the best!'
> The wind replies from dip to rise,
> 'Nay; towards her arms thou journeyest.'   (p. 494)

The prophetic machinery[16] in 'The Wind's Prophecy' contradicts
the import of 'no prophet durst declare' in 'When I Set Out for
Lyonnesse'. None the less, it does include the 'unexpected' in the
journey by challenging the poet's words with the wind's. The poet
is rebuked by his circumstances, but does not hear the rebuke.
Internal evidence for this is that the repetition of the wind's
response, which crescendos through stanza after stanza, is never
responded to by the self-communing poet, once again a self

---

[15] See Michael Millgate, *Thomas Hardy: A Biography* (Oxford, 1982, corr. repr.
1987), 121–2, 485.
[16] See Yvor Winters, *Forms of Discovery* (Chicago, 1967), 191.

unconscious. He does not hear or understand the wind's message because the wind conveys its prophecy in a voice which dramatically qualifies, to the point of obfuscating, its intent. The wind 'outshrieks'; it 'laughs'; the sky is 'hoarse': but the wind's prophecy which it strains its vocal chords to convey is, in part, affirmative. This is another unexpectedness in the poem. However, its stanza form with the refrain-like repetitions, and the internal rhyme on every fourth and every eighth syllable of every penultimate line enforce a sense, not of unexpectednesses but of absorbed, insistent self-delusion and of inevitability.

Hardy's technical pre-casting, his wilfully complex patterns, answer to his notion of the fated or predestined, what has been called his amateur philosophy. Hardy may be defended, and exonerated, by invoking words in Emma's manuscript which appear just prior to her account of their meeting:

At this date [1911] it seems as if all had been arranged in orderly sequence for me, link after link occurring in a chain of movements to bring me to the point where my own fortunes came on.

She had kept herself 'free until the one intended for me arrived'.[17] *Some Recollections* makes it clear that, despite the souring of their marriage in the 1890s, Emma Hardy continued to believe her conjugal life had been predestined, a belief formed from Christian faith and superstition, perhaps spiritualism even. 'A Man was Drawing Near to Me' accommodates into the female voice of the piece Emma's faith in the pre-ordained character of the poet's own journey to St Juliot Vicarage:

> There was a rumble at the door,
> A draught disturbed the drapery,
> And but a minute passed before,
>   With gaze that bore
>   My destiny,
> The man revealed himself to me.   (p. 580)

There is an unexpected degree of congruence between Hardy's fatalism and his wife's sense of her destiny—the difference being that while hers is lit by a curious glow of Christian romance, his is the expression of a melancholy atheism which comforts itself by regarding as spitefully inevitable events which may merely have

---

[17] Two citations from Emma Hardy, *Some Recollections*, 46, 50.

happened. Oddly similar too are the destiny represented by Hardy's looming larger, his inexorable approach to the Vicarage through stanza after stanza in 'A Man was Drawing near to Me', and the collision course of the iceberg and the *Titanic* in 'The Convergence of the Twain'. Not only is the iceberg called 'a sinister mate | For her', but its collision with the ship is described as though a wedding night:

> Till the Spinner of the Years
> Said 'Now!' And each one hears,
> And consummation comes, and jars two hemispheres.   (p. 307)

It would be a wild distortion to read the poem as a self-rebuke, on Hardy's part, for 'coldness'; but the writer's temperamental habits appear in the above descriptions and that of the *Titanic* on the sea-bed: 'stilly couches she'. Ever present is the possibility, in Hardy's sense of human experience rendered in poems, that what might have been 'unforeseen', and refreshingly so, becomes a poetically self-fulfilling prophecy.

IV

In 'The Wind's Prophecy' words between inverted commas spoken by the elements introduced the unforeseen. In Hardy's poems natural phenomena often utter advice, or criticize the poet: 'The Voice from the Thorn', 'The Wind Blew Words', 'The Voice of Things' are examples. To examine technical relations between a stanza form and quoted speech the ideal example is not a poem where nature talks, but one where a ghost speaks to the poet. 'Lausanne in Gibbon's Old Garden: 11–12 p.m.' is a homage to the author of *The Decline and Fall of the Roman Empire*, on the 110th anniversary of its completion at the same hour and place. *The Later Years of Thomas Hardy* relates the poem's occasion, with a collocation of place, time, another's words, and a writer's ghostly presence similar to that which the poet sought after his wife's death. Hardy

sat out there till midnight on June 27, and imagined the historian closing his last page on the spot, as described in his *Autobiography*: 'It was on the day, or rather the night, of the 27th of June 1787, between the hours of eleven and twelve, that I wrote the last line of the last page, in a summer house in my garden. After laying down my pen I took several turns in a *berceau,* or covered walk of acacias, which commands a prospect of the country, the lake and the mountains.'

Then the ghosted biography continues with another piece of obfuscatory speculation:

It is uncertain whether Hardy chose that particular evening for sitting out in the garden because he knew that June 27th was Gibbon's date of conclusion, or whether the coincidence of the dates was accidental.[18]

Hardy wrote to his wife, Emma, on 23 May 1892, at 9 p.m.—'We buried Osgood this afternoon. When we were in the cemetery chapel & the officiating minister was reading the words "O death, where is thy sting," &c. I looked at my watch, & it was exactly half past 4.'[19] It seems unlikely that Hardy would sit in Gibbon's garden for one hour exactly on the 110th anniversary by accident.

'Lausanne in Gibbon's Old Garden: 11–12 p.m.', despite its quoted words, is a poem with little of the unforeseen in it:

> A spirit seems to pass,
>   Formal in pose, but grave withal and grand:
>   He contemplates a volume in his hand,
> And far lamps fleck him through the thin acacias.
>
>   Anon the book is closed,
>   With 'It is finished!' And at the alley's end
>   He turns, and when on me his glances bend
> As from the Past comes speech—small, muted, yet composed.

>   (pp. 105–6)

The 'seems' in the first line alludes to a consciousness other than Gibbon's 'spirit'. This spirit is placed in the third person with 'He contemplates'—and thus the orientation of a lyric to first-person experience is implied. It is the object-pronoun in line 7: 'when on me his glances bend'. In 'Self-Unconscious' and 'The Self-Unseeing' this orientation to first-person experience could be limiting; self-communing cut the poet off from greater things that were present but not noticed. Hardy's attention to the punctuation and composition of his own voice can release him from such self-maiming absorption. In 'Lausanne . . . ', Hardy describes Gibbon's voice as 'small, muted, yet composed.' These commas produce a checked,

[18] F. E. Hardy, *The Later Years,* 68.
[19] Thomas Hardy, *Letters,* i. 269.

quietened tone and are a less consummate attempt at what Hardy
was to achieve in the concluding lines of ' "My Spirit will not
Haunt the Mound" '. The poem is again spoken by a woman who,
after describing how her spirit will travel to its favourite haunts,
carefully explains:

> And there you'll find me, if a jot
>   You still should care
> For me, and for my curious air;
> If otherwise, then I shall not,
>   For you, be there.   (p. 319)

Paulin notes: 'These pauses give the sense of an exact definition
being arrived at and their tone introduces a subtle, strange beauty,
for this is again a ghostly poem in both its content and sound.'[20]
The composition of his own voice as the speech of another conjures
a presence from the air; it incorporates an existence beyond his
own.

This apparently capacious, acknowledging activity can, however,
be put to diverse uses; for though such poetic behaviour is invoked
in the description of Gibbon's 'small, muted, yet composed' voice,
it is not true of the speech Gibbon makes:

> 'How fares the Truth now?—Ill?
> —Do pens but slily further her advance?
> May one not speed her but in phrase askance?
> Do scribes aver the Comic to be Reverend still?
>
> 'Still rule those minds on earth
> At whom sage Milton's wormwood words were hurled:
> *"Truth like a bastard comes into the world*
> *Never without ill-fame to him who gives her birth"*?'   (p. 106)

Paulin's description of another poem, 'A Broken Appointment',
catches the manner of these second two stanzas in speech marks:
'This is one of the few instances of Hardy's use of the grand style,
a style whose plangent sonorities are oddly combined with a
Donne-like intricacy where an essentially spoken sentence twists
over the stanzaic pattern'.[21] Plangent sonorities are oddly combined
in 'Lausanne . . .', but with an insistent questioning. How are the
final, italicized lines of the poem to be spoken? Should they be said

---

[20] Paulin, *Poetry of Perception*, 84.
[21] Ibid. 76–7.

as hurled 'wormwood words'—the statement within double quotation marks? Or as a small, muted, yet composed question—
framed with a question mark outside the double quotes, but inside
the single ones of Gibbon's speech? This quandary implies an
insecurity in the poem beneath its sonorous surface. When Hardy
ventriloquizes the voice of Gibbon, the speech that comes forth is
from 'the Past', but its source is not Milton so much as Sidney,
recalling the sestet of 'With how sad steps, ô Moone . . .' from
Astrophel and Stella:

> Then ev'n of fellowship, ô Moone, tell me
> Is constant *Love* deem'd there but want of wit?
> Are Beauties there as proud as here they be?
> Do they above love to be lov'd, and yet
> Those Lovers scorne whom that *Love* doth possesse?
> Do they call *Vertue* there ungratefulnesse?[22]

The repeated questions, the adoption of capitalized abstractions,
the use twice of the question form beginning 'do'—Hardy's lines
imitate these characteristics of Sidney's. The opening of Sidney's
poem 'With how sad steps . . . I How silently, and with how wanne
a face' touches Hardy's 'How fares the Truth now?—'. But why
does Hardy do this? There is animus behind the poem, an impetus
beyond the occasioned homage to Gibbon. J. O. Bailey points to
this poem's relation with the hostile critical reception of *Jude the
Obscure*:

Hardy's message is related to his feeling of need for courage as he wrote
Jude the Obscure and his sense of outrage when this attack upon pruderies
and social conventions was libeled as 'Jude the Obscene'. Gibbon and
Milton were in his mind as he wrote *Jude*.[23]

Sidney's poem is apt for Jude's tangled and taunted relations with
Sue, as is Milton's *The Doctrine and Discipline of Divorce* (from
which the quotation derives) for his relations with Arabella.
Moreover, the last word of Sidney's poem, 'ungratefulnesse', is the
poem's unheard complaint against the hostile reviewers, and his
upset public. In *The Older Hardy*, Robert Gittings dissuades his
readers from believing the 'persistent' 'legend' that 'Emma made a

---

[22] Sir Philip Sidney, *The Poems*, ed. W. A. Ringler (Oxford, 1962), 180.
[23] J. O. Bailey, *The Poetry of Thomas Hardy: A Handbook and Commentary*
(Chapel Hill, NC, 1970), 134. See also Millgate, *Biography*, 367.

special journey to Dr Richard Garnett, keeper of printed books at the British Museum, and asked him to suppress *Jude*, proposing herself to burn the manuscript'. The story, we are told, was started by 'the young Garnetts' and doubted, but spread by Ford Madox Ford. Gittings does, however, confirm that the novel caused 'a serious break' between Hardy and his wife; he cites the testimony of Gordon Gifford, Emma's nephew, living in their house at the time:

my aunt, who was a very ardent Churchwoman and believer in the virtues and qualities of women in general, strongly objected to the book, and, I think, to the outlook of some of the characters depicted therein. I should, however, mention that this was the first of the Hardy novels in which she had not assisted by her counsel, copious notes for reference, and mutual discussion.[24]

The interruption of another voice in 'Lausanne . . . ' doesn't criticize the self-absorbed poet but rebukes some of his readers, his reviewers, friends, and even his wife. The poem is not the chastening recognition of another, equally important, view; it is a consciously allusive self-justification.

Gibbon's voice is described as 'small, muted, yet composed'. 'Composed' is, of course, a pun; in the context it can mean both 'made calm or tranquil; properly adjusted, undisturbed by emotion; expressive of gravity or self-possession' (*OED*), senses relating to a person, and 'elaborately or well put together' (*OED*), referring to literary compositions. But if Gibbon's ventriloquized voice is composed because the writer has self-possession, it is also adjusted by Hardy to fit his stanza form. Recalling the character of the rigidly pre-cast, and the orientation of the lyric towards first-person experience, I feel the composition of the voice to fit the stanza is not a 'proper adjustment', but an elaborately elocuted insistence on the part of the poet that the novelist was justified in his stance against what Bailey called 'pruderies and social conventions'. Gibbon's 'self-possession' becomes a possession of Hardy's. Distortions required to make the words of an external authority fit the imposed stanza form appear among 'sage Milton's wormwood words'; for unlike the accurate quotation of the source both in the

---

[24] Robert Gittings, *The Older Hardy* (1978), 81. Millgate gives qualified confirmation to the anecdote, *Biography*, 320–1.

poem's manuscript and in *The Later Years of Thomas Hardy*, the poem does not adopt exactly Milton's words:

Truth is impossible to be soiled by an outward touch as is the sunbeam; though this ill-hap wait on her nativity, that she never comes into the world, but like a bastard, to the ignominy of him that brought her forth.[25]

Milton's 'brought her forth' sustains the image of sexual roles in the extramarital metaphor better than does Hardy's 'gives her birth'—required for the full rhyme with 'earth'. Hardy is putting words into the mouths of Gibbon and Milton, but he does remain faithful to the spirit of the original.

He was, however, capable of self-absorbed misquotation—as a cunning revision of Emma's words evidences. He edited the whole manuscript after his wife's death, and adapted a small portion of it as Chapter 5 of his ghosted biography. At the head of the chapter the author notes: '[the words in square brackets are added to make the allusions intelligible]', and throughout the printed text hiatuses are marked with rows of dots. But a comparison of the full text of *Some Recollections* with the biography shows that in the passage which introduces their first, unforeseen meeting, Hardy silently revised 'My life's romance now began'[26] into 'My life now began',[27] a change which enlarges manyfold the centrality of Hardy in Emma's narrative, and to the detriment of her first thirty years—the years upon which the manuscript largely dwells.

V

Emma's writing lends the colouring and authority of its words to some of Hardy's finest poems. The reading and imagination in his best work is of another order to that evidenced in Hardy's self-flattering revision of his wife's manuscript—and of another order to the only-too-cunning collocation of voices and external authorities in 'Lausanne . . .'. Davie's concept of Hardy the 'self-excelling' is crucial, but the continuities between his routine poems and his excellent ones are finely described by William Empson, who is attempting to catch what irritates him about the poet:

[25] Cited in F. E. Hardy, *The Later Years*, 69.
[26] Emma Hardy, *Some Recollections*, 50.
[27] F. E. Hardy, *The Early Life*, 90.

Probably it is the complacence of the man, which saw no need to try to reconcile the contradictions; the same complacence which could be satisfied with a clumsy piece of padding to make a lyric out of a twaddling reflection. No doubt he needed this quality to win through as he did. Most people who are admired for 'unpretentious integrity' have it.[28]

The largeness with which Empson turns from 'clumsy' and 'twaddling' to 'this quality' revises a mere weakness into a necessary condition of endurance and achievement. The final sentence implies that the tendency to praise Hardy for his honesty is as much a half-truth as the criticism of his unsophisticated style. Both these mischaracterized features contribute to a lifetime's effort. Among the 'Poems of 1912–13', recognized high points in the entire works, are some which adopt a rigidly insistent stanza form and a quoted criticism, as strategies of obligatory self-rebuke.

In 'Hardy's Virgilian Purples', Davie calls the sequence 'a long and climbing curve of spiritual apprehensions'.[29] The opening poems should then form a low point, and in a sense they do. 'The Going' and 'Your Last Drive' adapt the stylistic emphases that serve Hardy for a self-unseeing, a being wrapped up in himself, to bring home the irreparable fact of his wife's death, of irremediably missed opportunities in their last years together. 'The Going' concludes:

> Why, then, latterly did we not speak,
> Did we not think of those days long dead,
> And ere your vanishing strive to seek
> That time's renewal? We might have said,
>   'In this bright spring weather
>   We'll visit together
> Those places that once we visited.'
>
>   Well, well! All's past amend,
>   Unchangeable. It must go.
> I seem but a dead man held on end
> To sink down soon . . . O you could not know
>   That such swift fleeing
>   No soul foreseeing—
> Not even I—would undo me so!   (p. 339)

---

[28] William Empson, 'Selected Poems of Thomas Hardy', *Argufying: Essays on Literature and Culture*, ed. J. Haffenden (1987), 421.

[29] Donald Davie, *The Poet in the Imaginary Museum*, ed. B. Alpert (Manchester, 1977), 231.

Paulin declares that the poem has 'that cunning, Gothic irregularity, that spoken authenticity, which frees all of his best poems from the tyranny of a machine-made metrical regularity.'[30] The 'machine-made' analogy derives from Davie, who writes:

the hidden form of its unfolding, that form is (I think) not merely hidden and decently cloaked but positively *impeded* by the overt form with its intricate symmetries. Accordingly, though with the greatest hesitation, I find the imperious verbal engineer still, even here, thwarting the truly suffering poet.[31]

Though Davie's word '*impeded*' is apt (recalling 'Therefore if any man can show cause or just impediment why these persons should not be joined together in holy matrimony'), he misses the possibility that to be 'true' here, the 'truly suffering poet' ought to, and must, 'impede' his poem. Davie does not hesitate before the thought that the poet must thwart himself.

The element of cunning—that 'principle of spontaneity'—was what characterized Hardy as a mock-Gothic poet. Paulin recognizes the sense of irreparable finality in the poem, but, in defending it against Davie's criticism, does not relate that finality to the insisted-on irregularity of 'The Going'. Its two alternated seven-line stanza forms are characteristically complex, pre-cast forms whose insistent shape performs the poem's sense of a death's inexorability, the now unchangeable, while the pauses of the composed speaking voice (as Paulin observes) give the verse line its irregular stresses, played off against the form—a contrast which models the equally necessary 'unforeseen' in her death, about which the poem's penultimate line speaks. Of its concluding lines Paulin notes: 'This spontaneous, surprising declaration sounds like a rebuke. It is almost as though she has died to spite him or test his love and has succeeded only too well.'[32] The truth of this should be tempered by a qualifying rebuke in the poem, a self-rebuke partly there in the quoted words about what 'We might have said' and done. It is also there in the strict pre-casting of the form, which serves to dramatize Hardy's not noticing things. The last lines, 'such swift fleeing . . . would undo me so', are a curious rebuke to his wife, since, as it says, she could not know what her

[30] Paulin, *Poetry of Perception*, 90.
[31] Davie, *Thomas Hardy and British Poetry*, 59.
[32] Paulin, *Poetry of Perception*, 90.

death would do to him; and, read in the light of the poem's foreseeable rhymes, the 'no soul foreseeing— | Not even I' has a self-inflicting turn, just as the 'O you could not know' is an unnecessary, but by that token imaginatively needful, exoneration of his wife.

The second poem in the sequence, 'Your Last Drive', is an exacerbated 'self-unseeing' poem which mixes muted criticism of his wife, rebounding into self-criticism, in turn struggling with an attempted exculpation. The first two stanzas describe how she was herself unconscious of her approaching death, not seeing each sight on her drive as a 'last-time' view:

> Beholding it with a heedless eye
> As alien from you, though under its tree
> You soon would halt everlastingly.   (p. 339)

Hardy muted the poem's trace of criticism in revision; for the original 'cursory' eye, he substituted 'heedless', a word which, despite some suggestion that his wife was inattentive or careless, need not have the denigratory senses of skimping or taking short cuts present in 'cursory'. The three following stanzas of the poem, which include seven lines within quotation marks, turn the criticism of being 'unseeing' on to the poet. These lines begin with a further self-criticism. Hardy is 'unseeing' both in not noticing her approaching death, and in not accompanying her on her last drive. It is a vindictive self-torment since the poem also states that even had he accompanied her he would not have foreseen her death:

> I drove not with you . . . Yet had I sat
> At your side that eve I should not have seen
> That the countenance I was glancing at
> Had a last-time look in the flickering sheen,
> Nor have read the writing upon your face,
> 'I go hence soon to my resting-place;
>
> 'You may miss me then. But I shall not know
> How many times you visit me there,
> Or what your thoughts are, or if you go
> There never at all. And I shall not care.
> Should you censure me I shall take no heed,
> And even your praises no more shall need.'

True: never you'll know. And you will not mind.
But shall I then slight you because of such?
Dear ghost, in the past did you ever find
The thought 'What profit,' move me much?
Yet abides the fact, indeed, the same,—
You are past love, praise, indifference, blame.   (pp. 339–40)

Hardy's achievement in 'The Haunter', 'The Voice', and 'After a Journey', poems from the middle of the sequence, depends on a contrast with the elaborate rebuke in the quoted words 'written' on his wife's face, which, though unforeseen, are none the less absorbed like Gibbon's composed voice into the insistently regular stanza: a stanza formed not to justify the poet but to criticize him, and whose regularity is what makes the final line's irreparability so aching.

VI

Paulin describes the sequence as a progress 'towards [Hardy's and Emma's] "true dialogue"'.[33] Despite there being not only 'The Voice' which refers to the 'woman calling', but also three dramatic lyrics spoken by the 'Dear ghost', no colloquy occurs between the couple divided in death. The composed voices, external authorities Hardy needed to adopt, prove self-fulfilling prophecies of a justifying or criticizing kind, thwarting the truly unforeseen. Quoted voices will not serve to embody a reciprocity of words for Hardy, though they may occasion the need for such a reciprocity. Thus, the necessary paradox of 'Poems 1912–13': the poet and his dead wife, though they affirm each other by speaking, never speak to each other.

The first line of 'After a Journey' in manuscript and in the first three printings reads, 'Hereto I come to interview a ghost', finally becoming 'Hereto I come to view a voiceless ghost'. Hardy's reason for adopting the odd word 'interview' may derive from his reading of Virgil, to which Davie draws attention as in fact does Hardy in the sequence's epigraph, *Veteris vestigia flammae*. The word 'interview' is used by John Dryden in his translation of the meeting of Dido and Aeneas in the Underworld:

---

[33] Ibid.

["]Stay, stay your steps, and listen to my vows!
'Tis the last interview that Fate allows!"
In vain he thus attempts her mind to move
With tears and prayers, and late repenting love.
Disdainfully she looked; then turning round,
She fixed her eyes unmoved upon the ground;
And, what he says and swears, regards no more
Than the deaf rocks, when the loud billows roar . . .[34]

Hardy's is also an occasion of 'late repenting love'. Dido's silence speaks volumes here, and the passage shares with Hardy's 'After a Journey' waves attempting to make themselves felt: 'the unseen waters' ejaculations'. The superiority of the revised reading, 'view' for 'interview', resides in its removal of the apparently futile effort of interviewing a presence which may not have a voice—any possible trace of a radical etymology in *inter-view* (see and be seen) is banished by the contemporary sense present at the time of composition.[35] Revised, the line also echoes a phrase to be found three poems earlier in the sequence, 'The Voice': 'Can it be you that I hear? Let me view you then'. The improved opening line of 'After a Journey' reverses the emphasis of the earlier poem, contradicting its title with 'voiceless ghost'.

That 'The Voice' and 'The Haunter' are companion pieces has been noted by Yvor Winters, though both he and Davie, who alludes to Winters's discussion of the poems, feel the need to prefer one piece over the other. Whatever their relative merits, the two poems are necessarily sequential; they affirm each other by their different, juxtaposed voices. Here is the third stanza of 'The Haunter':

> Yes, I companion him to places
>   Only dreamers know,
> Where the shy hares print long paces,
>   Where the night rooks go;

---

[34] J. Dryden (trans.), *The Aeneid of Virgil*, ed. R. Fitzgerald (New York, 1965), 6. 11. 629–36, p. 195.

[35] *OED* indicates that in the 1870s and 1880s the verb 'to interview' meaning 'To have an interview with (a person); *spec.* on the part of a representative of the press: To talk with so as to elicit statements or facts for publication' was an American sense crossing the Atlantic and being resisted; hence *Daily News*, 13 Nov. 1880, 'The American custom of "interviewing" people of notoriety and of "drawing" them for opinions on all topics.' The meaning 'to catch a glimpse of, get a view of; to glance at, view' is last cited in 1624.

> Into old aisles where the past is all to him,
>   Close as his shade can do,
> Always lacking the power to call to him,
>   Near as I reach thereto!   (pp. 345–6)

If this is a voice from beyond the grave, it and its subject, the poet, remain separated by death; and they remain separated in this poem by the use of a third-person addressee: 'call to him', 'all to him'. It is only because 'The Haunter' introduces this rhyme and rhythm that the next poem in the sequence, 'The Voice', may open with an affirmative note so strong as almost to efface the bad faith of the poet, his partial deafness:

> Woman much missed, how you call to me, call to me,
> Saying that now you are not as you were
> When you had changed from the one who was all to me,
> But as at first, when our day was fair.   (p. 346)

'The Voice' may tacitly allude to the manuscript of *Some Recollections*, whose narrative restored to him the young Emma Gifford when he discovered and read it after her death. The poem's belief in ghosts is immediately questioned in the words 'Can it be you that I hear? Let me view you then', and it is not until 'After a Journey' that the anticipated 'spiritual apprehension', in Davie's phrase, occurs. As has often been remarked, 'The Voice' concludes with an unforeseen variation which embodies both the doubtful hesitation of the poet, in the stumbling short line, and also the unexpected affirmation of the voice's presence, an affirmation that is made by the poem and not the poet, whose doubts, while issuing him into the presence of the unforeseen, do not yet allow him to see and surely hear it. Even at this much-prized moment in the sequence, there is no dialogue:

> Or is it only the breeze, in its listlessness
> Travelling across the wet mead to me here,
> You being ever dissolved to wan wistlessness,
> Heard no more again far or near?
>   Thus I; faltering forward,
>   Leaves around me falling,
> Wind oozing thin through the thorn from norward,
>   And the woman calling.   (p. 346)

'The Haunter' prefigures the spiritual apprehensions of 'After a Journey' while it criticizes the poet for not revisiting with his wife the old haunts of their courtship when she was alive. Acknowledgements of each by each can be heard in an echo of the first stanza of 'The Haunter':

> How shall I let him know
> That whither his fancy sets him wandering
> I, too, alertly go?—   (p. 345)

'After a Journey' begins, 'Hereto I come to view a voiceless ghost, I Whither, O whither will its whim now draw me?' (p. 349) Even though the ghost is 'voiceless', her words appear to have reached the poet-protagonist, and whereas she was following his 'fancy', he, in turn, is now drawn by her 'whim'.

Hardy, on the evidence of revisions to 'The Haunter', wanted to strengthen this correspondence, recasting the last four lines to prefigure the end of 'After a Journey'. As first conceived, 'The Haunter' concluded:

> And if it be that at night I am stronger,
> Little harm day can do;
> Please, then, keep him in gloom no longer,
> Even ghosts tend thereto!

Hardy revised it to read:

> Tell him a faithful one is doing
> All that love can do
> Still that his path may be worth pursuing,
> And to bring peace thereto.

While neither of these entirely satisfies, Hardy prepares the reader for the celebrated final affirmation in 'After a Journey':

> Trust me, I mind not, though Life lours,
> The bringing me here; nay, bring me here again!
> I am just the same as when
> Our days were a joy and our paths through flowers.   (p. 349)

These echoes of one poem by another, these harmonies of rhythm and diction, embody the influence of the incorporeal on the living through the agency of one text's influence upon another; the authority for this strategy and the justice of it appear in the conclusion to *Some Recollections*. As from Gibbon's *Autobiography* and Sidney's sonnet in Hardy's 'Lausanne . . .', the message that the dead have for the living speaks (though with the absence of any direct speech here) from the 'small, muted, yet composed' sound of another's text informing the concluding lines to 'The Haunter' and 'After a Journey'. Emma's manuscript ends with the words, 'A strange unearthly brilliance shines around our path, penetrating and dispersing difficulties with its warmth and glow.'[36]

VII

I come back to 'touch' and 'fingering'. Davie described the rhythms of 'After a Journey' as 'not to be located in this "touch" or in that . . . we experience it as . . . manual skill, as "fingering"'.[37] Hardy's self-consciousnesses as a man and a poet contributed to his writing, in a notebook from the 1890s, 'Love lives on propinquity, but dies of contact.' The occasion of 'Poems 1912–13' promises a love making contact through irreducible propinquity. We hear of such near distance in 'The Haunter', where the woman says '[I] hover and hover a few feet from him | Just as I used to do'; or in 'After a Journey':

> Where you will next be there's no knowing,
>> Facing round about me everywhere,
>>> With your nut-coloured hair,
> And grey eyes, and rose-flush coming and going. (p. 349)

Though the man and wife are separated by death, each is affirmed by the other's speaking *of*, though not quite *to*, the other. The great poems of this sequence overcome the obstacle of Hardy's self-restricting epigram. This is achieved through the invigorating aptness, both technical and thematic, of the rhythms. Davie has noted of 'After a Journey', 'And yet there is a general reluctance to locate the convincingness of this poem in the aspect of it where, surely, the conviction is most carried—that is to say, in the meter.'[38] He does not spell out what the poem's convictions are, or how the rhythm which he perfectly senses confers this convincingness. It is the presence of his dead wife that the poem affirms, and yet that presence is a 'hovering' one. In 'After a Journey' her presence is 'spontaneous', 'unforeseen', 'irregular'; these same

[36] Emma Hardy, *Some Recollections*, 61.
[37] Davie, *Thomas Hardy and British Poetry*, 56.
[38] Ibid.

qualities appear in the rhythm: 'Where you will next be there's no knowing | . . . about me everywhere, | . . . coming and going.' The unforeseen and spontaneous or irregular distribution of the stresses, the poem's triumphantly erratic pulse, embodies the woman's being: for where the stresses fall 'there's no knowing', 'everywhere', 'coming and going'.

Touch and fingering in the making of art can be understood with regard to love and contact. 'After a Journey' is so covered with touches that it is not an example of mock-Gothic in-filling, but a responding to the woman's presence, effecting true spontaneities which may be judged to betray 'imperfection in every touch', and yet 'indulgently raise up a stately and unaccusable whole'. Davie adopts the word 'touch' from the visual arts: the sculptor or painter adding a touch here, a touch there; while 'fingering' he takes from the art of playing a musical instrument. These qualities may be distinguished, but they are not distinct, for both require a carefully modulated touch; just as each requires a tempered attack. 'Beeny Cliff', 'Places', and 'The Phantom Horsewoman', from towards the end of the sequence, demonstrate how Hardy himself had reinterpreted the thematic function of poetic rhythm. Gittings's relation of passages from *Some Recollections* to poems by Hardy is invaluable. 'Places' has two such correlations. Its second stanza describes Emma as she

> listened, just after the bedtime hour,
> To the stammering chimes that used to play
> The quaint Old Hundred-and-Thirteenth tune
>   In St. Andrew's tower
>   Night, morn, and noon.

The next stanza describes how,

> With cheeks whose airy flush outbid
> Fresh fruit in bloom, and free of fear,
> She cantered down, as if she must fall
>   (Though she never did),
>   To the charm of all.   (pp. 352–3)

The former of these derives from Emma's recollection of how 'that tune with its haltings and runs plays up in my head even now' and the latter from 'an unforgettable experience to me, scampering up and down the hills on my beloved mare alone, wanting no protection, the rain going down my back often and hair floating in the wind.'³⁹

What the wording of Emma's manuscript suggests, and 'Places' tends to make less clear, is the intimate family resemblances of human rhythm between bell-ringing, hymn tunes, horse-riding, poetic cadences of 'halts and runs' (true Gothic spontaneity) and a locally irregular form which thematically calls up the presence of the past hovering 'a few feet from him | Just as I used to do'. A critic in *The Saturday Review* (11 January 1902) had noted, 'Mr. Hardy has never written with flowing rhythms ... and his verse often halts'.⁴⁰ These rhythmic resemblances sponsor, authorize, and justly weigh the claim to a reciprocity of feeling in the opening lines from 'Beeny Cliff':

> O the opal and the sapphire of that wandering western sea,
> And the woman riding high above with bright hair flapping free—
> The woman whom I loved so, and who loyally loved me.
>
> (p. 350)

Similarly, the final stanza of 'The Phantom Horsewoman', with its eight halting short lines which are suddenly given rein in the exhilarating final run-on, makes good the belief that

> Time touches her not,
> But she still rides gaily
> In his rapt thought
> On that shagged and shaly
> Atlantic spot,
> And as when first eyed
> Draws rein and sings to the swing of the tide.   (p. 354)

In single words, individual lines, isolated poems, and through this sequence, a rhythmic, contentual, and thematic shape is made from haltings and runnings-on. It contains rebuke and recrimination, awareness of the irreparable, but also unforeseen presence, reparative affirmation that derives from acknowledged limitedness and imperfection. By incorporating rhythmic suggestions, incidents, and phrases from his first wife's memoir, Hardy's great poems exemplify how from the world of others' words—which are not the poem, not Hardy's regular art—comes the challenge, the check

---

³⁹ Two citations from Emma Hardy, *Some Recollections*, 12, 50–1.
⁴⁰ R. G. Cox (ed.), *Thomas Hardy: The Critical Heritage* (1970), 331.

to that art; yet, at the same time, they demonstrate how such checks may be responded to in a poem, may become a part of the poem, and part of Hardy's unforeseen excellence in poetry. By checking his art, another's words give the way to affirming it: 'We grew much interested in each other and I found him a perfectly new subject of study and delight, and he found a "mine" in me, he said.'

5

Robert Lowell and 'Moral Luck'

Harriet Lowell's response to modern music gave her father some
lines for his poem 'Fall 1961':

> A father's no shield
> for his child.
> We are like a lot of wild
> spiders crying together,
> but without tears.[1]

Lowell explained:

My daughter who was aged about five I think at the time happened to be
listening to a radio programme and Anton Webern's music came on and I
said, 'This is music you won't like, it's difficult, for grown-ups' and asked
her what it's like . . . then she said this amazing thing, 'It's like a lot of
wild spiders crying but without tears' . . . I stole it from her.[2]

Poets are prone to picking up poetic suggestions in loved ones'
words. Few would expect them to provide attributions, yet, as in
the example above, knowing the detail helps bind together further
the stanza's two sentences. When it comes to the adopting of
others' writings the conventions vary. Lowell would sometimes
casually acknowledge debts, as when he stated that ' "The Lesson"
picks up a phrase or two from Rafael Alberti.'[3] It may not always
be necessary to differentiate the words of others in a poem, and it
might be stifling to expect this of poets.

Marianne Moore and Elizabeth Bishop took the attribution of

---

[1] Robert Lowell, *Selected Poems*, rev. edn. (Farrar, Straus & Giroux, Inc., New
York, 1977 and Faber & Faber Ltd.), 105. I cite from this latest edition where
possible.

[2] Quoted from the television programme 'Robert Lowell', Voices and Visions,
Annenberg/CPB Project.

[3] Lowell, Note to *For the Union Dead* (1965), n.p. Alberti's poem is 'Retornos
del amor en los vividos paisajes', see J. M. Cohen (ed. and trans.), *The Penguin
Book of Spanish Verse*, 3rd edn. (Harmondsworth, 1988), 482–3. Lowell's poem is
more extensively shadowed with suggestions and phrases from Alberti than his note
indicates.

sources extremely seriously. Bishop notes in her memoir of the older poet: 'she *did* use a phrase of mine once without a note. This may be childish of me, but I want to reclaim it.'[4] Bishop was firmly opposed to Lowell's way with others' words in *The Dolphin* and wrote to the poet after seeing drafts of the sonnets: 'One can use one's life as material—one does, anyway—but these letters—aren't you violating a trust? If you are given permission—IF you hadn't changed them . . . etc. But *art just isn't worth that much.*'[5] There are then circumstances when considerations of behaviour towards the living are engaged by the absorption or individuation of others' words in poems, and in this Chapter I want to continue exploring some of them.

Gabriel Pearson remarks of Lowell's early poem 'In Memory of Arthur Winslow' that 'manic verbal control . . . conceals an impotence adequately to mourn.' How poets deploy their words and the words of others is an aspect of how they value the existences of other people. Pearson also notes that such poems 'displace emotion from the ostensible subject' on to the poem, so that it becomes an image of 'the poet's own project of poetry-making'. The poet's sense of vocation, or perhaps career, has clouded his eye to the other lives he composes into his tokens of success. The importance attached to a successful professional career as a poet is hardly unique to Lowell, though his friend Elizabeth Bishop behaved as one who thought differently. One of Lowell's undoubted significances is that he did identify the project of *his* making poetry with the value of poetry as such, simultaneously enabling and imperilling his ambitious project. Pearson saw that 'Lowell offers his own literary career (implicitly of course) as an augury and illustration of some possible ultimate cultural good health or good management or good luck.'[6] In what follows I am attempting to develop Pearson's insights into the relations in Lowell's work between his emblematic career, his process of composing others' words and viewpoints into his poems, and his awareness of their separate existences in and beyond his lines and

[4] Elizabeth Bishop, 'Efforts of Affection', *The Collected Prose*, ed. R. Giroux (1984), 141.

[5] Bishop cited in David Kalstone, *Becoming a Poet: Elizabeth Bishop with Marianne Moore and Robert Lowell*, ed. R. Hemenway (1989), 241.

[6] Four citations from Gabriel Pearson, 'Lowell's Marble Meanings', *The Survival of Poetry*, ed. M. Dodsworth (1970), 60 (three times), 56.

phrases: 'one life, one writing!' Lowell exclaimed in 'Night Sweat' and yet the fineness of this poem lies in its second stanza's recognitions. He sees 'Behind me! You!' and begs his wife to 'absolve me, help me, Dear Heart'.[7] Unfortunately, it was not always so.

I

In the conclusion to 'Exorcism', Lowell wrote:

> My words are English, but the plot is hexed:
> one man, two women, the common novel plot.
> what you love you are. . . .
> *You can't carry your talent with you like a suitcase.*
> *Don't you dare mail us the love your life denies;*
> *do you really* know *what you have done?*[8]

The lines which seem to be attributed by the italics were probably first written by Elizabeth Hardwick, the poet's second wife, taken from a letter in reply to one of Lowell's. When she says that he can't carry his talent with him like a suitcase, she may mean that a writer's talent is a compacting of qualities which are located in a choice of life; that a writer's gift is, at least in part, an effusion of who he or she is, and who a person is involves a history of choices which cannot be undone by making another choice that does not take into account the weight of a history already accrued. Letters are writing, of course, but writing love in a letter cannot merely substitute for presence: '*Don't you dare mail us the love your life denies*'.

What happens when a poet puts these problems into a poem, also writing, though with a different history of cultural usage, of contexts both public and private, of relations between interlocutors and readers? The question itself requires contexts, wanting to know what happens to the text, or to the readers, or to the lives from which these words come and to which they return in words

---

[7] Lowell, *For the Union Dead*, 68–9. In Lowell, *Notebook*, 3rd edn., rev. and expanded (New York, 1970), 175–6, the poem appears as only the first stanza. It returns in *Selected Poems*, 134, but without what I have taken to be a stanza break at l. 14.

[8] Lowell, *The Dolphin* (1973), 48.

from the public domain on a page. These questions are also about poetic technique, and technique as a form of care, of attention directed towards an object. Since the poem may contain others' words and occasions of others' lives, the care cannot be conceived of as purely aesthetic, cannot find its end in the poem created, for it moves through this object to return, in the words, to the world from which it arose. This may seem a truism, though not one accepted or observed by all. Where does technique find its end: is it in the work of art, or through that in lives from which the art derives, and to which it returns? In 1928 T. S. Eliot wrote, 'we cannot say at what point "technique" begins or where it ends'.[9] Perhaps it is possible to say where it has been, and where it stopped. Since one place to which Lowell's poem returns is the private life of others, may criticism be concerned with what the work of art does there? Seamus Heaney implies it must, when, commenting on Plath's 'Daddy', he notes that it 'rampages so permissively in the history of other people's sorrows that it simply withdraws its right to our sympathy'.[10]

Principles of aesthetic autonomy, of artistic impersonality, affirm that the poem detaches itself from the emotions, and lives, which brought it into being. Readers may contemplate a poem about harm without finding it harmful. Yet the aesthetic transformation which makes this possible, and which achieves it by concentrating attention on the work of art may, simultaneously, be a form of care for the poet's self and the selves of others: interlocutors, protagonists, relatives, friends, and readers. William Empson touches on the problems in a stanza cut from 'Aubade' after its magazine publication:

> This is unjust to her without a prose book.
> A lyric from a fact is bound to cook.
> It was more grinding; it was much more slow,
> But still the point's not how much time it took,
> It seemed the best thing to be up and go.[11]

When Lowell said of *Life Studies* that 'There's a good deal of tinkering with fact' and yet that 'the reader was to believe he was

  [9] T. S. Eliot, 'Preface to the 1928 Edition', *The Sacred Wood* (1928), p. ix.
  [10] Seamus Heaney, *The Government of the Tongue* (1988), 165.
  [11] Quoted in Philip and Averil Gardner, *The God Approached: A Commentary on the Poems of William Empson* (1978), 164.

getting the *real* Robert Lowell'[12] he is more confidently recognizing poetry's inevitable transformations in selectivity, shaping, and, often, inventing. A difference is the object of reference. Empson thinks of the girl in his poem; Lowell sees his book as a self-portrait, though it contains pictures of many other people. Pearson noted of *Life Studies* that Lowell 'was not making his poetry more personal but depersonalizing his own life'.[13] Is this true of the others in it as well?

Whether a poem is good enough in this light would be another way of giving a meaning to Lowell's success as a poet. The term 'success' is also subject to conflicting contexts of definition. What influence does Lowell's successful career as a poet have on the subject-matter and technique of his mature and later poems? These issues can be focused more by looking at the arguments in Bernard Williams's essay 'Moral Luck'.[14] It takes, as two of its illustrative examples, an artist deciding to leave his wife and family for the sake of his art; and a woman deciding to commit suicide because the adulterous affair which she has embarked upon has failed to achieve in her life the meaning intended when it was undertaken.

II

Williams writes against the belief that the moral values of actions and individuals can be judged by removing from their circumstances the contingent impurities of luck, so that rational justification may be achieved. Poets can be conscious of the role played by luck in their inspiration, their practice, and successes, both of writing and reputation. Bishop told Lowell that she thought him 'The luckiest poet I know!—in some ways not so lucky, either'.[15] Thinking of himself and his second wife, Lowell began 'It Did (Elizabeth)':

> Luck, we've had it; our character the public's—
> and yet we will ripen, ripen, know we once

---

[12] Lowell, *Collected Prose*, ed. R. Giroux (1987), 246–7.

[13] Pearson, 'Lowell's Marble Meanings', 58.

[14] Quotations from this essay are followed by page nos. in parentheses which refer to Bernard Williams, *Moral Luck: Philosophical Papers 1973–1980* (Cambridge, 1981).

[15] Elizabeth Bishop cited in Kalstone, *Becoming a Poet*, 191.

did most things better, not just physical
but moral—[16]

Why Williams reflects on luck is illustrated by his Gauguin case. He says: 'Let us take first an outline example of the creative artist who turns away from definite and pressing human claims on him in order to live a life in which, as he supposes, he can pursue his art.' (p. 22) To make his example relate to moral reflection, he must assume a Gauguin who is 'concerned about these claims and what is involved in their being neglected (we may suppose them to be grim), and that he nevertheless, in the face of that, opts for the other life'. (p. 23) Heaney affirms that Lowell was such an artist: 'His obsessive subjectivity did not signify an abandonment of the usual life with its attendant moral codes and obligations.'[17] Lowell's bouts of mania may have diminished his sense of responsibilities in relation both to life and art, but they were followed by phases of crumpled gravity, of shame, and the need to make amends: 'I am tired. Everyone's tired of my turmoil.'[18] It is possible to become damagingly restive from an exhaustion with such moral awareness.

'My own father was a gentle, faithful, and dim man. I don't know why I was agin him. I hope there will be peace.'[19] So the poet concludes 'Near the Unbalanced Aquarium', a prose fragment of autobiography about one of his breakdowns, written in 1957. Lowell was afflicted by the three-adjective sequence. Unlike the *mot juste*, where revisions, if there are any, disappear with the arrival of the one right word, the Ciceronian triad provides opportunities for visible self-revision. Commander Lowell was 'gentle' and 'faithful': these are acts of reparation, a coming to see that the father had his qualities. Yet he was also 'dim'. Ezra Pound refers to the word in a phrase from one of Ford Madox Ford's poems; he is exemplifying a 'Don't': 'Don't use such an expression as "dim lands *of peace*". It dulls the image.'[20] Lowell thinks his father is 'dim' and hopes 'there will be peace.'

Yet even the word 'dim' may be making its contribution to a

---

[16] Lowell, *For Harriet and Lizzie* (1973), 46; 3 years earlier, in the 3rd edn. of *Notebook*, this read 'Knowledge, we've had it', 249.

[17] Heaney, *The Government of the Tongue*, 130.

[18] Lowell, *Selected Poems*, 109.

[19] Lowell, *Collected Prose*, 363.

[20] Ezra Pound, *The Literary Essays of Ezra Pound*, ed. T. S. Eliot (1954), 5.

reparative act, for if his father is kind and forgetful, slow-witted, but without vicious stupidity, then he can be forgiven for the mistakes he made, as, for example, when he intervened in the young Lowell's love affair with Anne Dick by writing a letter to her father:

> we were nomad quicksilver and drove to Boston;
> I knocked my father down. He sat on the carpet—
> my mother calling from the top of the carpeted stairs,
> their glass door locking behind me, no cover; you
> idling in the station wagon, no retreat.[21]

Is there a concealed accusation of the addressee in Lowell's transfer of the epithet 'idling' from station wagon to girl? Elegies contemplate the writer's own mortality. An adjective applied to another may also describe the applier. As well as reckoning the fullest implications for the life of Mr Robert Levett, the quack doctor, in Johnson's 'Officious, innocent, sincere',[22] a reader can interpret the significance of their force for Levett's life by considering them for Johnson's—a life not always characterized by forward efficiency and incapacity to wound, or unviolated by impurities. When Lowell remorsefully describes his father as 'a gentle, faithful, and dim man', the adjectives express an awareness of his father's difference: Lowell knew from painful experience that he could be aggressive, unfaithful, and faithless, as well as dangerously bright.

The poet's manic aggression is described in 'Near the Unbalanced Aquarium':

By some crisscross of logic, I reasoned that my cruel boorishness would be an act of self-sacrifice. I would be bowing out of the picture, and throwing Roger into the arms of Anna. Without warning, but without lowering my eyes from Anna's splendid breastplate blouse, I seized Roger's yellow ankles and pulled. Roger sat on the floor with tears in his eyes.[23]

Lowell reconstructs his hitting on what he imagined was winning by losing. He tried to demonstrate a power, show himself as if magnanimously the better man, and was escorted out of the picture

---

[21] Lowell, *Selected Poems*, 194; for an earlier version, see the 3rd edn. of *Notebook*, 67. Philip Cooper considers the literary afterlife of this event in *The Autobiographical Myth of Robert Lowell* (Chapel Hill, NC, 1970), 19–21.

[22] Samuel Johnson, *The Poems of Samuel Johnson*, ed. D. N. Smith and E. L. McAdam, 2nd edn. (Oxford, 1974), 234.

[23] Lowell, *Collected Prose*, 352.

by the head nurse to be sedated with round-the-clock injections of chloropromazene. The confrontation with his father resulted in a similarly self-disgusted bathos: 'I knocked my father down. He sat on the carpet'. Lowell's narration of the incident with Roger foreshadows that broken line, 'I seized Roger's yellow ankles and pulled. Roger sat on the floor'. In both cases obscure acts of competitiveness go awry: the winner loses. Lowell's three-adjective chains demonstrate a building up of verbal power and its dissipation.[24] They can make a triumph of defeat, or be defeated by their triumph. The conclusion to 'Home after Three Months Away' presents a figure aware once more of responsible connections with others: 'the time I put away I was child's play'. It also laments the loss of manic stature in being well again: 'Cured, I am frizzled, stale and small.'[25] Lowell's concern for 'pressing human claims', and for the moral consequences of these claims 'being neglected', is in 'Dolphin':

> I have sat and listened to too many
> words of the collaborating muse,
> and plotted perhaps too freely with my life,
> not avoiding injury to others,
> not avoiding injury to myself—
> to ask compassion . . . this book, half fiction,
> an eelnet made by man for the eel fighting—
>
> my eyes have seen what my hand did.[26]

Jonathan Raban noted: 'This is Lowell's most personal and profound statement about his life and work. It commands more attention than exegesis.'[27] Itself withdrawing the expectation of sympathy, the poem places its poet in the circumstances of moral awareness. Lowell's lines do not expect to vindicate him there. They prevent Thomas Nagel's[28] criticism of the Gauguin example being applied to Lowell. Nagel suggests that there is nothing in the case to demonstrate that Gauguin, deciding to leave his wife and

---

[24] For Bishop's comments on Lowell's adjective problems, see Kalstone, *Becoming a Poet*, 207.
[25] Lowell, *Selected Poems*, 89, 90.
[26] Ibid. 78.
[27] Jonathan Raban, Note to 'Dolphin', Lowell, *Selected Poems*, ed. J. Raban (1975), 186. I doubt if you can have more attention without any exegesis. Raban is giving voice to unqualified awe.
[28] See Thomas Nagel, *Mortal Questions* (Cambridge, 1979), 28–9.

five children in order to paint, has acted within the realm of moral considerations, and that if he has not, then the 'luck' involved in his proving to be a great artist is not 'moral'.

Williams introduces the consideration that a person making the decision to turn away from definite and pressing human claims may not be doing it with the sole aim of pursuing his or her art: 'This other life he might perhaps not see very determinately under the category of realising his gifts as a painter, but, to make things simpler, let us add that he does see it determinately in that light—it is as a life which will enable him really to be a painter that he opts for it.'(p. 23) When Lowell writes in 'It Did . . . ': 'Luck, we've had it; our character the public's—', he suggests that luck has played its part in the successes of himself and Hardwick, and he must have career success in mind because he mentions the public. Yet, when adding, 'and yet we will ripen, ripen', he indicates that the decisions of life made by artists are unlikely only to involve the pursuance of an art and of success in that art. Lowell's poem leans on the laurels of his previous books, of his achieved stature as a poet; but when its author, a young man, went to Tennessee in 1938 and camped on the lawn of Allen Tate's house to be with the writers, a 'terrible piece of youthful callousness',[29] he could not be sure in advance that he was going to become the figure who, for example, came controversially second to Edmund Blunden in the Oxford Professorship of Poetry vote for 1966.

Williams's idea of 'moral luck' requires such situations in life where, as he says of his Gauguin: 'Whether he will succeed cannot, in the nature of the case, be foreseen.'(p. 23) Williams's sense that luck is operative, requires that the decision to act, founded upon an absence of certainty, can only be retrospectively justified by the success of the project undertaken. He is aware of the problems involved in defining what success in such circumstances might be:

Gauguin, in our story, is putting a great deal on a possibility which has not unequivocally declared itself. I want to explore and uphold the claim that in such a situation the only thing that will justify his choice will be success itself. If he fails—and we shall come shortly to what, more precisely, failure may be—then he did the wrong thing, not just in the sense in which that platitudinously follows, but in the sense that having done the wrong thing in those circumstances he has no basis for the

[29] Lowell, *Collected Prose*, 257.

thought that he was justified in acting as he did. If he succeeds, he does have a basis for that thought.   (p. 23)

Williams has not invented the idea of justification by results. In a letter postmarked 30 August 1846, Browning wrote to Elizabeth Barrett: 'having once decided to go to Italy with me, the next thing to decide is on the best means of going: or rather, there is just this connection between the two measures, that by the success or failure of the last, the first will have to be justified or condemned.'[30] Browning is concerned about Elizabeth's health: if she dies on the journey, the decision to go will seem wrong. Since they are determined on a *life* together in Italy the success of the venture depends crucially on Elizabeth Barrett's living. This is a requirement of success. Williams gives a parallel, but contrasting, case for Gauguin:

If Gauguin sustains some injury on the way to Tahiti which prevents his ever painting again, that certainly means that his decision (supposing it now to be irreversible) was for nothing, and indeed there is nothing in the outcome to set against the other people's loss. But the train of events does not provoke the thought in question, that after all he was wrong and unjustified. He does not, and never will, know whether he was wrong.   (p. 25)

This is to show a distinction between extrinsic and intrinsic, or constitutive, luck. Because Robert and Elizabeth are discussing living together it is a question of constitutive luck that, having made the decision and the arrangements as best they can, the couple survive the journey as a couple. If the question is whether great works of art are going to be produced, then the constitutive luck refers to whether the person making the decision has the aptitude, or capacity, or determination to make works which then prove capable of being called great, so that the decision will retrospectively seem right because success has ensued.

Williams is not countenancing, as grounds for making the decision, *enthusiasm* in Dr Johnson's sense: 'A vain belief of private revelation; a vain confidence of divine favour or communication.' Williams's artist as moral agent must be aware that no satisfactory guarantee of success could be provided in advance, and thus that he is able to see the true risk to himself and others:

[30] Robert Browning, *Letters of Robert Browning and Elizabeth Barrett Barrett, 1845–1846*, 2 vols., ed. E. Kintner (Cambridge, Mass., 1969), ii. 1022.

It could not be that one is morally justified in deciding to neglect other claims if one is a great creative artist: apart from doubts about its content, the saving clause begs the question which at the time one is in no position to answer. On the other hand, '. . . if one is convinced that one is a great creative artist' will serve to make obstinacy and fatuous self-delusion conditions of justification, while, '. . . if one is reasonably convinced that one is a great creative artist' is, if anything, worse. What is reasonable conviction supposed to be in such a case? Should Gauguin consult professors of art? (p. 24)

If it is mistaken to expect justification from professors before, at what point is it not mistaken? The decision to begin to try to make works of art, which may involve sacrifices to be endured by the artist and those near, has to be made internally on the basis of limited evidence for its outcome. Nevertheless, whether success or failure has occurred cannot be decided purely internally. Yet nor can it be referred entirely outside, to those who are assumed to be competent to judge. Furthermore, in art, there is a long-standing distinction between career success, which Lowell certainly had, and success removed from the area of immediate recognition—the growing conviction (or might it be delusion?) that lasting pieces of art have been made.

Nor is it true that if a professor of art is convinced by a new piece of work the young artist would be justified in ignoring the appreciation of the professor on the grounds that such a person could not know. However, he or she might be justified in remaining sceptical. There is flattering subjectivism in assuming that the distinction between career success in a life and ultimate success in art is clear and absolute. A young artist would have this much justification in submitting to the judgement of a professor of art. Once a body of work has been created, and has been lucky enough to reach the public domain, professors have more to go on, so that 'obstinacy and fatuous self-delusion' might become substantial issues when 'the art world' rejected these products. Many instances could be provided of such rejections taking place, and the artist being vindicated in the longer run. The reverse must be a much more common occurrence. It could also be self-punitive entirely to discount one's career successes as indications of some possible lasting achievement.

These problems about knowing that an artist has succeeded bear upon a further issue of rational justification, namely, that the people who have been hurt by the Gauguin figure's conscious neglect of pressing human claims have every right to reject the justifications offered. Even if the artist succeeds, in whatever terms, success in itself will not remove the reproaches levelled:

> One should be warned already, however, that, even if Gauguin can be ultimately justified, that need not provide him with any way of justifying himself to others, or at least to all others. Thus he may have no way of bringing it about that those who suffer from his decision will have no justified ground of reproach. Even if he succeeds, he will not acquire a right that they accept what he has to say; if he fails, he will not even have anything to say   (pp. 24 5)

Williams's essay indicates that the more qualms proliferate the more does the decision to commit oneself to art, or even to make a single work of art, involve a necessary hardening of considerations, a simplification of aim, so that the various and complex issues can come into play. When the moral complexity becomes inhibiting or debilitating of any action at all, then it has failed in its purpose of helping readers and writers to live, work, or be better.

In writing with an autobiographical content, such as much of Lowell's, whether success has occurred involves the presence within the work itself of moral issues concerned with the neglecting of claims, the sufferings of others, and the irremovability of grounds for reproach. Williams sees these as intrinsic to rational justification when, thanks to luck, the artist has succeeded, but extrinsic to whether success can be granted to have occurred. Thus success always involves a context; it implies a number of viewpoints or sets of terms which will be counted as signalling achievement, and which will allow other viewpoints or terms to be, in some degree, disregarded.

If an artist is involved in what Williams calls a 'project', by which he means something like a 'life's work', then success is a consideration that only has a limited significance. Most artists *in medias res* straddle both of the alternatives Williams gives: 'if he succeeds, he will not acquire a right that they accept what he has to say; if he fails, he will not even have anything to say'. The conditions have not arisen, and most probably will not arise where such 'success' or 'failure' could be clearly or categorically decided. They would not be able to demand the right, even if there were one. This does not mean that the moral claim can be discounted.

III

Heaney has drawn attention to a style in Lowell's mature work which 'relaxed the method of decisive confrontation'.[31] 'The Old Flame' is one such poem:

> My old flame, my wife!
> Remember our lists of birds?
> One morning last summer, I drove
> by our house in Maine. It was still
> on top of its hill—[32]

The difference between 'My old flame, my wife!' and 'Remember our lists of birds?' is that the second incorporates the wife as a familiar figure, where the first, with its exclamation mark, must be addressed to readers, or, at least, not quite to the old wife. This uneasiness is at the heart of the poem; the wife is his first, Jean Stafford (married to Lowell 1940–8), divorced long before the poem was written. 'The Old Flame' is an act of recovery, set on uncertain grounds. The uneasiness is in 'our house in Maine', where the pronoun re-established their marital status with regard to the old house. With the poem's second line, the previous wife is invited into the project of reparative recall.[33]

The poet's wry nostalgia for a relationship which the poem later signifies was not ideal, is framed by a different nostalgia, that of the new inhabitants of 'our house'; theirs, however, is a gimcrack confection:

> Old Glory with thirteen stars
> hung on a pole. The clapboard
> was old-red schoolhouse red.
>
> Inside, a new landlord,
> a new wife, a new broom!
> Atlantic seaboard antique shop
> pewter and plunder
> shone in each room.

[31] Heaney, *The Government of the Tongue*, 146.
[32] The text of 'The Old Flame' which I quote from in this and the following paragraphs is that in Lowell, *Selected Poems*, rev. edn., 101–2.
[33] Cooper points out the debt 'The Old Flame' owes to Jean Stafford's 'A Country House Story', in *Autobiographical Myth*, 25–6.

The poem begins to focus around the words 'old' and 'new': 'new wife', 'new broom', to set against 'old flame, my wife', 'Old Glory' and 'old-red'. At the beginning of the next stanza there is 'A new frontier!', with the exclamation mark once again hinting at a distance between the vaunted sentiment and the poet's own stance with regard to it. The word 'old' is deployed by Lowell to encompass conflicting retrospections: there is the attempt to see the marriage as a substantial and significant fact of both people's histories, and this climaxes in the penultimate stanza with 'Poor ghost, old love, speak I with your old voice'. This request is not answered in the poem. Its deployments of 'old' try to give a project which has not endured a value like one that has, at least in the recalling mind, and the marriage has thus a dignity of experience by contrast with the lifestyle of the 'new' people. Stanzas 6 and 7 give the new people's domestic orderliness set against Lowell and Stafford in their unendurable, unenduring intensity:

> Health to the new people,
> health to their flag, to their old
> restored house on the hill!
> Everything had been swept bare,
> furnished, garnished, and aired.
>
> Everything's changed for the best—
> how quivering and fierce we were,
> there snowbound together,
> simmering like wasps
> in our tent of books!

The contrast with the ersatz oldness of the new people may allow the poet to give an authenticity to his own 'old love', but the poem does not fail to recall that the relationship was foundering. The 'old flame' of the title turns sour in the 'voice I of flaming insight I that kept us awake all night'. A blazing row and a fiery intelligence are hinted at here. This poem revises a previous relationship to achieve a cherishing of the past against the grain of irreparable events. It deploys the skills of Lowell at their best, to revalue the experience of the younger, less technically flexible writer. 'The Old Flame' is an attempt to set the past in place, reparatively ordered and with a resignation towards what cannot be changed.

Williams comments on how a project might come to be seen as a failure. He uses Anna Karenina's affair with Vronsky to introduce a type of regret. What he calls 'agent-regret' is concerned with how active protagonists think about the effects of their actions on their own and others' lives. Williams writes that 'Agent-regret requires not merely a first-personal subject-matter, nor yet merely a particular kind of psychological content, but also a particular kind of expression' (p. 27) and then adds: 'The sentiment of agent-regret is by no means restricted to *voluntary* agency.' (pp. 27–8) You can feel agent-regret if a marriage goes wrong but you are not wholly or solely to blame. You feel it as a case of 'how much better if it had been otherwise', where your own actions are a part of its being how it is, but where causation is too complex or too widely dispersed to lay the blame singly at your door. You feel responsibility for the outcome of events, and your role in those events is a constituent of their moral value and significance.

Williams is concerned with agent-regret because it can illuminate the distinction between intrinsic and extrinsic luck:

It would have been an intrinsic failure, also, if Vronsky had actually committed suicide. It would not have been that, but rather an extrinsic misfortune, if Vronsky had been accidentally killed. Though her project would have been at an end, it would not have failed as it does.   (p. 27)

Anna's project fails intrinsically. This can be said of a marriage even if the couple faced problems which were not only of their own making so long as the failure to deal with these problems did reflect responsibility on them as agents. The agent-regret which arises in cases where luck has played a part indicate that the elements outside the agent's control are nevertheless intrinsic to the context, not entirely external accident or chance. There has to be something that might just possibly have been done to prevent it, however remote the possibility.

Lowell's is a case where a marriage fails, and produces feelings of agent-regret, which in turn prompt the making of a poem, one which has succeeded in that other people, though almost certainly not all people, like it and their liking is a response to something intrinsic to the work, for which the artist can take responsibility. Here again are Williams's sentences about such occurrences:

In other cases, again, there is no room for any appropriate action at all. Then only the desire to make reparation remains, with the painful consciousness that nothing can be done about it; some other action, perhaps less directed to the victims, may come to express this. What degree of such feeling is appropriate, and what attempts at reparative action or substitutes for it, are questions for particular cases, and that there is room in the area for irrational and self-punitive excess, no one is likely to deny. (p. 29)

Lowell's 'The Old Flame' constitutes 'some other action, perhaps less directed to the victims'. It is tempting to assume that the wife is the victim, but perhaps more accurate and fairer to sense that both poet and wife are victims, and that the poem is also less directed to the poet, the other victim. Evidently, too, in many human situations, being the victim does not preclude being one of the agents:

> In one bed and apart,
>
> We heard the plow
> groaning uphill—
> a red light, then a blue,
> as it tossed off the snow
> to the side of the road.

It is terrible to be alone together 'In one bed and apart'. The snow has trapped them, 'quivering and fierce'. They both hear the plow as it struggles to free them from each other. There is an attempt to view the past in an equal light, to accept that it was 'for the best'. Lowell's poem achieves a grace and tonality which seems able to do this without further fault.[34]

IV

Geoffrey Hill, in 'Poetry as "Menace" and "Atonement"', broods on the work of art as a substitute or compensation, when 'there is no room for any appropriate action', and on how such situations may produce self-defeating activity: 'let us postulate yet another impure motive, remorse, and let us suggest that a man may continue to write and to publish in a vain and self-defeating effort to appease his own sense of empirical guilt'.[35] The impurity of the

---

[34] David Roberts recounts a version of the events behind this poem in the chapter 'A Country Love Story', from *Jean Stafford: A Biography* (1988), 223–48. For a less satisfactory retrospection on Lowell's part, see 'Jean Stafford, a Letter', in *Day by Day* (1978), 29.

[35] Geoffrey Hill, *The Lords of Limit: Essays on Literature and Ideas* (1984), 7.

remorse is increased by 'vain' in its punning self-regard, and by 'appease', suggesting not the making of emblematic reparations towards others, or oneself viewed altruistically, but a self-placation. Elsewhere, in 'What Devil Has Got Into John Ransom?', Hill sees revision as a temptation to imagine that actual reparation is, in fact, possible: 'the "devil" that has got into John Ransom at this late stage is a decent little devil whose highly moral whisper is that one can genuinely make amends for some actual or supposed betrayal in "real life" by tampering years later with the evidence of the fiction'.[36] To imagine that poetic revision can literally make amends is to underestimate the fact of damage, physical or mental; but to assume that the poem is independent of life, a pure fiction, is to remove some of the co-ordinates for making purposeful revision. The composing poet would then not be swimming against a tide but treading water. Revision may indicate a finer co-ordination of points. It may display a loss of contact: 'To Allen Tate, working a later tack and writing in a different vein, Ransom was not so much possessed of a devil as gripped by a "mania" which drove him in later years to the ruinous rewriting, the "compulsive revisions" of poems written in early middle age.'[37]

Lowell too was a compulsive reviser, and in *The Dolphin* described himself as 'a writer still free to work at home all week, | reading revisions to his gulping wife'. (p. 73) There is a vertiginous groundlessness in 'the endless days revising our revisions' (p. 63) as if the purposive direction had been lost to view. In 'Summer Between Terms' he complains 'I waste hours writing in and writing out a line, | as if listening to conscience were telling the truth'— having already punned himself into difficulties: 'Surely good writers write all possible wrong' (p. 28). The activity of revision is relevant to luck, regret, and reparation, because it links the initial decision to behave in a particular manner with how it can be viewed as a success or failure. Williams's constitutive luck may operate within the interstices of a line of verse; the revision is prompted by agent-regret, and with the need to make reparative actions towards the work, or the life, or both.

Williams touches on revision when arguing against a model of rational deliberation which would see each decision in terms of all

---

[36] Ibid. 135.
[37] Ibid. 121.

the implications that it could have for a whole life. Not only does this *life-plan* picture of moral thought embody 'the ideal fulfilment of a rational urge to harmonize all one's projects', it also seeks to protect the self against 'reproaches from our future self if we act with deliberative rationality' (p. 34). Writers in the process of composition, reading, re-reading, and revision may be attempting to harmonize their projects, to work with deliberative rationality in order to relieve their future selves of reproach.

However, is it creatively possible to bear in mind all the implications of each compositional act, both on what is already produced and on what has yet to be made? By 'creatively' is meant: consistent with the habits of mind, the combinations of guided impulse and reflection which are focused in making art. It is possible to distinguish between work done by writers who 'know what they are doing' and others who do not; it is another matter to suggest that knowing what one was doing meant being rationally conscious of everything that could be brought to bear on the question of what to do next. There is room for moral luck and judgement in every word.[38]

Williams states that: 'The standpoint of that retrospective judge who will be my later self will be the product of my earlier choices.' (p. 34) Similarly, the whole text cannot be known in advance, and even during revision it does not exist as a whole possessed singly by the mind, for the self altered in working on a text is not quite the same as the one that began it. The separateness and wholeness of a finished work thus retains its interest for the one who made it. These remarks are at a tangent to the idea of the poet as a catalyst, in T. S. Eliot's 'Tradition and the Individual Talent', because the self of the writer is also being altered by the compositional decisions made in the act of writing and revising, just as, differently, it will be later by the publication and reception of the work.[39]

Luck is introduced into moral considerations at so many levels that in making art, as far as autobiography and relations with other living persons are concerned, to leave well alone may seem the best policy. This is the view adopted by W. H. Auden in later life, which surfaces in one of the sonnets from *The Dolphin*. Auden

[38] There is an instructive discussion of these issues through an analogy between translating and making moral decisions in Stuart Hampshire (ed.), *Public and Private Morality* (Cambridge, 1978), 31–4.

[39] Eliot, *The Sacred Wood*, 53–4.

is reported[40] to have said that he would not speak to Lowell on hearing of the 1973 book:

> The scouring voice of 1930 Oxford,
> 'Nothing pushing the personal should be published,
> not even Proust's *Research* or Shakespeare's *Sonnets*,
> a banquet of raw ingredients in bad taste . . .　　　(p. 67)

An intelligible point of view, with a moral value of its own, has been made to appear exaggerated posturing. Auden's outlook defines a simple rectitude. Yet many may consider Auden's policy as expressed here, less valuable than the works which would be lost if it had been adopted. None the less, Lowell cannot expect to make his position impregnable by making another's view, in adapted quotation, look absurd. In the first part of 'Doubt' he asks:

> Should revelation be sealed like private letters,
> till all the beneficiaries are dead,
> and our proper names become improper Lives? (p. 42)

The question is hardly asked neutrally. Is 'beneficiaries', with its allusion to the reading of a will, the right word for the others involved? Is 'improper' focused? Does the capital letter on 'Lives', with its suggestions of biographies and scandalous revelations, carry a conviction that the individuals involved have the right to set their record straight before they become the public's property? Is 'setting the record straight' what art can do?

It is hard to feel that Lowell handles these issues with enough skill and tact in his sonnet which touches on Auden's opinions. Yet Auden cannot have the monopoly on the truth. Lowell may neither dismiss Auden's view, nor force Auden to accept his. Williams notes:

The idea that there has been a moral cost itself implies that something bad has been done, and, very often, that someone has been wronged, and if the people who have been wronged do not accept the justification, then no-one can demand that they should. It is for them to decide how far they are prepared to adopt the perspective within which the justification counts. This is just one of the ways—the distancing of time is another—in which,

---

[40] See Ian Hamilton, *Robert Lowell: A Biography* (1983), 425, and, on the opinions expressed in Lowell's poem following, see W. H. Auden, *Forewords and Afterwords* (1973), 88–108.

if the moral sentiments are to be part of life as it is actually experienced, they cannot be modelled on a view of the world in which every happening and every person is at the same distance.   (p. 37)

The Dolphin is about people and happenings that are taking place at different distances. It is shadowed with the understandable desire to vindicate Lowell's decisions in his life and in his art, but weighed with stark instances of how such vindication cannot be achieved by attempting to provide a single 'distance' for the registration of these instances:

> My words are English, but the plot is hexed:
> one man, two women, the common novel plot.
> what you love you are. . . .
> *You can't carry your talent with you like a suitcase.*
> *Don't you dare mail us the love your life denies;*
> *do you really* know *what you have done?*

If the italicized lines criticizing the poet act independently of the literary context in which they find themselves, then they are instances of these intractable and various ethical distances which Williams affirms to be part of the inhabited moral landscape. But if the lines are deployed by the poet in literary self-justification, then all the words from whatever quarter appear to stand at the same distance from the author. Lowell's technique at this stage in his life (the italicized other's words deployed without explanation, reflection, or mediation) seems not flexible and flexed enough for a reader to be sure.

The technical problems of Lowell's sonnets are summarized in a letter responding to the first *Notebook* from I. A. Richards to the poet. After professions of faith in Lowell's 'immense vividity', 'phrase-making explosiveness', 'originality of slant', and 'triumphantly compelling cadences', Richards adds:

you disturb me with, well: the FORM (how to get out what you really need most: i.e. deeper self-examination as to what you have, and want, to say). TONE (far too assured). ADDRESS (?to your following?); reiterations in sentiment; *lacunae* in connexity . . .[41]

These seem accurate qualms, and relevant to 'Exorcism' because it is attempting some 'deeper self-examination' from within the

---

[41] I. A. Richards, *Selected Letters of I. A. Richards*, ed. J. Constable (Oxford, 1990), 181.

circumstances of moral problems and values. This is more than might have occurred if Lowell had conformed to Auden's prohibition. Lowell's risk is necessary for an entry into the moral landscape; there are, nevertheless, several versions of this pastoral.[42]

Though he may not be able fully to justify his actions, they are neither amoral nor immoral. They may, though, have been mistakes, and Lowell never lost the capacity to pause and reconsider. In an exchange of letters during July 1973, Lowell and Bishop comment on the morality of publishing *The Dolphin* and on the endurance of the irreparable. Lowell reflects: 'My sin (mistake?) was publishing. I couldn't bear to have my book (my life) wait inside me like a dead child.' To this, Bishop replies: 'We all have irreparable and awful actions on our consciences . . . I just try to live without blaming myself for them *every* day at least . . .'.[43] 'Epilogue', the last poem in Lowell's final book, delivers a harsh criticism on much of his work which seems 'heightened from life, | yet paralyzed by fact'. The poem concludes with a partial self-justification and intercession:

> Pray for the grace of accuracy
> Vermeer gave to the sun's illumination
> stealing like the tide across a map
> to his girl solid with yearning.
> We are poor passing facts,
> warned by that to give
> each figure in the photograph
> his living name.[44]

Lowell sees pictured the effect of love crossing mapped distances to arrive in the mail. Invoking Vermeer's painting of a girl reading a letter by the light of a window, calling to something or someone beyond himself, the poet approaches his best vein once more a final time.

---

[42] See Hill, 'Lives of the Poets', *Essays in Criticism*, 34 (July 1984), 262–9.

[43] Cited in Kalstone, *Becoming a Poet*, 247.

[44] Lowell, *Day by Day*, 127. At the end of a recent interview, E. J. Scovell cites these lines and associates them with Vermeer's *An Artist in His Studio* in the Kunsthistorisches Museum, Vienna. I had assumed the painting referred to was *Woman in Blue Reading a Letter* in the Rijksmuseum-Stichting, Amsterdam. For a discussion of these possibilities, see Helen Deese, 'Lowell and the Visual Arts', S. G. Axelrod and H. Deese (eds.), *Robert Lowell: Essays on the Poetry* (Cambridge, 1986), 180–91.

'Du musst dein Leben ändern'[45] [You must change your life],
Rilke wrote, and the concern with luck in Bernard Williams's essay
fixes on cases where decisions have been made to change a life.
Intrinsic luck and agent-regret are concepts to increase the scope of
moral consideration for who and what is involved in decisions to
change. Lowell's compulsive sonnet writing and revising, what has
been called 'An automatism of constant repair',[46] were to focus
and fulfil a damaged and damaging life. At best they have the
desperation of Randall Jarrell's woman at the Washington Zoo
who cries 'You know what I was, I You see what I am: change me,
change me!'[47] In her elegy for Lowell, his friend Elizabeth Bishop
laments the failing hope to improve your life by revising your
work, the sorry realization that to reiterate is not to make
reparation. 'Nature repeats herself, or almost does: I *repeat, repeat,
repeat; revise, revise, revise*', she states in 'North Haven', then
concludes:

> And now—you've left
> for good. You can't derange, or re-arrange,
> your poems again. (But the Sparrows can their song.)
> The words won't change again. Sad friend, you cannot change.[48]

---

[45] Rainer Maria Rilke, 'Archaïscher Torso Apollos', *Gesammelte Werke*, 7 vols.
(Leipzig, 1927), iii. 117.
[46] Karl Miller, 'Some Names for Robert Lowell', *Doubles: Studies in Literary
History* (Oxford, 1985; rev. paper edn., 1987), 316.
[47] Randall Jarrell, *The Complete Poems* (1981), 216.
[48] Bishop, *The Complete Poems 1927–1979* (1983), 188, 189.

6
Geoffrey Hill's Position

Where does the perennial interest in debates concerning relations between poetry and politics lie? For poets it may involve a simultaneous frustration with their marginal status or purchase on public life, and belief in the authority of their art. The urgency with which such debates are conducted is fed by complex insecurities and a real impotence. In 'What Devil Has Got Into John Ransom?', Geoffrey Hill notes that 'Public occasions may be poetry but the poem, or, more precisely, the modern poem, is not a public occasion' (p. 131).[1] Division between the public world and the world of the modern poem presents to the critic a double focus. Hill writes in admiration of Matthew Arnold, that he was not 'unconcerned with politics but rather . . . saw literature as containing politics within a sphere of more precisely adjusted anxieties' (p. 107). The activity of containing and adjusting is performed by the modern poet against the prevailing conditions. In 'Poetry as "Menace" and "Atonement"' he 'is engaged in vicarious expiation for the pride of the culture which itself rejects him' (p. 4); and, concerned with the sin of pride in modern artists' senses of themselves, Hill confronts the problem 'that it is made more objectively difficult to confess if no one apart from oneself believes that there is anything which needs to be confessed' (p. 8). It is as if, convinced he has committed a crime, the modern poet in this culture is forced to admit that no policemen can be bothered to arrest him.

Hill's attention to social, political, and cultural conditions takes place in an extreme isolation: 'no one apart from oneself believes'. Others may come to experience concern about the culture in which they live through their work or unemployment, family attachments and separations, friendships maintained or allowed to decay. They

---

[1] Unless otherwise stated, citations of prose by Geoffrey Hill are from *The Lords of Limit: Essays on Literature and Ideas* (André Deutsch Ltd., 1984), to which page nos. in parentheses refer.

compare and contrast their conditions with those of other people
or, with more detachment, view their own lives as like those of
others, altruistically. Even this detachment is located in a moral
landscape with other figures at varying distances. Hill's work is
exercised by social and cultural issues in an intensely moral light.
It is also strikingly isolated. The question asked of his work is how
these moral, literary concerns with the life of a culture are to be
inhabited if the ordinary conditions in which moral experience
occur are such attenuated ones in his work?

I

'Difficult friend' (p. 81)[2]—so Hill's poem dedicated to Osip Mandelstam begins. In 1921, T. S. Eliot wrote: 'it appears likely that
poets in our civilization, as it exists at present, must be *difficult*'.[3]
Twelve years later, finding reasons why poets have been thought,
rightly or wrongly, difficult, Eliot gives advice on how to become
the 'more seasoned reader, he who has reached, in these matters, a
state of greater *purity*, does not bother about understanding; not,
at least, at first'.[4] In encountering new poetry, receptivity is
essential and 'greater *purity*' may mean an attentive openness to
the ways in which a poem makes itself felt. Irritably reaching after
the meaning may prevent the reader from attending to it. Such
openness, alert but not defensive, is also required for making a
person's acquaintance: a necessary stage in becoming, and finding
out if you want to become, someone's friend.

Most people have friends. Why does the poet not turn to his
friends, to those who are naturally close to him? In 'About an
Interlocutor', Osip Mandelstam argues that addressing living interlocutors 'takes the wings off the verse, deprives it of air, of flight.
The air of a poem is the unexpected. Addressing someone known,
we can only say what is known.'[5] Mandelstam's sense of risk in

[2] Citations of poems or notes to poems by Geoffrey Hill are taken from *Collected Poems* (André Deutsch Ltd., Harmondsworth, 1985, and Oxford University Press, Inc.), to which page nos. in parentheses refer.

[3] T. S. Eliot, 'The Metaphysical Poets', *Selected Essays*, 3rd edn. (1951), 289. Hill alludes to Allen Tate on Eliot's difficulty in *The Lords of Limit*, 131.

[4] Eliot, *The Use of Poetry and the Use of Criticism* (1933), 151.

[5] Osip Mandelstam, *Selected Essays*, trans. S. Monas (Austin, Tex., and London, 1977), 61, 62–3, and 61.

choosing interlocutors has not been the experience of many poets in English; nor, beyond a casual sense of 'to know someone', will what may be addressed to living interlocutors remain restricted to the known, for even those to whom we are closest remain distinctly unknowable. 'There is no lyric without dialogue', Mandelstam continues; but it is dialogue with an unknown interlocutor. He accepts a reductive presumption about other people, resisting a style of poetry bound to reiterate trite lessons for an identified audience. If those closest to us are felt to be unknowable, there is truth in Mandelstam's statement that 'Fear of a concrete interlocutor, a listener from the same "epoch," that very "friend in my generation," has persistently pursued poets at all times.' The attraction of hearing our words in the consideration of another's light, and the fear of what that light may show—such feelings between poets and interlocutors, poems and readers, as between potential friends, are among the impulses which encourage attachment.

Hill rarely addresses his poems to identified living interlocutors.[6] The familiar style, one of whose virtues is to foster attachment and equality, was defined by Donald Davie, writing on Shelley, as 'a quality of tone, of unflurried ease between poet and reader', and Davie notes that Shelley's poems in the familiar style were 'inspired by "the companions around us"'.[7] He implies that the admired tonal relations between poet and reader may be substantiated and exemplified by relations between poet and interlocutor. Davie argues that this style of poetry flourishes in societies with settled conventions of behaviour, and a homogeneous literary culture. Poetry of a similar kind has survived into our day when the conditions for a public familiar style—if ever other than ideal— barely exist. There are poets now, and Davie is among them, who

[6] The dedication of poems to living people, where the dedicatee is not addressed in the poem, should not be confused with the poetry of living interlocutors. Geoffrey Hill often dedicates his poems to relatives, friends, and colleagues; occasionally dedications included in magazine publications are later dropped, and vice versa; see Philip Horne, 'A Bibliography . . .', in P. Robinson (ed.), *Geoffrey Hill: Essays on his Work* (Milton Keynes, 1985), 237–46.

[7] Donald Davie, *Purity of Diction in English Verse* (1952), 138, 159, where Davie is quoting a phrase of Mary Shelley's. For a criticism of Davie's application of Augustan poetic manners to the contemporary poet's relations with readers, see William Empson, 'Monks and Commissars', *Argufying: Essays on Literature and Culture*, ed. J. Haffenden (1987), 112.

seek to compose a transition between public and private. The poet adopts an intimate tone where integrity of voice can be sustained, while remaining aware that the poem is intended to be overheard by people other than those to whom it is addressed. Hill has admired Swift's poetry for making such transitions, though in conditions more approaching an ideal. He singles out

> in particular its power to move with fluent rapidity from private to public utterance and from the formal to the intimate in the space of a few lines. At times, in the letters to Bolingbroke and Oxford, what is private is simultaneously public in its implications. It is of course true that when one has a few good friends and those friends happen to be the most important men in England, E. M. Forster's injunction 'only connect' has a particularly happy significance.   (p. 68)

Swift's ability to 'represent personal predicaments emblematically and turn private crisis into public example'(p. 68) is attractive because it overcomes the division Hill notes in the essay on Ransom. Relations between Hill's poetry and its readership are difficult, involving suspicion and enthralment, attraction and fear, different from Shelley's Pisan circle, or, again, from Swift's 'few good friends'.

Hill has repeatedly touched on the artist's historical subservience to men of power. In 'Annunciations, 1' from *King Log*, troubadours appear at such men's banquets as 'all who attend to fiddle or to harp | For betterment' (p. 62). Hill's own gloss explains: 'they listen to violin and harp, because the function of art is to instruct by delight ("for betterment" = "for moral improvement"). At the same time they fiddle and harp, in the vulgar sense of the term, they pull strings to get on (they try to "better themselves").'[8] Hill's object, despite the remote setting, is to exemplify a dilemma in poetry's commerce with contemporary social usage and abusage. The poem's concluding line contains the word 'gobbets' which the *Oxford English Dictionary* gives as 'Piece, lump, esp. of raw flesh or food; extract from a text set for translation or comment.' If society is a conspiracy of the mutually self-advancing, the poet's higher calling may make him want to have nothing to do with it.

Resistance to the banquet values has inspired the creation of particularly succulent morsels for 'comment'. Difficult poetry has

---

[8] Hill, cited in K. Allott (ed.), *The Penguin Book of Contemporary Verse*, 2nd edn. (Harmondsworth, 1962), 390–3, for this and the two citations which follow.

been defended on the disputable grounds that in a society which advances by conspicuous consumption the harder it is to swallow the better. Once again, poetry's moral quality is defined by its isolation. A poem too may be *in* the world, but not *of* it. The 'unflurried ease' that Davie found in the familiar style is secured upon implicit agreement between reader and writer, similar to that which may exist between friends, to take what is given on trust. The familiar style trusts to the good intentions of both sides in the literary exchange. Hill, in writing sceptically of the 'poetry-banquet', has identified for modern poetry a context of mutual exploitation and suspicion, a context of separated people in linguistic difficulties.

Hill's commentary on 'Annunciations' was prompted by Kenneth Allott's problem when attempting to anthologize him for a revised edition of *The Penguin Book of Contemporary Verse*. Allott recounts how his own choice from *For the Unfallen* dissatisfied the poet and Hill's preferences were unintelligible to the anthologist:

> The alternatives then are to omit Mr Hill altogether from the anthology or to represent him by the most recent work with which he is content. I have chosen the latter course because I think Mr Hill is a poet. I understand 'Annunciations' only in the sense that cats and dogs may be said to understand human conversation (i.e. they grasp something by the tone of the speaking voice), but without help I cannot construe it. Mr Hill has kindly supplied the following comment on the poem . . .

Hill's self-defence and self-exegesis is acutely dubious about poetry consumers. It converts Allott's politely mocking confessions of faith and perplexity into a picture of social relations between English speakers:

> I suppose the impulse behind the work is an attempt to realize the jarring double-takes in words of common usage: as 'sacrifice' (I) or 'Love' (II)— words which, like the word 'State', are assumed to have an autonomous meaning or value irrespective of context, and to which we are expected to nod assent. If we do assent, we are 'received'; if we question the justice of the blanket-term, we have made the equivalent of a rude noise in polite company.

By recognizing a desire to assume the meanings of words 'irrespective of context' this passage implies what a context is. T. S. Eliot, it may be recalled, wrote that the music of a word 'arises from its relation first to the words immediately preceding and following it, and indefinitely to the rest of its context; and from another relation, that of its immediate meaning in that context to all the other meanings which it has had in other contexts'.[9] Eliot applied the word 'context' first in an intrinsic sense (the parts of speech that precede and follow a word and so restrict its meaning), then extrinsically to mean both other places in texts where the word is used, and other milieux, other occasions in which the word arises. Where context means milieu or occasion, speech is more context-specific than writing.

We mostly speak to more or less identified auditors in more or less recognized contexts, and the meanings of our words are defined accordingly. A writer who works to situate the text by invoking a named or indicated interlocutor, and describing or implying an occasion, seeks to carry over into the intrinsic context some of the external constraints which help to secure the meanings of words. For Mandelstam this was to 'take the wings off the verse', to ground it. By attention to syntactic and semantic ambiguity, to intrinsic context, 'the jarring double-takes in words of common usage' may be realized in the poem. To follow that impulse, as Hill's reference to 'a rude noise in polite company' suggests, is to grow distant and difficult with regard to extrinsic contexts, to particular situations, circumstances, interlocutors, and, by extension, readers.

In *The Lords of Limit*, Hill describes the human situations in which his authors find themselves so as to identify precisely their virtues in literary contexts. 'Situation', as a critical term, combines a neutral descriptive sense with a highly charged, but imprecise, evaluative meaning. When Hill revised 'it seems to be a modern scholastic fallacy that "living speech" can be heard only in the smoke-room or in bed'[10] to 'modern fallacy . . . only in intimate situations' (p. 39), he deployed the word's vagueness and neutrality. Hill was being evasive about the problem concealed by this so-called 'fallacy' since he himself writes that 'the modern poem, is not a public occasion'. He observes that Ransom's 'are poems of "situation" where the nuances range from simple "setting" to the fullest implications of being in a devil of a fix' (p. 126). Swift attracts the word too, enduring the whole range in his life:

⁹ Eliot, 'The Music of Poetry', *On Poetry and Poets* (1957), 32–3.
¹⁰ Hill, 'The World's Proportion: Jonson's Dramatic Poetry in "Sejanus" and "Cataline" ', *Jacobean Theatre*, ed. J. Russell Brown and B. Harris (1960), 114.

Given the current English political attitude, to be in Ireland, the 'depending kingdom', as a member of the so-called governing class was to be in a 'situation' of considerable difficulty. Swift polemically rejected the situation as a principle in the fourth *Drapier's Letter* but encountered it daily as a fact. His sensitive reaction to this situation, both personal and national, resulted in a release of creative energy ... (p. 83)

Hill's valuable appreciation of Swift stands upon his being able to move from '*situation*', meaning specific predicament, to *situation*, meaning daily experience of it, to *situation* meaning historical impasse both personal and national; and also upon the direct correlation of those different situations to 'situations' in works of art: 'Rochester peoples a situation with actors who themselves grasp that they are "situated" and must therefore act to live.' (p. 71) Swift's ability, at times, to make 'what is private ... simultaneously public in its implications' (p. 68), to move between types of situation, is located by Hill within Swift's political defeat, and he suggests the importance for Swift of the defeated man: 'Defeat restores Unity of Being, if only hermetically and in isolation.' (p. 75) Such isolation resembles the context of the modern poet as Hill sees it, and there is a compensation for the lonely figure identified in what might have been Shakespeare's situation when composing *Cymbeline*: 'it is possible for serious artists to elicit a private freedom from the fact of not being received as they deserve' (p. 55).

A public freedom is elicited for the artist by converting 'situations' into contexts where volition can be sustained: ' "Situation" is inescapable; "stance" or "attitude" is vital' (p. 126), Hill notes in the essay on Ransom. St Robert Southwell, facing the Privy Council, achieves 'stance' and 'attitude' in the 'most searching of contexts' (p. 26); his stand is 'vital', both alive and necessary. Wordsworth achieves it in a poem: 'The "magical change" between stanzas eight and nine of the "Immortality" Ode is vital' (p. 95). Hill contrasts this with Richard Oastler's declamatory style and a phrase of Matthew Arnold's: 'Oastler's speech and Arnold's "has anyone reflected" are inert.' (p. 95) Here are further correlations of situations and contexts. Southwell's vital stance refers both to his conduct in life and his style of writing. Wordsworth's is a poetic transition. Oastler's is a case of demagoguery. Arnold's is a gesture in an essay. The imaginative and ethical comparability of contexts within literary writing and outside it gives life to Hill's work. The

identities of saying and doing, and of writing and saying, are
necessary for the grounding of his judgements. He acknowledges
that it is disputed ground, but adds, 'I would respond that
"utterance" and "act" are not distinct entities.' (p. 11) The writers
he most admires in *The Lords of Limit* and his poetry have all
enacted 'this sense of identity between saying and doing' which, in
'Our Word Is Our Bond', he suggests 'Modern poetry . . . yearns
for' (p. 153). A freedom of movement between situations and
contexts allows an argued identity of saying and doing; it also
makes possible the contrast of writers' exemplary behaviour with
the negative and contagious verbal and moral conditions in 'a devil
of a fix' (p. 126).

   Placing together 'Difficult' and 'friend' in the opening line of his
poem addressed to Mandelstam, Hill correlates disparate contexts
and situations. Mandelstam, to whom the poem is '*A Valediction*
. . .', was at times a difficult man as well as a 'difficult' poet. The
memoir by his widow Nadezhda, *Hope against Hope*, begins
memorably: 'After slapping Alexei Tolstoy in the face, M. immediately returned to Moscow.'[11] In homage to his subject, Hill's poem
is difficult, though not impossible—a word Davie applies to
Mandelstam and his contemporary Marina Tsvetayeva: 'Impossible persons, both of them.'[12] Hill's poem employs meanings of
'difficult' applied to poetry and behaviour, but also draws to the
word implications from its relation to, and distance from, 'hard':

> Tragedy has all under regard.
> It will not touch us but it is there—
> Flawless, insatiate—hard summer sky
> Feasting on this, reaching its own end.   (p. 81)

That summer sky can be unfeeling, painful to bear, difficult to
understand, strenuous, severe, and strict in its performance of
tragedy's selective gluttony. Mandelstam was also a hard poet (his

---

[11] Nadezhda Mandelstam, *Hope against Hope*, trans. M. Hayward (1971), 3.
Seamus Heaney reflects on this sentence in 'Osip and Nadezhda Mandelstam', in
The Government of the Tongue (1988), 71–3.
[12] Davie, *The Poet in the Imaginary Museum*, ed. B. Alpert (Manchester, 1977),
268. See also Davie, *Collected Poems* (Manchester, 1990), 356–7: here Davie
considers Mandelstam's 'hardness', taking a cue from Mandelstam's 'About the
Nature of the Word', where he writes, 'man should be the firmest thing on earth'.
Henry Gifford has informed me that the Russian word translated as 'firm' has the
sense of 'hard', 'steadfast', and 'resolute'.

poems are not easy, and they can be firmly resolved): his '[Stalin Epigram]'[13] contributed first to his exile and then to his death when in transit to a labour camp. The relation of 'Difficult friend' to 'hard summer sky' implicates Mandelstam in his predicament, without lessening a tacit condemnation of his treatment: Mandelstam may have had a tragic flaw in his difficulty as a social being and a hard poet, but the tragedy that did for him is 'Flawless'. Stalin's state, however evil it was, could not conceive itself capable of culpability. Mandelstam's poetic difficulty was self-protective; he could imply criticism of the state by indirection. Yet such obliquity was itself regarded by the state as antisocial. Hill's poem is called 'Tristia . . .' because Mandelstam too wrote a poem of that name, and, naming his poem, he associated himself with Ovid, who, when in exile, sent a work of that title back to Rome. Both poets were banished from the capital by their respective rulers.

Closer to home, the subtitle to 'Tristia . . .', '*A Valediction to Osip Mandelstam*', remembers Donne's title 'A Valediction Forbidding Mourning',[14] for Hill's poem is also a refusal to mourn:

> The dead keep their sealed lives
> And again I am too late. Too late
> The salutes, dust-clouds and brazen cries.   (p. 81)

He is too late because Mandelstam is dead, and because others have leapt on his hearse as if it were a bandwagon. The 'brazen cries' might be trumpet blasts, hard because they are made of the alloy brass. Both its obduracy and impurity might account for 'brazen' in its idiomatic sense; the cries are shameless in feeding off his fate. Hill is aware that Mandelstam's social and poetic context is not his, and that his is not perilous. Tragedy may have 'all under regard' but 'It will not touch us'—we will not be moved by it, and will not suffer it. Hill implies a relation between that regard and his own with the title he gave to the group from which 'Tristia . . .' comes: 'Four Poems Regarding the Endurance of Poets'. The difficulty of Hill's poem inheres in the adjustment of its regard: it must be hard, for, though distant from the events it is alert to, it is

---

[13] Osip Mandelstam, *Selected Poems*, trans. C. Brown and W. S. Merwin (1973), 69–70.

[14] Hill's title associates the well-known English love-poem of parting with Mandelstam's own poem of departure, which begins, in the Brown and Merwin translation, 'I have studied the science of good-byes' (*Selected Poems*, 23–4).

conscious of their violent reality. However, it must not too readily visualize violence, taking its hardness from the forces it resists. Nor can it be too close to its subject, assuming thus an unfounded intimacy with such suffering.

Hill's general title is concerned with 'the Endurance of Poets', with the pains that some poets have had to bear, and how they have outlived their lives in the poetry which survives them. 'Difficult friend, I would have preferred I You to them', Hill begins, as if the speaker were himself a remote Augustus 'preferring' candidates for literary posts; thus, *they* may be Stalin's politically acceptable poets and critics. Yet 'prefer' has its less specialized meaning here too, and *they* may also be the late mourners and followers. Osip Mandelstam died when Geoffrey Hill was 6. The first person singular may also be the poet speaking. Mandelstam is a 'Difficult friend' of Hill's only in and through the poetry which survived him, thanks largely to the agencies and memory of his widow. If we are not too difficult, too brazen, or too hard, the poet in his poetry may be able to fulfil 'the great end I Of poesy, that it should be a friend'.¹⁵

II

Ben Jonson's 'Inviting a friend to supper' promises a fine social occasion through the skill with which it adopts and vivifies a literary context. It consolidates social trust by exercising trust-worthiness in, for instance, the freedom and constraint, the liberty of its couplets:

> No simple word,
> That shall be vtter'd at our mirthfull boord,
> Shall make vs sad next morning: or affright
> The libertie, that wee'll enjoy to night.¹⁶

To refuse such an invitation would be a social and literary solecism, for it would suggest that the receiver could understand neither the poem's worth nor the good faith in which it had been issued to the friend. 'Solecism' is a word which combines a writer's behaviour in

---

¹⁵ John Keats, *The Poems of John Keats*, ed. M. Allott (1970), 80.
¹⁶ Ben Jonson, *Ben Jonson*, 11 vols., ed. C. H. Herford, P. and E. Simpson (Oxford, 1925–52) viii. 65.

his words with points of social behaviour. The *Oxford English Dictionary* gives definitions and exempla under three main headings: '1. An impropriety or irregularity in speech or diction; a violation of the rules of grammar or syntax; properly, a faulty concord. 2. A breach or violation of good manners or etiquette; a blunder or impropriety *in* manners, etc. 3. An error, incongruity, inconsistency, or impropriety of any kind.' It is a word Hill has had recourse to more than once, for it holds together, in its social and grammatical meanings, related values which the distancing or separation of extrinsic context, occasion, or situation from intrinsic textual context attenuates or threatens to break. The word keeps literary behaviour in touch with behaviour on other occasions, even when the literary context does not concern itself directly with non-literary behaviour.

In his radio script for 'The Living Poet', Hill refers to the problem of banishing these literary rude noises from one's work:

The most painstaking attention to detail does not necessarily preclude the perpetration of 'howlers'; grammatical or referential solecisms. It is arguable that, in the notorious 'middle years', the impulse to persist in writing poetry (and indeed certain kinds of meditative prose) is an impulse to restitution. There is an obligation to get the facts right; and when one has failed, one must seek to amend.[17]

In the postscript to *King Log*, Hill printed a revised text of 'In Memory of Jane Fraser' subtitled 'An Attempted Reparation', and with a note saying: 'I dislike the poem very much and the publication of this amended version may be regarded as a necessary penitential exercise.'[18] His versions are identical apart from three commas in the first stanza, the change of a comma to a full stop at the end of the penultimate line, and the final line—which originally read 'And a few sprinkled leaves unshook'[19] and became 'Dead cones upon the alder shook.' (p. 22) The phrasing is more resolute,

---

[17] Broadcast talk, 'The Living Poet', BBC Radio 3, 6 Aug. 1979.
[18] Hill, *King Log* (1968), 70.
[19] In the first two printings of the poem (1953, 1954) the punctuation at the end of the penultimate line is a full stop. This became a comma in the first edition of *For the Unfallen* (p. 23) and reverted to a full stop in *King Log* (p. 69). In the third impression of *For the Unfallen*, the revised version with the dates '[1953–1967]' is printed, but the three commas from the first stanza which have been removed in the *King Log* text have returned, or remained. The poem appears on p. 22 of *Collected Poems* in the text of *For the Unfallen* (3rd edn.) but without the dates in brackets.

the rhythm more conclusive, and the nonce verb 'to unshake' has been removed.

'"They say that genius is an infinite capacity for taking pains," he [Sherlock Holmes] remarked with a smile. "It's a very bad definition, but it does apply to detective work."'[20] In 'Poetry as "Menace" and "Atonement"', where aggressive and reparative impulses are examined in socio-political and theological terms, Hill considers Simone Weil's proposal for 'a system whereby "anybody, no matter who, discovering an avoidable error in a printed text or radio broadcast, would be entitled to bring an action before [special] courts" empowered to condemn a convicted offender to prison or hard labour' (p. 8). He introduces the reasonable doubt that the remorse a writer might feel about failures of due care and attention resulting in misprints and solecism, or which anyone might feel about committing a *faux pas*, are not of the same order as those human errors and irresponsible oversights that cause pain and death. It is true, and practical ethical considerations would preserve both a sense of proportion in judgement and not stint on forgiveness. Yet careless talk can cost lives. As Hill has said of the sinking of the *Titanic*, about which he has written a terse ode, it was the hubristic claim of the designers that falsely lulled the passengers and crew; they were, Hill observes, 'swamped by a slogan'.[21]

Charles Péguy was 'a meticulous reader of proof' (p. 206), and *The Mystery of the Charity of Charles Péguy* includes this *pièce de résistance*:

> To dispense, with justice; or, to dispense
> with justice. Thus the catholic god of France,
> with honours all even, honours all, even
> the damned in the brazen Invalides of Heaven.   (p. 190)

The stanza shows how an inattention to commas in proof-reading could mean the difference between a legal process founded on ethical discrimination, and a judiciary that can do what it wants, such as 'to dispense | with justice'—where the quandary of the line-end gives pause or just hurries on down injudiciously. The poet, bearing in mind a judging reader such as Simone Weil with

---

[20] Sir Arthur Conan Doyle, *A Study in Scarlet, The Complete Sherlock Holmes Long Stories* (1929), 29–30.
[21] Hill, 'The Poetry of Allen Tate', *Geste* (Leeds) (Nov. 1958), 9.

her proposed power of citizen's arrest, manifests by attention to
the state of the text a resistance to a sloppy world. It is a world
with which his mock solecisms signify a measure of complicity.
The aloofness of resistance and embrace of complicity are both
contained in the conclusion of 'Annunciations, 2':

> 'O Love,
> You know what pains succeed; be vigilant; strive
> To recognize the damned among your friends.'   (p. 63)[22]

These lines combine conflicting desires: to identify those who are
'damned', and happen to include our friends, in order to shun
them; and to acknowledge 'the damned' as also friends, to pray for
or tend them. Combining these, Hill dramatizes a struggle between
self-interested and self-sacrificial impulses; he also settles the strife
into the irreducible and singular presence of the words themselves.
The extended ambiguities present a conflict of motives and balance
of opposed pressures, the combination of a further conflict. Played
upon by diverse forces and driven to seek amends by writing more
poems, further occasions for culpability, the poet continues to be
impelled by what Hill has called 'yet another impure motive,
remorse' (p. 7).[23]

John Purkis, in a footnote on the imaginary Spanish poet Hill
'translated' for 'The Songbook of Sebastian Arrurruz', considered
that 'Although this poet is a "spoof"—his name sounds like
"arrowroot" and he is said to have been banished for committing
a grammatical solecism so that his work was removed from all the
anthologies—Hill takes him very seriously as an *alter ego*.'[24]
Sebastian Arrurruz is a fictional instance of similarities and differences between suffering for the sake of your art and martyrdom
for others' sakes. In a 'Homage to Henry James', entitled 'The
Martyrdom of Saint Sebastian', readers are called to 'Consider

---

[22] Hill's concluding line may be a reminiscence of Eliot's famous remark about
Pound's 'Hell Cantos', Cantos xiv–xv, that they are a 'Hell for the *other people*, the
people we read about in the newspapers, not for oneself and one's friends', in *After
Strange Gods* (1934), 43.

[23] Hill's phrasing and his qualm here may derive from Eliot's 'About Donne
there hangs the shadow of the impure motive; and impure motives lend their aid to
a facile success', in 'For Lancelot Andrewes', *Selected Essays*, 345; and, perhaps,
'the purification of the motive I In the ground of our beseeching', 'Little Gidding',
Collected Poems 1909–1962 (1963), 220.

[24] John Purkis, *Donald Davie, Charles Tomlinson, Geoffrey Hill*, A306 Twentieth Century Poetry, The Open University (Milton Keynes, 1976), unit 31, p. 55.

such pains "crystalline": then fine art I Persists where most crystals accumulate.'(p. 51) The solemn joke about Arrurruz's banishment and removal from the anthologies hints at agreement with Simone Weil's proposed punishment for verbal crimes as well as awareness of Mandelstam's fate. At the risk of bathos and banality, Hill keeps exemplary sufferings in contact with more mundane errors to which all are prone:

'A knitting editor once said "if I make a mistake there are jerseys all over England with one arm longer than the other".' Set that beside Nadezhda Mandelstam's account of the life and death of her husband . . . and one can scarcely hope to be taken seriously. Men are imprisoned and tortured and executed for the strength of their beliefs and their ideas, not for upsetting the soup. And yet one must, however barely, hope to be taken seriously. (pp. 7–8)

In a broadcast talk, Hill said: 'I write very much by intuition and work hard, by means of scholarship and self-criticism, to satisfy myself of the validity of that intuition',[25] and in the sonnet sequence, 'An Apology for the Revival of Christian Architecture in England' he employs the scholarly temptation to wax nostalgic so as to chart a history of falsification and neglect. '6. A Short History of British India (III)' half mourns a half-truth:

> the life of empire like the life of mind
> 'simple, sensuous, passionate', attuned
> to the clear theme of justice and order, gone.
>
> Gone the ascetic pastimes, the Persian
> scholarship . . .   (p. 157)

The most consistently presented scholarly passion is Sebastian Arrurruz's attenuated meditation on a lost *amour*. He has been called by his translator 'a shy sensualist with a humour that could be said to balance the sensuality except that the finer nuances have been lost in translation'[26]—and his work has the self-confessed manners of an academic poet:

> Already, like a disciplined scholar,
> I piece fragments together, past conjecture
> Establishing true sequences of pain;

---

[25] 'The Living Poet', BBC Radio 3, 6 Aug. 1979.
[26] J. Haffenden (ed.), *Viewpoints: Poets in Conversation with John Haffenden*, (1981), 95.

For so it is proper to find value
In a bleak skill, as in the thing restored:
The long-lost words of choice and valediction.   (p. 92)

A 'disciplined scholar' is an academic trained in a certain discipline; also one who has been chastised, perhaps for scholarly error or 'past conjecture' which has proved untrue, and, mortifying himself by penance, takes pains to establish 'true sequences of pain'—a compacting of both his disappointments and his recalling them. Attempting to restore what was 'long-lost' (as in 'long-lost friend', of one re-encountered), he remains perpetually desirous while perpetuating his longings through his work.

In the fifth fragment of Arrurruz's sequence of pain, his scholarly taste for exactitude conspires with the desolate emptiness of his yearning; this familiar conflation of reading and eating (another instance of the suspicious 'poetry-banquet') makes Arrurruz sound gluttonous, choosy, and more than half-starved:

> I find myself
> Devouring verses of stranger passion
> And exile. The exact words
>
> Are fed into my blank hunger for you.   (p. 97)

The phrase 'I find myself' has Arrurruz surprised at who he discovers himself to be; he has uncovered himself by study, given substance and sustenance to his feelings by reading poetry. That exact word 'blank' he might have chanced upon in a number of not unsuitable English poems, or his translator might have done. Coleridge, suffering from unrequitable extra-marital passion, gazes on the heavens 'with how blank an eye!'; Tennyson, recalling a dead friend, sees how 'On the bald street breaks the blank day'; while William Empson—though strictly speaking Arrurruz could not have known this—begins a poem about no longer writing poetry with 'It is this deep blankness is the real thing strange.'[27] With his 'blank hunger' Arrurruz, a poet with an empty piece of

---

[27] S. T. Coleridge, *The Complete Poetical Works of Samuel Taylor Coleridge*, 2 vols., ed. E. H. Coleridge (Oxford, 1912), i. 364, and see also William Wordsworth, *The Poems*, 2 vols., ed. J. O. Hayden (Harmondsworth, 1977), i. 528; Alfred, Lord Tennyson, *The Poems of Tennyson*, 3 vols., ed. C. Ricks (1987), ii. 326; William Empson, *Collected Poems* (1955), 81; and see Hill, *Collected Poems*, 68, and *The Lords of Limit*, 151.

paper before him, is also suffering from a writing block; he reads to feed his inspiration. He is a skeleton at the feast.

III

Writing of the 'Lachrimae' sequence, Jeffrey Wainwright notes that the sonnets 'are also a profound discussion and demonstration of artifice in expression. Truly it is a dangerous game. Our language has woven several connotations around the words "artifice" and "artificial" for good reasons.'[28] This credits the cumulatively collaborative efforts of English-speaking people with beneficial results; Wainwright's statement trusts the common tongue, whereas Hill—despite and because of his ear for the colloquial—cannot put his trust in it or them. He has written that 'In handling the English language the poet makes an act of recognition that etymology is history. The history of the creation and the debasement of words is a paradigm of the loss of the kingdom of innocence and original justice.'[29] Hill feels the shudder of the Fall in words, words that are *of* this world, and sees acts of composition as a resistance to, and a seeking to amend for, sins and shame. Employing the same old words, he attempts to restore to the world of usage, and to the world that usage makes ours, distinguishable senses and values embedded in them. Victor Erlich asked,

could not this unique command of the ambiguity of human experience, this adeptness at conveying the 'formidable density' of the world's body (John Crowe Ransom), be construed as a counterpart of that density of the medium, which, according to the Formalists, is typical of poetry?[30]

Hill has a theological view of the medium's density, 'a sense of language itself as a manifestation of empirical guilt'(p. 7). Amid the slipperiness, confusion, sloppiness, and active deceit of language-users (and, Hill would add, in words themselves), it is always advisable to read the small print closely.

Speaking of the 'debasement of words', Hill reiterates a time-honoured analogy between poetry and money. 'To debase' means

---

[28] Jeffrey Wainwright, 'Geoffrey Hill's "Lachrimae" ', *Agenda*, 13 (Autumn 1975), 37–8.
[29] Haffenden (ed.), *Viewpoints*, 88.
[30] Victor Erlich, *Russian Formalism* (The Hague, 1955), 180.

to 'lower in quality, value, or character', and to 'adulterate' coins. Some unequivocally admire rich imagery and like their poets to have the Midas touch. The weakness of the pure gold of poetic speech,[31] however, is that it is brittle and particularly vulnerable to debasement. Osip Mandelstam (whose conflicting uses of monetary imagery led Clarence Brown to note 'a profound indecision of spirit'),[32] argued in his 'Notes about Poetry' (1923) for the place of alloy in verse:

Colloquial language loves accommodation. Out of hostile chunks it creates an alloy. Colloquial speech always finds the middle, convenient way. In its relationship to the whole history of language it is inclined to be conciliatory and is defined by its diffuse benevolence, that is to say, by its opportunism. Poetic speech on the other hand is never sufficiently 'pacified,' and in it, after many centuries, old discords are revealed.[33]

The sceptical weighing of colloquial language's attributes in this passage does not extend to a preference for poetic speech over them; Mandelstam is in favour of colloquial language which, he argues, 'brings good to the language, that is longevity, and helps it, as it might help the righteous man, to perform its ordeal of independent existence in the family of dialects'. Such speech, originating in exchanges between people, shows the values Mandelstam attributes to it, because its various and hidden senses allow the expression of one idea or feeling while implying another, seeking in the explicit and implicit meanings of speech a tacit goodwill in the hearer, and offering room for his or her reply in confirmation or disagreement. It is the medium in which differences of opinion, value, idea, and belief can understand each other and themselves through the maintenance of amicable relations by mutual accommodation.

For Hill, colloquial language with its clichés and dead metaphors, idioms, jargon, and slang is a matter for vigilant adjustment. This involves attachment and resistance: 'because the nature of true poetic speech is the attempt to transfigure some of the negative liabilities of speech into more positive form'.[34] When Jesus went up

---

[31] See Hill, 'Gurney's Hobby', *Essays in Criticism*, 34 (Apr. 1984), 106–8.
[32] Clarence Brown, *Mandelstam* (Cambridge, 1973), 104. See also Heaney on this imagery in *The Government of the Tongue*, 81–2.
[33] Osip Mandelstam, *Selected Essays*, 80.
[34] Haffenden (ed.), *Viewpoints*, 86.

into a high mountain with three of his disciples 'he was transfigured before them. And his raiment became shining, exceeding white as snow'. Peter suffered from one of the negative liabilities of speech when he blurted out 'let us make three tabernacles', for 'he wist not what to say' (Mark 9:2–3, 6). Hill wants to maintain the independent and active involvement of art in its 'situations'. Confronting a predicament and rendering it as a literary context, a poem converts a given 'fix' into a volitional stance. In *The Lords of Limit,* Hill describes this rendering and converting in the language of a mystical theology: 'as a moral artist' Swift 'can transfigure his patterns'; Southwell's is 'an art of "transfiguration".' The term connotes both "metamorphosis" and "elevation"'; Wordsworth, in the 'Immortality' Ode, 'transfigures a fractured world', a world 'redeemed by the silence between stanzas eight and nine'. The transfiguration foreshadows redemption.

Hill's word 'transfigure' makes a high claim for what poetry can do. Poetic and colloquial speech are understood by an analogy between man's Fall into the Christian hope (Donne's 'Therfore that he may raise the Lord throws down')[35] and the debasement then redemption of words. Hill's difficulty lies in convincing himself, and the reader, that the 'transfiguring' and 'redeeming' work of the artist is not a mere 'leap of metaphor' but 'a process of reasoning' or, were it only a leap of metaphor, that the poem remain an act of faith from within 'the data' and not 'a pious wish', terms he applies to Sidgwick and T. H. Green. James Joyce can make the Wall Street Crash into an archetype of the Fall of man,[36] but the activities of bankers and economists may make it harder for them to enter the kingdom of heaven. Can poetic strategies, with their ancillary theoretical underpinnings, do the work of a redeemer? Is this not inevitably the realm of metaphor, metaphor which stands either as a sign of a faith maintained elsewhere, or as a memory of the given but no longer sustaining theological mystery?

The New Testament offers neither a simple nor a single attitude to money and coin. The money-lenders in the Temple, the parable of the talents, and the lilies of the field are not so much contradictory as complexly complementary. When certain Pharisees and

[35] John Donne, *Poetical Works,* ed. H. J. C. Grierson (1933), 337.
[36] See 'The fall . . . of a once wallstrait oldparr is retaled early in bed and later on life down through all christian minstrelsy', James Joyce, *Finnegans Wake* (1939), 3.

Herodians tried to 'catch him in his words', Jesus asked, 'Whose is this image and superscription?' His reply to their answer may be interpreted as reaffirming, out of an attempt to corner him into a treasonable utterance, the metaphorical similarity and the categorical difference between the power men have in controlling a currency, and God's power: 'Render to Caesar the things that are Caesar's, and to God the things that are God's' (Mark 12: 13, 16–17).

Of *Mercian Hymns* XI-XIII, Jon Glover remarks: 'Offa's coins appear as objects of wonder, symbols of power, relics, objects of curiosity and contempt.'[37] The first of these prose-poems, rendering to Offa the things that are Offa's, advances the analogy between minting a coin and making a work of art:

> Coins handsome as Nero's; of good substance and weight. *Offa Rex* resonant in silver, and the names of his moneyers. They struck with accountable tact. They could alter the king's face.

Nero, who torched Christians, 'fiddled while Rome burned', considered himself an artist. The poem touches on exchange values for which an artist may be responsible. There is a regicidal aggression in 'They struck', somewhat pacified and weighed by 'tact'—where social delicacy is in contact with touch. The pressures behind and against the two senses are nicely judged in the ambiguity of 'accountable'—the treasury's books balanced, the king's vanity about his profile understood:

> Exactness of design was to deter imitation; mutilation if that failed. Exemplary metal, ripe for commerce. Value from a sparse people, scrapers of salt-pans and byres. (p. 115)

The other side of the coin to that risky artistic freedom to alter the king's face is his punishment for counterfeiters: the criminal disfigured, altered by mutilation. A poet too may design poems in the hope of preserving their 'originality', their difficulty of imitation. 'Exemplary' is one of Hill's much-loved and needed words. He has applied it to his art: 'Poetry is responsible. It's a form of responsible behaviour, not a directive. It is an exemplary exer-

---

[37] Jon Glover, 'The Poet in Plato's Cave: A Theme in the Work of Geoffrey Hill', *Poetry Review*, 69 (Mar. 1980), 63.

cise.'[38] His prose-poem's diction is also 'Exemplary metal, ripe for commerce'.

Are Hill's words an alloy of hostile chunks, a coinage more durable than pure metal, made in the spirit of Mandelstam? Instances in this prose-poem, despite the allusion to colloquial language, suggest that a pure poetic speech has been carefully designed to retain value. The phrase 'scrapers of salt-pans and byres' gains resonance by having the colloquial 'scraping by', and the familiar 'buyers', implied in the design; but these words are not in the poem. It preserves its own originality of diction against the debasement of such phrases—phrases which have the world too much with them.

Hill has been exercised by how 'the lyric maintains a perilous autonomy against mundane attrition'.[39] This suggests that it is as perilous to be independent of the world's attrition, as to be worn down by a too familiar and lengthy contact with it. Hill keeps colloquial language within hearing distance of his poems because he is aware of the danger; it does not appear in his poems as colloquial speech because such language is too debased by the compromises embedded in it through the centuries:

> Swathed bodies in the long ditch; one eye upstaring.
>   It is safe to presume, here, the king's anger. He
> reigned forty years. Seasons touched and retouched
>   the soil.
>
> Heathland, new-made watermeadow.   (p. 115)

The expression 'safe to presume'—which, like 'I dare say', has lost touch with the physical vulnerability in 'safe' and 'dare'—is contextualized with a violence and authority that sets safety mortally in question, makes presumption a dangerous arrogance. You too could end up in the ditch. The comma'd-off 'here' points to the historical context of Offa's coins, to the place in the prose-poem reached, and so to a present moment in history, from which it is safe to presume, I dare say—a safety for which to be grateful. Here, recalling Mandelstam's distinction, Hill has 'transfigured' the pacified colloquialism into a fearfully poetic phrase, a reminder of our bloody past in the language.

---

[38] Haffenden (ed.), *Viewpoints*, 99.
[39] Hill, 'Robert Lowell: Contrasts and Repetitions', *Essays in Criticism*, 13 (Apr. 1963), 193.

Yet how the seasons in their alterations imitate the valuing and revaluing of coins and words: 'touched' is cognate with 'tact'; 'to retouch'[40] is what painters do to improve the finish of their work. The collocation of touches gives a delicacy and persistence to the seasonal cycle, the circulation of currency, the exchanges of words. The epithet 'new-made' applied to 'watermeadow' brings to mind Pound's renovative poetic slogan and the title of a 1934 collection of essays, *Make it New*. Just as the seasons retouch the earth, does transfiguring a language redeem the sensible world?

IV

If poetry could achieve this miracle it would be demonstrating enormous, perhaps omnipotent, power. Where does the power that language does have come from? Pound believed that the poetic vitality of a language lay in the identity of word and thing, in preciseness of definition, and that it was the poet's job to promote and maintain this vitality. When T. S. Eliot wrote that 'Language in a healthy state presents the object, is so close to the object that the two are identified',[41] Pound's influence on the idea and its phrasing may be heard. These thoughts encouraged a timely, radical attention to poetic technique at the beginning of the twentieth century by emphasizing the pre-eminence of the poet in the creation of meaning, the demonstration of power.

In 'Redeeming the Time', Hill quotes Hopkins's speculation that if a writer will express 'a sub[t]le and recondite' thought on a difficult subject in a mimetic style 'something must be sacrificed, with so trying a task, in the process, and this may be the being at once, nay perhaps even the being without explanation at all, intelligible.' (p. 94) Hill believes it a sign of decadence to sacrifice density to intelligibility, or respond to what he calls a 'very dubious

---

[40] See Eliot, *Collected Poems 1909–1962*, 36, where Eliot, rhyming 'pose' and 'repose', gives to the latter a flickering sense of 'pose again' as well as its accepted meaning; the device is similarly employed in 'a hundred visions and revisions' (p. 14).

[41] Eliot, *Selected Essays*, 327; I may be exaggerating Pound's influence, but Eliot's statement does not accord with the view of poetic language in 'The Music of Poetry' (1942), and cited above. For Pound's pronouncements on poetic language at the time of Eliot's essay on Swinburne, see 'A Retrospect', *The Literary Essays of Ezra Pound*, ed. T. S. Eliot (1954), 4–5.

philosophy of authorial responsibility to the "reader"' (p. 10). He offers instances to support the contention that writers are ruined by considering the demands of an audience. T. S. Eliot, in his later plays, 'could genuinely mistake "the fashionable requirements" of Shaftesbury Avenue or the Edinburgh Festival for the needs of "a wider audience"' (pp. 135–6). Hill calls Eliot's situation here 'that degree of worldly temptation'; and, while John Crowe Ransom did not have to endure it, he was 'inclined to confuse "consensus" with "language" and the consensus is increasingly that of the "dull readers"' (p. 136).

Resisting such temptations there is a modernist nostalgia for rudimentary conditions:

In tables showing primitive Chinese characters in one column and the present 'conventionalized' signs in another, anyone can see how the ideogram for man or tree or sunrise developed, or 'was simplified from', or was reduced to the essentials of the first picture of man, tree or sunrise.[42]

Pound's three divergent possibilities for the relation of the primitive to the conventional indicate the unlikeness of his English, and anyone's English, to the Chinese characters as here conceived in their representational relation to things. The strain involved for Pound in writing poetry in English made him long for a state where the poetic language came ready-made: 'Fenollosa was telling how and why a language written in this way simply HAD TO STAY POETIC; simply couldn't help being and staying poetic in a way that a column of English type might very well not stay poetic.'

Davie, discussing a distinction between fundamental identity and conventional relation of words and things, cites the French poet St-John Perse reporting a conversation with André Gide:

He told me of the attraction that an exhaustive study of the English language was beginning to exert over him. I, for my part, deplored the denseness of such a concrete language, the excessive richness of its vocabulary and its pleasure in trying to reincarnate the thing itself, as in ideographic writing; whereas French, a more abstract language, which tries to signify rather than represent the meaning, uses words only as fiduciary symbols like coins as values of monetary exchange. English for me was still at the swapping stage.[43]

[42] Ezra Pound, *ABC of Reading* (1951), 21, 22.
[43] St-John Perse, cited in Davie, *Articulate Energy: An Inquiry into the Syntax of English Poetry* (1955), 97; Hill alludes to Davie's discussion, and in particular ibid. 121, in *The Lords of Limit*, 140.

Pound's primitivism is impossible for English. Neither St-John Perse's view of the language, nor his discrimination between it and French seem quite accurate. The richness of English—not only its seams of near-synonyms, but also the compounded ambiguity, the alloy of its plainest words—makes it a language which can be made to manifest in its ambiguous density an emblem of, a metaphoric experience of 'the thing itself', but because of this ambiguity its users are equally obliged to exchange it as a structure of fiduciary symbols. The absence of absolutely and eternally fixed relations between words and things, or between speakers and interlocutors, obliges English speakers to give and take words in trust. Moreover, it is context, both within writing and in the implied circumstances of utterance, that contributes to the definition of meanings and values in the exchange, that helps to settle the conditions of trust.

Quoting Péguy's words, Hill incidentally tests St-John Perse's distinction between the French and English languages:

> 'Encore plus douloureux et doux.' Note how
> sweetness devours sorrow, renders it again,
> turns to affliction each more carnal pain.   (p. 196)

The word 'renders' in Hill's stanza recalls St-John Perse's fiduciary symbols, paying and paying back, but finds in the French for sweet and sorrowful a texture of incarnate being and an opportunity for a 'transfiguration' which the paper-currency metaphor would disallow. Shakespeare's Juliet can express a continuity of pleasure in approaching separation because her English 'Parting is such sweete sorrow' has an initial alliteration which the vowels and terminal consonant of 'sorrow' depart from;[44] in 'douloureux et doux' the long drawn out suffering of the three vowels in 'douloureux' is compacted into the brief pout of 'doux', with its more closely related vowel sounds and consonants. These differences are one reason why the *Oxford English Dictionary* illustrates 'render', meaning 'translate': 'poetry can never be adequately rendered in another language'. Hill's renderings demonstrate two interdependent characteristics of poetic language. The first is that both French and English, with their different means, combine to give auditory

---

[44] W. Shakespeare, *The excellent and lamentable Tragedie, of Romeo and Juliet*, sc. 7, 960.

substance to signification; the second, that both depend on trusting exchanges between writer and reader. A dense style invites a reader's engagement, Hill indicates by citing Coleridge, who 'required "the attention of my reader to become my fellow-labourer"' (p. 119). The reader cannot simply be 'required' to do this, though; a relationship has to be established in trust.

V

The transfiguration foreshadows redemption. In *The Lords of Limit*, 'Jonson redeems what he can' (p. 54) and Hopkins's 'vocation was to redeem the time' (p. 103), while, less confidently, Hill writes of his own critical vocabulary: 'If these terms appear portentous and suggestive of a "certain laxity", they may be partly redeemed by close illustration.' (p. 95) This touches once more on relations between a situation in historical experience and the theological significance attributed to it. Mediating between these is the transfiguring power of poetic language.

An extract from Péguy's writings entitled 'Politics and Mysticism' dwells on the term 'mystique' in its conclusion: 'Everything begins in mysticism and ends in politics.—The interest, the question, the essential is that in each order, in each system, mysticism be not devoured by the politics to which it gave birth.'[45] Péguy's life and work gave Hill occasion to enact, in his own poetic language, the attrition of 'la mystique' by 'la politique' while seeking to transfigure that too-worldly process into the absolutes of an irreducible piece of art. In the phrase 'douloureux et doux' cited above, it is as though the French for 'sweet' had eaten the heart out of 'sorrow', leaving the husk of two consonants and a vowel. Those words, like 'la mystique' and 'la politique' are set in an aggressive feeding embrace; but the word 'renders' in the same passage, calling upon translation and artistic portrayal, recalls that other discrimination concerning politics and mysticism: 'Render to Caesar the things that are Caesar's, and to God the things that are God's.'

Early in *The Mystery of the Charity of Charles Péguy*, questions are asked about the responsibility of a writer for his words:

[45] Charles Péguy, *Basic Verities*, 'Rendered into English by Anne and Julian Green' (1943), 107.

> Must men stand by what they write
> as by their camp-beds or their weaponry
> or shell-shocked comrades while they sag and cry?   (p. 183)

The question frames diverse circumstances in which it is difficult and conceivably inadvisable to 'stand by'; nor is it always possible to avoid being merely 'bystanders'. If men do not or cannot ever be thought to 'stand by' their words (in those senses relating to vigilance, loyalty, and accountability), can poetry be considered, in Hill's words, 'a form of responsible behaviour'? One reason why it is difficult to stand by the words in a poem is because they move; they have a rhythmical momentum which, with their interplay of meanings and associations, creates an emotion:

> But still mourn,
> being so moved: éloge and elegy
> so moving on the scene as if to cry
> 'in memory of those things these words were born.'   (p. 196)

The bracketing, outer rhymes of the stanza conjoin poetry's sweetness to the subject's sorrows, while the sardonic play on 'moved' and 'moving' holds that up for inspection. There's a hint of piling on the agony to grab the stage. Wordsworth thought that,

from the tendency of metre to divest language in a certain degree of its reality, and thus to throw a sort of half consciousness of unsubstantial existence over the whole composition, there can be little doubt but that more pathetic situations and sentiments, that is, those which have a greater proportion of pain connected with them, may be endured in metrical composition, especially in rhyme, than in prose.[46]

A poet of Hill's scrupulous scepticism could recognize the value of what Wordsworth observes, but suspect rhyme and rhythm for rendering sorrow sweet, making pain enjoyable beyond endurance. Such musical powers can be viewed in the light of Péguy's belief that 'la politique' would devour 'la mystique', that suffering is exploitable by poet and politician; and 'to divest language ... of its reality' may render the suffering redemptive and the language transfiguring, but also invite the exploitation of suffering for the encouragement of a spurious national unity by 'church and civic dignitaries' (p. 206).

In early work, Hill devised a compacted syntax and complex

---

[46] Wordsworth, 'Preface to *Lyrical Ballads*', *The Poems*, i. 885.

diction which almost brought his poetry to a standstill. Edward
Lucie-Smith found it 'difficult to avoid the word "costive"',[47] while
Christopher Ricks felt that 'the poems, though they still have force,
no longer have so much momentum'.[48] Reading 'The Lowlands of
Holland', a reader may

> Witness many devices; the few natural
>
> Corruptions, graftings; witness classic falls . . .   (p. 47)

The short clauses, single words, parted and sutured by the punctuation and lineation, require a dwelling on each word, while to read
on is to follow the staggering moves. Being moved from 'Corrup-
tions' to 'graftings' involves bearing in mind that the former are
'decompositions', 'moral deteriorations', 'corrupt practices', 'perv-
ersions of languages'; and the latter are 'transplanted tissue',
'hybrid plant growth', 'illicit spoils'. The halting rhythm was
purposefully conceived. Hill wrote at the time about Allen Tate's
'Ode to the Confederate Dead': 'The Union cavalry . . . are like
Milton's angels, who cannot be injured. Parting before the blow,
they flew together again. The self-healing properties of Capitalism
are, of course, renowned.'[49]

Hill is still exploring the collusions of military, commercial,
governmental, and religious visions and actions. No longer balking
their careering progress while miming their processes, in *The
Mystery* . . . his music answers to the sorrows, doing what it can:

> The line
>
> falters, reforms, vanishes into the smoke
> of its own unknowing; mother, dad,
> gone in that shell-burst, with the other dead,
> 'pour la patrie', according to the book.   (p. 192)

That line-break 'the smoke | of its own unknowing' recalls the
anonymous medieval mystical text *The Cloud of Unknowing*, as if
to go through the smoke of battle were to penetrate the Divine
mystery. The distance between that title and Hill's rephrasing of it,
the faintly clumsy 'its own unknowing', echoes the settled, colloquial, and even sceptical 'its own undoing'—where the men merely

---

[47] E. Lucie-Smith (ed.), *British Poetry Since 1945* (Harmondsworth, 1970), 240.
[48] Christopher Ricks, 'Cliché as "Responsible Speech": Geoffrey Hill', *London
Magazine* 4 (Nov. 1964), 101.
[49] Hill, 'The Poetry of Allen Tate', 10.

meet their death. They die 'according to the book', which may be a Bible, a training manual, and a historical account. The relation of 'dad' to 'patrie'—by way of 'other dead', which itself remembers 'mother'—finds connection and conflict between loyalties to the home and the homeland; and the movement of the lines, in their laconic and mundane routine, bear one of those 'more pathetic situations' which Wordsworth recognized as needing the consolation of a 'still, sad music'.

Hill's paradigm of language as debased and to be redeemed is not infused with Christian hope. The Fall may be fortunate, but only poetry appears to offer consolations and dubious ones at that. Hill's high agnosticism infuses his poetry with the need for, and the suspicion of, something beyond poetry. '7. Loss and Gain' in 'An Apology . . .' takes its title from Cardinal Newman's novel of Catholic conversion, an event with losses and gains of its own. Condensed into Hill's sonnet is a balance-sheet of English nineteenth-century history: losses and gains for 'the ruined and the ruinously strong'. Conceiving the two together conjures labyrinthine bafflements. Is there self-delusion in the one who gains a vision of salvation, and, caught in Keats's quandary ('Was it a vision, or a waking dream? . . . Do I wake or sleep?'[50]), imagines that history may be atoned for?

> Vulnerable to each other the twin forms
>
> of sleep and waking touch the man who wakes
> to sudden light, who thinks that this becalms
> even the phantoms of untold mistakes.   (p. 158)

These 'untold mistakes', which are both unadmitted and so vast in number as to be uncountable, include a world of different blunders: self-deception, solecism, fatal error of judgement. Hill's scruple and discipline suggest a further paradigmatic substitution: the state of the text for the state of the world, by which the poems become patterns of an uncorrupted body politic.[51] Hill's careful rhythmic adjustments would regulate trustful, though not credulous, exchanges of meaning within the lines' contexts, their responsibly moving words models for the circulation of an ideal currency. But this would be to indulge the 'pious wish' that Hill's poems, or

---

[50] Keats, *The Poems of John Keats*, 532.
[51] See Hill's discussion of this way to read a poem in *The Lords of Limit*, 143–4.

anyone's, were capable of becalming 'even the phantoms of untold mistakes'. It would be to miss the risk of becoming 'becalmed'. The scepticisms are not to be outstripped. Could a poem ever atone for history? Could it alone redeem the time?

VI

When Mandelstam characterized colloquial language, he came to the conclusion that 'Poetic speech on the other hand is never sufficiently "pacified," and in it, after many centuries, old discords are revealed.' Hill too knows how poems preserve 'old discords' and can be menacing; he has also proposed that 'it may sometimes be necessary to mimic a dilemma' in a poem—hearing discords, to contain them.[52] *Mercian Hymns* XVIII includes a piece of poetic speech which reveals old discords after many centuries, and it mimics a dilemma to examine the uses and abuses of scholarship and imagination. It discreetly alludes to a political furore involving quotation out of context and the referencing of sources:

> At Pavia, a visitation of some sorrow. Boethius'
> dungeon. He shut his eyes, gave rise to a tower
> out of the earth. He willed the instruments of
> violence to break upon meditation. Iron buckles
> gagged; flesh leaked rennet over them; the men
> stooped, disentangled the body.
>
> He wiped his lips and hands. He strolled back to the
> car, with discreet souvenirs for consolation and
> philosophy. He set in motion the furtherance of
> his journey. To watch the Tiber foaming out
> much blood.   (p. 122)

The prurient visualization of violence for dubious ends begins with an elevation of Offa's tourism ('Offa's Journey to Rome', the hymn is entitled) by employing the ostentatiously Latinate 'visitation', while 'some' implies a connoisseurship of emotion, a simultaneous indulgence and withdrawal. The sentence which mimics a crucial moral slip is 'He willed the instruments of violence to break upon meditation.' It is menacingly unclear whether Offa wills the instru-

---

[52] Hill, '"The Conscious Mind's Intelligible Structure": A Debate', *Agenda*, 9–10 (Autumn–Winter 1971-2), 21.

ments to be broken by the power of meditation, identifying with Boethius; or, he wills them to break Boethius' meditation; or, he exploits meditation to will that a body be broken.

Seamus Heaney has observed that in *Mercian Hymns* 'the Latinate and local also go hand in glove',[53] but, rather than conspiring together, here a conflict between etymologies is impacted in the movement from 'instruments', 'violence', and 'meditation' to 'Iron buckles gagged; flesh leaked rennet'—a body tortured on the rack, to which the Latinate, though it commands the proceedings, does not, as the men do, stoop. Hill's style here is indebted to Pound's *Homage to Sextus Propertius*, which also deploys confrontations of words with diverse etymological origins. About Pound's lines 'The moon still declined to descend out of heaven, | But the black ominous owl hoot was audible', Davie wrote:

The absurdly misplaced formality of 'declined to', and the ludicrously stilted passive, 'was audible', exemplify the English of the bored schoolboy lazily construing his Latin homework, but equally the proud pompous clerk (Pakistani, Cypriot or whatever) using the language of those who were lately his imperial masters ... Thus it appears that by wholly transposing 'imperialism' into language, into the texture of style, by forgetting his own existence 'for the sake of the lines', Pound has effected a far more wounding and penetrating critique of imperialism in general ...[54]

Hill, whose essay 'Our Word Is Our Bond' painstakingly traces Pound's untold mistakes, has praise for *Homage to Sextus Propertius*: 'The status fought for, and accomplished, within the comedy and melodrama of this sequence, is, therefore, that of standing by one's words in a variety of tricky situations' (p. 156).

The difficulty for the poet is that to enter the 'tricky situations' he must 'mimic a dilemma'; this might involve transposing 'imperialism' into raw translatorese. Simultaneously, the poet must stand by his words; must compose them so that his lines resist their diction's susceptibility to being the inert phraseology of the shibboleths that constitute the dilemma. Hill must exhibit the dilemma without succumbing to Yvor Winters' 'fallacy of imitative form:

---

[53] Heaney, *Preoccupations* (1980), 160.
[54] Davie, *Pound* (1975), 59, 61; the lines Davie comments on are in Ezra Pound, *Collected Shorter Poems* (1952), 240.

the attempt to express a state of uncertainty by uncertainty of expression'.[55] A poem which mimics a dilemma will necessarily show signs of what it offers for inspection. This partly explains Pound's troubles with critics over the supposed schoolboy howlers in *Homage to Sextus Propertius*.[56] Or, as Hill replied to those who found nostalgia in 'An Apology . . .', 'To be accused of exhibiting a symptom when, to the best of my ability, I'm offering a diagnosis appears to be one of the numerous injustices which one must suffer with as much equanimity as possible.'[57] Such critical misunderstanding blunts the strategic ironies that seek to mimic and remain responsible for the mimicking words. It is one consequence of detaching inner context, where the words ambiguously work, from an outer context of named or implied interlocutors.

The second verset of *Mercian Hymns* XVIII associates Offa with Pontius Pilate and the Pharisees; he enjoys washing his hands of a moral problem. 'He set in motion the furtherance of | his journey' hints at a self-interested furthering and careering from place to place in his tourism—which takes him, in the final clause, as far as Rome, the underworld, and the prophecy of the Cumaean Sybil to Virgil's Aeneas. Hill's footnote points to this; and the prose-poem's final clause turns out to be a gobbet of poetic speech: ' "To watch the Tiber foaming out much blood": adapted from Virgil, *Aeneid*, VI. 87, "et Thybrim multo spumantem sanguine cerno".' (p. 202) In this line old discords are revealed after centuries, referring to the prediction of war given to Aeneas, and fulfilled later in his epic.

The same Latin differently rendered appeared in Enoch Powell's speech of 20 April 1968: the year in which Hill began *Mercian Hymns*. The speech was given to the Annual General Meeting of the West Midlands Area Conservative Political Centre at the Midland Hotel, Birmingham; that is to say, in the modern-day regional capital of Offa's Mercia. Nearing his end, Powell said:

As I look ahead, I am filled with foreboding. Like the Roman, I seem to see 'the River Tiber foaming with much blood'. That tragic and intractable phenomenon which we watch with horror on the other side of the Atlantic but which there is interwoven with the history and existence of the States

---

[55] Yvor Winters, *In Defence of Reason* (Denver, 1956), 87.
[56] See E. Homberger (ed.), *Ezra Pound: The Critical Heritage* (1972), 155–71.
[57] Haffenden (ed.), *Viewpoints*, 93.

itself, is coming upon us here by our own volition and our own neglect. Indeed, it has all but come.[58]

To allude to bloodshed is not necessarily to invoke it; but Powell moves from 'I seem to see', through 'it has all but come', to 'All I know is that to see, and not to speak, would be the great betrayal'—from mock-hesitant prophecy to expectation, justified by adopting a phrase from Virgil without its context of a war that will found an imperial power: he gives substance to his enmities. The allusion to Virgil is the only particular instance of bloodshed given: 'after many centuries' he reveals the 'old discords' to invite an emotive concurrence. Thus, he would set in motion the further-ance of his journey: to change British immigration policy, and, more immediately, to affront the shadow cabinet leader Edward Heath.

Elsewhere, Powell said:

A classical scholar is equipped with the pre-digestion of a great range of human experience, political and also non-political, so that among non-classics he is rather like a man who knows the times-table, compared with people who don't . . . The classical scholar already knows that eight times seven are seventy-two [*sic*] because that's in the *Antigone*, as it were.[59]

This is to suppose, whether the mistaken multiplication is deliber-ate or not, that the application of past literary experience to contemporary lived experience is as unambiguous as doing your sums. It cannot be: because words, and words in different lan-guages, do not perform with the transparent utility of numbers. Powell's classical scholarship visualizes violence to gain emotional assent for what is desired by invoking its opposite; in the phrase 'we watch with horror', the alarm in 'with horror' fails to conceal the glee at having that example to enforce his own case—'we watch'. Powell's words, many believed at the time, appeared to encourage social discord in the name of alleviating or preventing it. In his opening paragraph, Powell released himself from injunc-tions to caution when referring to possible conflicts—a caution which distinguishes the responsible public speaker from the rabble-rouser:

[58] Speech by Rt. Hon. J. Enoch Powell, MP, printed in T. E. Utley, *Enoch Powell* (1968), 190.
[59] John Goodbody and Robert Silver, 'Politicians and Other Artists: An interview with Enoch Powell', *Trinity Review* (Summer 1977), 12.

Above all, people are disposed to mistake predicting troubles for causing troubles and even desiring troubles: 'If only', they love to think, 'if only people wouldn't talk about it, it probably wouldn't happen'. Perhaps this habit goes back to the primitive belief that the word and the thing, the name and the object, are identical.[60]

Hill, unlike the young T. S. Eliot in his essay on Swinburne, is not drawn to this 'primitive belief'. When he speaks of poetry as 'a form of responsible behaviour', his phrase summons belief in speaking and writing as acts to be judged like any other physical actions. Hill's phrase implies that because words and things, speakers and interlocutors are not bound in fixed relations their fine adjustment, a form of responsible behaviour, is urgent and necessary. Powell's introductory remarks do not release him from the obligation to speak with tempered caution; they locate him in a linguistic context where such care and attention is essential to prevent 'predicting troubles' from inviting or 'causing troubles'. When Hill asks: 'Did Péguy kill Jaurès? Did he incite | the assassin?' (p. 183) he is pondering this vexed relation between the use of certain words and the foreseeable consequences.

By enacting in *Mercian Hymns* XVIII a show of scruple which veils the unscrupulous, and in a literary context where adjusted regard makes the engagement of scruple possible, Hill restores, through the language of the prose-poem and the example of the notes, moral attention to an occasion for accurate and responsible behaviour. A final detail about Powell's speech illuminates Hill's pointed scholarly tact: '"for consolation and philosophy": the allusion is to the title of Boethius' great meditation, though it is doubtless an excess of scruple to point this out.' (p. 202) Enoch Powell, a professional academic philosopher, lost his place in Edward Heath's shadow cabinet for a speech which was 'racialist in tone and liable to exacerbate racial tensions';[61] he had offended against the protocol for Members of Parliament by quoting at length a letter from Northumberland about the behaviour of immigrants in his Wolverhampton constituency. Powell neither gave precise details of his source—though he stated that it was not an anonymous letter—nor did he offer evidence for the assertions

---

[60] Utley, *Enoch Powell*, 179.
[61] Ibid. 18; see also B. Smithies and P. Fiddick, *Enoch Powell on Immigration* (1969), 59–60, 133–4.

made there. The protocol of not quoting private correspondence derives from two conflicting obligations: it is right to protect the privacy of those who write to their Member of Parliament; it is also right, when material is quoted, to give details of the sources and evidence so that they can be independently examined.

VII

Mercian Hymns hardly appears to concern itself with the linguistic behaviour of contemporary politicians. If it does, its presentation of symptoms in aid of diagnosis is particularly oblique. When Hill praised the 'fluent rapidity' of movement in Swift's poems 'from private to public utterance and from the formal to the intimate', he recognized the necessary context for that fluency in Swift's social relations. Such conditions do not, for the most part, exist for poets who today want to address their work to the conditions of public life.[62] Had Hill addressed Enoch Powell in his prose-poem, it would have drastically reduced meaning and implications, limiting it to making a point about a particular act in the late 1960s, and would have involved assuming a relation between speaker and inter-locutor in either the public or the private sphere—and, if the latter, of the private made public, an assumption which, as far as I know, does not have substance in the lives of either poet or politician. Nevertheless, oblique strategies, the absence of named living inter-locutors for instance, enable his work to render some of the ethical matter of political life without the tonal falsifications that an assumed familiarity or public address could entail. Eric Griffiths has noted that Hill 'knows better than to rely simply on the bare underpinnings of imagined auditors';[63] and, in the absence of extrinsic contexts in which such acts of imagination may be substantiated, the intrinsic contexts of his words exemplify lan-guage as a thing which, like 'The wooden wings of justice', is 'borne aloof' (p. 161)[64] into the considerable realm of the poem.

[62] See Hill, *The Lords of Limit*, 131.

[63] Eric Griffiths, 'Standing in the Shadows', *Perfect Bound*, 6 (Cambridge) (Autumn 1978), 79; I am indebted to Eric Griffiths for drawing my attention to possible relations between *Mercian Hymns* XVIII and Enoch Powell's so-called 'Rivers of Blood' speech.

[64] Hill's 'borne aloof' recalls 'a wailful choir of small gnats' which is 'borne aloft I Or sinking as the light wind lives or dies' in Keats, *The Poems of John Keats*, 654.

The colloquial speech which Mandelstam valued as a constituent of poetry's language cannot appear in lyric poetry as simply itself. The word 'colloquial' indicates at least two speakers who are also listeners, and implies exchanges of words. Hill has written on more than one occasion that lyric poetry's composition is 'dramatic'.[65] When he describes how a writer may enact the 'drama of reason' by including the 'antiphonal voice of the heckler' (p. 90), his word 'antiphonal', the church-music term, converts into a composed counterpointing of voices a nettled inruption of dissent in another's seamless mid-flow. It has been reported of leading politicians that as young men they sometimes asked 'supporters to heckle them to enliven dull meetings'.[66] The composition of heckling voices is vulnerable to such party management; the poet may feel the need to 'enliven' his work, and the divide between an antiphony that is merely veiled accord and the true challenge of confronted differences resides, for poetry, in a composed stylistic rawness. This is a quality Hill praised in Wordsworth's 'Resolution and Independence', where his 'creative gift was to transform the helpless reiterations of raw encounter into the "obstinate questionings" of his meditated art without losing the sense of rawness' (p. 109). Wordsworth's gift is beyond Hill's scope; but Hill, who is drawn, as Keats could be, towards 'the high claims of poetry itself' (p. 5), has stretched for 'rawness' by attempting some resistance to those higher reaches. Of Swift as a poet, Hill wrote:

there will be a temptation to claim that a timely encounter with popular verse 'redeemed' Swift as a poet. But there is no simple and obvious way in which this could be affirmed. Some of Swift's poems may have achieved immediate popular success, but one still has reservations about calling him a 'popular' poet; he did not so much use as demonstrate the colloquial; the very kind of accuracy he achieved was the result of a certain aloofness. (p. 82)

Those last two clauses are also true of Geoffrey Hill; and that 'very kind of accuracy' is his greatest strength. However accurate though, there is no redemption here. Not only is there 'no simple and obvious way in which this could be affirmed', there is no way.

The fourth section of 'The Songbook of Sebastian Arrurruz' has:

---

[65] See ' "The Conscious Mind's Intelligible Structure": A Debate', 75, and Hill, *The Lords of Limit*, 90.
[66] *Sunday Times*, 16 Oct. 1983, p. 16.

A workable fancy. Old petulant
Sorrow comes back to us, metamorphosed
And semi-precious. Fortuitous amber.
As though this recompensed our deprivation.
See how each fragment kindles as we turn it,
At the end, into the light of appraisal.   (p. 95)

Here, 'as though' is prepared for with 'workable fancy' and sardonically scrutinized by 'appraisal'; besides which, its combination of the wishful and the sceptical is ontologically precise. It defines the loss, 'our deprivation', and marks the need to repair, which it rejects as a 'fancy'. Though indeed 'semi-precious', Hill's lines bear comparison with lines from 'The Female Vagrant' about which, as noticed earlier, he remarks: 'In "as if" and "because", pedantically isolating her, we glimpse the remoteness of words from suffering and yet are made to recognize that these words are totally committed to her existence.' (p. 117) Hill's obliquity can release him into felicity, but, as comparison with Wordsworth's encounter poems indicates, his rarefied occasions attenuate the human purposes of his lines.

There is a difference in kind between addressing lyric poetry to a living, trusted interlocutor and capitulating to a consensus. How indebted are the many readers like us to Coleridge's presence as apostrophized addressee, the friend of the 1805 *Prelude*, or to Sara Hutchinson for the first, passionately vulnerable, version of what became 'Dejection: an Ode'. Literary behaviour between people authenticates the implied general relation between reader and poet. It is because Hill is suspicious of the reader to a fault, and includes the reception of literary work in a writer's 'situation', that poetic achievement is defined by mystical analogies: atonement, transfiguration, redemption. However credible this account of literary value, it does not describe why, for the most part, people read worthwhile books; and, because Hill does not consider the reception of literature as context for its positive qualities, the works he admires are attributed with few of the virtues for which they may be sought. Poetry can only give the pleasure Wordsworth ascribes to it in his 'Preface to *Lyrical Ballads*', or be that friend in Keats's 'Sleep and Poetry', if it is first received. Once received, its benign influences may be variously helpful, as the situations from which it arises are infectious variously and to differing degrees.

What is distanced in the achievement of Hill's exemplary accuracy is the sound of other specified people being spoken to, or uttering the grain of their lives. His poems recognize this distance and judge it by demonstrating, through the composing of voices which is his poetry, tones which have become far cries from people:

> Not as we are but as we must appear,
> Contractual ghosts of pity; not as we
> Desire life but as they would have us live,
> Set apart in timeless colloquy.
> So it is required; so we must bear witness,
> Despite ourselves, to what is beyond us,
> Each distant sphere of harmony forever
> Poised, unanswerable. If it is without
> Consequence when we vaunt and suffer, or
> If it is not, all echoes are the same
> In such eternity. Then tell me, love,
> How that should comfort us—or anyone
> Dragged half-unnerved out of this worldly place,
> Crying to the end 'I have not finished'.   (p. 77)

Plangent and exacerbated, a voice calls upon a living, nameless interlocutor to answer. Only, in reply, no word comes. Hill's 'florid grim music broken by grunts and shrieks' (p. 199) dramatizes the achievement of poetry's harmonies—colloquial, answerable speech transposed into 'timeless colloquy'; it also contains the dramatic exchanges of a discordant world, nevertheless and necessarily attuning them. Though friends are not contracted to each other, as the married are, and though Hill has been principally concerned with words as 'bonds', he has alluded to the bonds of friendship. Of his Oxford years he has said, 'I remained ill-at-ease socially, but made and kept several good friends.'[67] One of Offa's school friendships is sorely tried in *Mercian Hymns* VII: 'Coelred was his friend and remained so' (p. 111) even after being flayed for losing a toy aeroplane. Friendship's bonds can be heard to break in 'While friends defected, you stayed and were sure' (p. 159), or 'your friendship so forsaken';[68] and also in Péguy's life, where Hill notices 'the harsh severing of old alliances and friendships in the years that followed' (p. 206). A benefit of the attuned language of

---

[67] Haffenden (ed.), *Viewpoints*, 77; Hill discusses literary friendship in 'Letter from Oxford', *London Magazine*, 1 (May 1954), 72–3.

[68] This is how the line 'as seeker so forsaken' (p. 141) appeared in the second of 'Three Mystical Songs', *Agenda*, 11–12 (Autumn–Winter 1973–4), 54.

poetry is that it stays faithful and remains true. In the long run it will be a friend. As well as for the liberty and fidelity of our friends, we can be grateful for Geoffrey Hill's work with all its broken music and concords for ever on the mend.

7
Envy, Gratitude, and Translation

Far cries may reach here through the sounds of verses in translation. The activity of rendering texts in another language is a process
of creating similarity in difference. Bernard Bergonzi has recently
affirmed the desirability of studying poems from different cultures,
'not only because of the basic "otherness" of foreign poetry, but
because such knowledge gives one a better sense of what English
poetry can and cannot do'.[1] Writing and studying translations is
one way of gaining a sense of what English poetry can and cannot
do. Yet it may also be a means of blurring the sense, of reducing
the 'otherness'. Helen Vendler has affirmed that 'By rewriting poets
from Horace to Pasternak in his own irregular, idiomatic, and
forceful American voice, Lowell announced that American poetry
henceforth would possess the past in a commanding, not subordinate, manner.'[2] This forcefulness, possessing and commanding,
endangers a sense of the original and its translator.[3]

---

[1] Bernard Bergonzi, *Exploding English: Criticism, Theory, Culture* (Oxford,
1990), 197.
[2] Helen Vendler, 'Contemporary American Poetry', in Vendler (ed.), *The Harvard Book of Contemporary American Poetry* (Cambridge, Mass., 1985), 10.
Perhaps the most persistently firm objection to this view came from Vladimir
Nabokov, who wished 'that he would stop mutilating defenceless dead poets—
Mandelshtam, Rimbaud, and others'. *Selected Letters 1940–1977*, ed. D. Nabokov
and M. J. Bruccoli (San Diego, New York, London, 1989), 387; and for a detailed
criticism of Lowell rendering Mandelstam, see 'On Adaption', *Strong Opinions*
(New York, 1973), 280–3. Placing Bergonzi and Vendler together might give the
impression that the argument is between English and American poetry. This is not
the case. There are English poets who have translated with the conscious appropri-
ativeness of Lowell. See e.g. Jeremy Reed's versions from Montale in his *Selected
Poems* (Harmondsworth, 1987), 199–240; and, for his version of 'La casa dei
doganieri', ibid. 208. For other translations of the poem, see Eugenio Montale,
Selected Poems (New York, 1965), 72–5; 'Twenty Seven Poems', trans. K. Bosley,
G. Singh, and B. Wall, *Agenda*, 9–10 (Autumn–Winter 1971–2), 115; and Edwin
Morgan, *Rites of Passage: Selected Translations* (Manchester, 1976), 70. Many
American translators have not forcefully taken possession. Nor is this simply a
question of that misleading idea, literal accuracy. Ezra Pound's 'The River-
Merchant's Wife: A Letter' is not literally accurate, but nor is it written into the
poet's own idiom. Rather Pound's forms are recreated and stretched by the need to

Gabriel Pearson has seen *Imitations* as both 'the exercise of a vast tact' and a 'determination to make Parnassus under his own steam'.[4] Lowell's methods can inflict damage on his image of the poem, or poet even, as Vendler has it. Yet the process of translating a poem begins in every case with an infliction of damage. The first draft is a painfully distorted shadow of its original in which the characteristics that give the poem shape are weakened or lost by changes of word order, dictional register, loss of texture, rhyme, and rhythm. 'So, in the end, for any live translator,' Charles Tomlinson observes, 'it is not a question of approaching a text with a defined method, but of eliciting definition from, and restoring to clarity that chaos which occurs, as, line by line, the sounds and patterns of the original crumble to pieces in the mind of the translator.'[5] Such crumblings can feel like an envious spoiling, even if not so motivated. The translator's work of composition and revision may then be a reparative one, in which the new version is lent qualities in the second language that differentiate it, give it a separate existence, and restore some of its original otherness.

---

find a style for poetry of an extremely different character and civilization. See Sanehide Kodama, *American Poetry and Japanese Culture* (Hamden, Conn., 1984), 74–84.

[3] James Kirkup has noted: 'I dislike those modern poets who seek to impose their own (often inferior) individual style and vocabulary on some helpless foreign poet. I try to let the foreign poet speak out in his own way, with his own voice, at the risk of my English occasionally sounding a little strange.' See 'Translating Penna and Ceruda: Working Papers', in D. Weissbort (ed.), *Translating Poetry: The Double Labyrinth* (1989), 83. My chapter is written from broadly this viewpoint, though I doubt that the two methods are so simply distinguished. The foreign poet's voice may have to be repaired from a confusion of the two in drafts of a translation.

[4] Gabriel Pearson, 'Lowell's Marble Meanings', *The Survival of Poetry*, ed. M. Dodsworth (1970), 81.

[5] Charles Tomlinson, 'Introduction: *The Poet as Translator*', in Tomlinson (ed.), *The Oxford Book of Verse in English Translation* (Oxford, 1980), p. xxi. Tomlinson enlarges on translation and otherness in Bruce Meyer, 'A Human Balance: An Interview with Charles Tomlinson', *Hudson Review*, 43 (Autumn 1990), 441–3.

I

Envy, says Francis Bacon in his essay on the subject,

is also the vilest affection, and the most depraved; for which cause it is the proper attribute of the devil, who is called *The envious man, that soweth tares amongst the wheat by night*: as it always cometh to pass, that envy worketh subtilly, and in the dark, and to the prejudice of good things, such as is the wheat.[6]

Literary envy sows tares amongst its own wheat: it deforms and takes away even that capacity for work which the envying person may possess. In such a state, I would, like the speaker of Shakespeare's Sonnet 29,

> looke upon myself and curse my fate,
> Wishing me like to one more rich in hope,
> Featur'd like him, like him with friends possest,
> Desiring this mans art, and that mans skope,
> With what I most injoy contented least . . .[7]

Writing to Elizabeth Barrett on 21 April 1846, Robert Browning misremembered it: 'So Shakespeare chose to "Envy this man's art and that man's scope" in the Sonnets.'[8] There is no clear-cut distinction between envy and jealousy, but the two words do not overlap in all their uses. Envy is the grudging contemplation of some more fortunate person. Jealousy involves being solicitous for the preservation of something, or resentful towards another on account of a known or suspected rivalry. I can envy a person for his or her advantages. If I were God my jealousy would be an intolerance of unfaithfulness where faith is my due. A jealous

[6] Francis Bacon, *Essays*, ed. M. J. Hawkins (1972), 28.

[7] W. Shakespeare, *The Complete Works*, Original Spelling Edition, ed. S. Wells, G. Taylor, *et al.* (Oxford, 1986), 853. For discussion of relations between social envy, money, art, and love in this sonnet, see 'Editing Out: The Discourse of Patronage and Shakespeare's Twenty-Ninth Sonnet', in John Barrell, *Poetry, Language and Politics* (Manchester, 1988), 18–43.

[8] R. Browning, *Letters of Robert Browning and Elizabeth Barrett Barrett, 1845–1846*, 2 vols., ed. E. Kintner (Cambridge, Mass., 1969), ii. 638. Daniel Karlin comments on the allusion in *The Courtship of Robert Browning and Elizabeth Barrett* (Oxford, 1985), 129. T. S. Eliot also altered the line in *Ash-Wednesday*, I: 'Desiring this man's gift and that man's scope', *Collected Poems 1909–1962* (1963), 95. Christopher Ricks comments on the alteration in *T. S. Eliot and Prejudice* (1988), 223–4.

husband, similarly, is suspiciously vigilant in defence of what he takes to be his own.

Both the *Oxford English Dictionary* and *Webster* give 'envious' as a synonym of 'jealous' in one of its meanings. They suggest that to be jealous of another's art or scope is to envy that person. This muddies both streams. Jealousy of others' gifts may mean wishing to preserve their right and capacity to use them, or their fame in possessing them, as when William Hazlitt, in his essay on envy, writes:

No one envies the *Author of Waverley*, because all admire him, and are sensible that admire him how they will, they can never admire him enough. We do not envy the sun for shining, when we feel the benefit and see the light. When some persons start an injudicious parallel between him and Shakspeare, we then may grow jealous and uneasy, because this interferes with our older and more firmly rooted conviction of genius, one which has stood a severer and surer test.[9]

The jealous husband and the person jealously protective of another's gifts or reputation both have some good fortune to celebrate: a desirable wife, or talented friend, or a just conviction of merit to maintain. The God of the Old Testament is a jealous God because he expects fidelity from his chosen people. God may be jealous, but he cannot envy because he is the omnipotent deity of a monotheism.

Melanie Klein seeks to discriminate between envy, jealousy, and greed in her 1956 paper 'A Study of Envy and Gratitude'.[10] She observes that 'Envy is the angry feeling that another person possesses and enjoys something desirable—the envious impulse being to take it away or to spoil it.'[11] On the other hand, jealousy, she suggests, 'is mainly concerned with love which the subject feels is his due and which has been taken away from him'. Jealousy can

[9] William Hazlitt, 'Envy', *The Complete Works*, 21 vols., ed. P. P. Howe (1930–4), xx. 314.

[10] This Chapter's title acknowledges a debt to Klein's writings on this subject, with which I came into contact through reading poems by Adrian Stokes. See *With All the Views: Collected Poems of Adrian Stokes*, ed. P. Robinson (Manchester, 1981), 49–51, 94, 102.

[11] M. Klein, *The Selected Melanie Klein*, ed. J. Mitchell (Harmondsworth, 1986), 212. It is, of course, possible to use the word envy with positive implication, as in the compliment or expression of good wishes: 'How I envy you!' Yet even this may be the sign of a negative impulse overcome in good feeling. Here I am concerned with the vice and one psychological account of it.

be positive in its operations. Envy, in particular, may cause conditions which invite reparative action; it is also an obstacle to such action. As I have suggested, translation is an activity peculiarly vulnerable to the suspicion of envy expressed in damage done to the original, prompting perhaps the making of reparation.

Hazlitt says of Sir Walter Scott that 'We do not envy the sun for shining, when we feel the benefit and see the light': we don't envy the writer because we feel gratitude. The analogy with the sun removes him from a context of opinion and comparison: no one would think of envying the sun the fact that it shines and gives warmth. The sun doesn't have a reputation for shining which could be taken away: it doesn't derive its value from the social stock exchange of relative and shifting judgements. Shakespeare begins his sestet:

> Yet in these thoughts my selfe almost despising,
> Haplye I thinke on thee, and then my state,
> (Like to the Larke at breake of daye arising)
> From sullen earth sings himns at Heauens gate . . .

His speaker escapes from envy by thinking of another's love for him, a love praised by associating its gift with the effects of dawn, the sun again, lifting the speaker's state out of the earthly realm of status and luck. Shakespeare is no one's fool: 'my state' reminds us of courts, of who's in and who's out, as does the sonnet's couplet:

> For thy sweet loue remembred such welth brings,
> That then I skorne to change my state with Kings.

Bacon says that 'envy is ever joined with the comparing of a man's self; and where there is no comparison, no envy; and therefore kings are not to be envied but by kings'.[12] Bacon seems not to reckon with ambition or the devil here, and Shakespeare's word 'skorne' conceives of the possibility that commoners might envy kings. The sonnet's concluding compliment works by running against a real possibility. Introducing the king's different 'states', the sonnet equivocally invites disbelief in what its conclusion says. This makes the bravura gesture of the compliment all the more winning; yet the hyperbole can sound hollow. The sonnet may be saying that, hard as it is to credit this escape from an outcast state,

---

[12] Bacon, *Essays*, 26.

the poet and interlocutor had better believe it because both interests are served by doing so. The escape from envy may be a sleight of hand, but it's a necessary trick the writer plays on himself, and, since the friend is the focus of his fortune's looking up, the poem turns its compliment.

II

What can writers do to ease their envy of others? Haply think on someone. It will be especially difficult to mitigate and transform envy if it deforms or takes away the capacity for work possessed by the envying person. Melanie Klein believes that 'Greed is an impetuous and insatiable craving, exceeding what the subject needs and what the object can and wishes to give.'[13] She calls it 'destructive introjection'—not a receiving of what is given, but a robbing thoroughly, cleaning out the safe. However, 'envy not only aims at robbing in this way, but also at putting badness, primarily bad excrements and bad parts of the self, into the mother—first of all into her breasts—in order to spoil and destroy her; in the deepest sense this means destroying her creativeness.' Many have flinched at the perverse violence in Klein's description of infantile envy, yet her speculations can be constructive in considering how damage is done to literary creativeness.

Take success, for example. You cannot be destructively jealous of another's success, because the attention given is not yours to have. Your jealousy would be directed to protecting the other's reputation. Nor could you reproduce the work of another which has brought the success you lack, though this has not prevented some from trying. Envying another's success, you want to 'take it away and spoil it'. Bacon wrote that 'whoso is out of hope to attain to another's virtue will seek to come at even hand by depressing another's fortune',[14] and noted how 'he that cannot possibly mend his own case, will do what he can to impair another's'. A reviewer or critic might besmirch the reputation of another. It is not that you want the other's success; rather you

[13] Klein, *Selected Klein*, 212–13. Klein gives examples of envy from the Bible, Chaucer, Spenser, Shakespeare, and Milton in *Envy and Gratitude and Other Works 1946–63* (1975), 182, 202–3.
[14] Bacon, *Essays*, 24, 25.

cannot bear to see it being enjoyed. Richard Wollheim has praised, or acknowledged the good fortunes of, Ashbery and Updike as art critics: 'Their own eminence allows them to be free of envy, and this is a rarity in a critic.'[15]

Envy deforms and takes away the talents its sufferers may possess. How does it do this? The person envied grips my imagination. It is this imagined figure who is spoiled by envy, not necessarily the person in life. Since the figure within is involved in the type of work I do, damage to this other within me eats up part of my inner life. Spoiling a figure within, Klein observes, 'is experienced as particularly dangerous because it has the effect of hampering all attempts at reparation and creativeness'. She continues: 'Envy interferes most of all with these constructive attempts because the object which is to be restored is at the same time attacked and devalued by envy.'[16] To do creative work might involve regaining a generous feeling towards those writers who have been envied.

Also opposing reparation is idealization of other writers. Idealization, Klein notes, 'becomes also an important defence against envy, because if the object is exalted so much that comparison with it becomes impossible, envy is counteracted'.[17] Hazlitt's analogy of Sir Walter Scott and the sun does this, or Shakespeare's 'Like to the Larke at breake of day arising'; and idealization counteracted may figure in the calculated hollowness of the sonnet's hyperbolic conclusion. A further danger in idealization is that it can debilitate the writer through an escape from envying comparison, which generates feelings of constitutional unworthiness or incapacity, when the self is viewed in the distorting light of comparison with an idealized figure.

Envy and idealization are wrestling in 'A Letter to—.', Coleridge's first version of 'Dejection: an Ode'. The object of these mixed feelings is Wordsworth, not only because of his poetic gifts, but also for his domestic happiness:

> To *visit* those, I love, as I love *thee*,
> Mary, William, and dear Dorothy,
> It is but a temptation to repine!

[15] Richard Wollheim, 'Objects of Love', in *TLS* 4547 (25–31 May 1990), 553.
[16] Klein, *Selected Klein*, 224–5.
[17] Ibid. 217.

The Transientness is Poison in the Wine,
Eats out the Pith of Joy, makes all Joy hollow!
All Pleasure a dim dream of Pain to follow!
My own peculiar Lot, my household Life
It is, and will remain Indifference or Strife—
While ye are well and happy, 'twould but wrong you,
If I should fondly yearn to be among you—
Wherefore, O! wherefore, should I wish to be
A wither'd Branch upon a blossoming Tree?[18]

Coleridge understands that his presence and his love for Mary's sister Sara Hutchinson is like envy in its action, destroying goodness, it 'Eats out the Pith of Joy'. Because of the self-abasement, and self-pity too, references elsewhere in the poem to Wordsworth's art ('dear William's Sky-Canoe!' or 'As William's self had made the tender lay!'[19]) idealize the other poet's powers as an escape from the envy which aggravates Coleridge's sense of unworthiness and incapacity. In 'Poetry as "Menace" and "Atonement"' Geoffrey Hill praises Coleridge's 'To William Wordsworth: composed on the night after his recitation of a poem on the growth of an individual mind' (1807), for: 'the quality of disinterested stoicism with which this habitually self-pitying man was able to bring his own broken life and aspirations into the focus of meditation'.[20] The achievement of balanced critical judgement is also a reparation, even temporarily, of individual wholeness.

III

In the *Premessa* to his selected translations, *Il musicante di Saint-Merry*, Vittorio Sereni cites an observation of the poet and translator Sergio Solmi about the desire to translate:

La traduzione nasce, a contatto col testo straniero, con la forza, l'irresistibilità dell'ispirazione originale. Alla sua nascita presiede qualcosa come un

---

[18] S. T. Coleridge, *Coleridge's Dejection: The Earliest Manuscripts and the Earliest Printings*, ed. S. M. Parrish (Ithaca, NY, and London, 1988), 28–9. See also Parrish's Introduction (pp. 1–20) in which he notes 'Wordsworth's marriage gave him the joy Coleridge longed for and envied', 20.

[19] Ibid. 24, 30.

[20] Geoffrey Hill, *The Lords of Limit: Essays on Literature and Ideas* (1984), 12.

moto di invidia, un rimpianto d'aver perduto l'occasione lirica irritornabile, di averla lasciata a un più fortunato confratello di altra lingua.[21]

The translation is born, in contact with the foreign text, with the power,
the irresistibility of the original inspiration. At its birth there presides
something like a feeling of envy, a regret at having missed the irrecoverable
lyric occasion, to have lost it to a more fortunate confrère in another
language.

This envy of another's lyrical occasion resembles that admitted by
Alun Lewis in 'To Rilke': 'if you had known that I was trying | To
speak to you perhaps you would have said . . .' and the German
poet replies that 'they never lack an occasion, | They, the devoted'.
Lewis rejoins with the grimly circumscribed 'But I have to seek an
occasion' and later,

> I hungered for the silence you acquired
> And *envied* you, as though it were a gift
> Presented on a birthday to the lucky.[22]

Poets in difficult circumstances, Lewis in India during 1943 for
instance, can feel robbed of occasion. Sereni, in the same year
Lewis was transferred to India Command, suffered a comparable
loss. It proved irrecoverable except through acts of translation and
a creative devotion to converting the lack into an occasion itself.
He was captured by the invading American army in Sicily on 24
July 1943, and spent the next two years in prisoner-of-war camps
in North Africa. He was separated from the contexts of his early
poetry, and excluded from the experiences of the Civil War in Italy
during those same years.

Again in the *Premessa* to his selected translations, Sereni notes:
'A tradurre da testi altrui non avevo mai pensato fino a quando un
compagno di prigionia, che leggeva l'inglese molto meglio di me
ma non aveva esperienza di versi, mi passò una sua versione
letterale da una poesia di E. A. Poe pregandomi di farne una poesia
italiana'[23] [I had never thought of translating others' texts until a
fellow prisoner, who read English better than I but did not have
any experience of making poetry, passed me his literal version of a
poem by Edgar Allan Poe asking me to make an Italian poem of

---

[21] Vittorio Sereni, *Tutte le poesie*, ed. M. T. Sereni (Milan, 1986), 290.

[22] Three references to Alun Lewis, *Selected Poems*, ed. J. Hooker and G. Lewis
(1981), 67–8.

[23] Sereni, *Tutte le poesie*, 287.

it]. Sereni tells this anecdote to indicate in his translating an impulse towards overcoming isolation, to relocate limits in relation with another.

The urge to translate may prove more powerful, more nagging than an original creative impetus; it may be of the same strength as the original, but it cannot be of the same type. While the original lyric occasion may arrive in the form of an unforeseen encounter with experience, that of the translation involves contact with a text, another's work. This engages responsibilities of a different kind. The impulse to make a poem will probably have extra-literary sources; so too the desire to translate can have impulses in the translator's life which form links with the work attempted.[24] Sereni's translations of René Char may have helped him counteract his sense of exclusion from a fulfilling encounter with experience.

Char was a leader of a resistance group in the Vaucluse area of France during the years when Sereni was imprisoned in Algeria. The 'moto d'invidia' which Solmi cited as arising from having missed the occasion, can occur with the most desolating of situations, the 'Horrible journée!' of *Feuillets d'Hypnos* 138, for example, where 'J'ai assisté, distant de quelque cent mètres, à l'exécution de B.' The prose-poem describes how B, who is about to be shot by a group of SS, could have been saved if Char had given the order, but

> Je n'ai pas donné le signal parce que ce village devait être
> épargné à *tout prix*. Qu'est-ce qu'un village? Un village pareil
> à un autre? Peut-être l'a-t-il su, lui, à cet ultime instant?[25]

I did not give the signal because this village had to be saved at *all costs*. What's a village? A village like any other? Perhaps he understood, he himself, at that final moment?

When, on the facing page, this has become: 'Orribile giornata! Ho assistito, qualche centinaio di metri distante, all esecuzione di B',[26] the translator's exclusion may be felt, but also his imaginative assistance in this horrible day, this horrible occasion. The accuracy

---

[24] Tomlinson has commented similarly: 'Clearly there was common ground, a common sense of impending inner chaos perhaps, that drew Elaine Feinstein to Tsvetayeva. This personal aspect is a paramount one', *Oxford Book of Verse in English Translation*, p. xii.

[25] René Char, *Fureur et mystère* (Paris, 1962), 122.

[26] Ibid. 314–15, and see also Sereni, 'I Feuillets d'Hypnos', *Letture preliminari* (Padua, 1973), 97–113.

of tone and restrained dignity of Sereni's rendering, the inclusion of the translator in the process of remembrance and transformation, converts the 'moto di invidia' into a living gratitude. A passage in 'The Dry Salvages' contemplates 'the agony of others, nearly experienced'.[27] This insight into the community and isolation of suffering is applicable to *Feuillets d'Hypnos* 138, and its 'distant de quelque cent mètres', far enough to experience nearly the death of B. It also bears upon Sereni's translation, for the translator too is at a distance, across a frontier of language, person, history, but he too, through imaginative involvement, may come to have nearly experienced the agony of others in making a translation.

IV

Envy can accompany the desire to translate a text. It may not be the author who is envied, but the lyric occasion, and that does involve the author's historical specificity, speaking a different language, being there at the time, often before the translator was born. It is irrecoverable, not to be experienced, except to a lesser and mediated extent through reading the poem. The poem represents the translator's disadvantage, for, were it not remarkable, there would be no interest in its birth, which is why it can be the object of envy. Eugenio Montale's 'Eastbourne', from *Le occasioni* (1939), begins with a strangely familiar phrase:

> 'Dio salvi il Re' intonano le trombe
> da un padiglione erto su palafitte
> che aprono il varco al mare quando sale
> a distruggere peste
> umide di cavalli nella sabbia
> del litorate.   (p. 170)[28]

> 'God save the king', the trumpets intone
> from a pavilion erected on piles
> which open a way for the sea when it rises
> to obliterate wet

---

[27] Eliot, *Collected Poems 1909–1962*, 209.
[28] Citations from the poetry of Eugenio Montale are from *L'opera in versi*, ed. R. Bettarini and G. Contini (Turin, 1980), to which page nos. in parentheses refer.

> hoof-prints of horses in the sand
> of the seashore.

The occasion is a walk along the shore of an English seaside town, but experienced as no English person could ever experience it, because of the particular political and cultural implications in what is seen and heard by an Italian, the poet Montale, at this time. 'Eastbourne' was first published in January 1937, but takes place on August Bank Holiday 1933, and is dated by the poet '1933 e 1935' (p. 922).

The four years between the poem's occasion and its publication were ones in which the fate of Italy in the 1940s was shaped, a shaping which involved relations between Mussolini and the British Government. Hitler had come to power in January 1933, and by the summer had secured dictatorial powers. In 1935 Italian troops invaded Abyssinia, and that autumn the League of Nations, urged on by Anthony Eden, introduced sanctions against Italy. Mussolini's imperial expansion was interpreted as a threat to British interests in the near east, while from the Italian Government's point of view the British could be seen as hypocritical. By the time 'Eastbourne' was published, the Spanish Civil War had broken out and Italian troops were fighting on Franco's side.

In 'Intenzioni (intervista immaginaria)', an interview with himself from 1946, Montale describes his attempt to live in Florence during these years as under a glass bell-jar, 'col distacco di uno straniero, di un Browning'[29] [with the detachment of a foreigner, of a Browning]. The Italian interest in English and American literature during these years was a search for alternatives to the imposed neo-imperial culture. Franco Fortini has situated Montale among 'quelli dei letterati e dei loro seguaci, anche dei migliori, nei caffè e nelle case dove l'antifascismo era sospiro verso Cambridge o Harvard, versi di Eliot e prose di Gide'.[30] [those of the literati and their followers, even the best, in cafés and houses where antifascism was a sigh towards Cambridge and Harvard, Eliot's poetry and Gide's prose.] 'Eastbourne' has its own patriotic sigh:

---

[29] Eugenio Montale, *Sulla poesia*, ed. G. Zampa (Milan, 1976), 566. For translations of this interview, see Montale, *Selected Essays*, ed. G. Singh (Manchester, 1978), 205–10, and *The Second Life of Art: Selected Essays of Eugenio Montale*, ed. and trans. J. Galassi (New York, 1982), 295–304.

[30] Franco Fortini, *I cani del Sinai* (Turin, 1979), 43.

> ed io in ascolto
> ('mia patria!') riconosco il tuo respiro,
> anch'io mi levo e il giorno è troppo folto.   (p. 170)

> and listening
> ('my country!') I recognize your breathing,
> I also rise and the day is too crowded.

In a letter to Silvio Guarnieri of 22 May 1964, Montale explains that 'Mia patria è my fatherland, l'inno. Il giorno è folto di cose e di memorie. La voce è il solito messaggio dell' assente-presente. La festa non ha pietà perché non cancella il vuoto, il dolore ecc.' (p. 923) [Mia patria is my fatherland, the anthem. The day is crowded with things and memories. The voice is the usual message from the absent-present. The feast has no pity because it does not remove the emptiness, sorrow, etc.] The things and memories include political reflections, suggested by the British national anthem Montale hears played by the band. In 'Eastbourne', an Italian poem of the mid-thirties, the phrase 'God save the King' need not only be alluding to George V but also Vittorio Emmanuele III who in early 1923 had conferred on Mussolini his powers. Italian middle-class antifascists could look with longing towards the British system where a monarchy gave legitimacy and continuity to a parliamentary democracy. Vittorio Emmanuele, twenty years after recognizing Mussolini's political supremacy, helped engineer the Duce's downfall.

Immediately before the lines about his own country, are these:

> Come lucente muove sui suoi spicchi
> la porta di un albergo
> —risponde un'altra e le rivolge un raggio—
> m'agita un carosello che travolge
> tutto dentro il suo giro . . .   (p. 170)

> As, flashing on its segments,
> a hotel door moves
> —another replies and returns a ray—
> a roundabout disturbs me that overturns
> everything within its revolving . . .

The circular movement of the hotel door gives rise to an image of worsening political conditions: 'Vince il male . . . La ruota non s'arresta.' (p. 171) [Evil conquers . . . The wheel does not stop.] Stopping the wheel could mean preventing the triumph of evil, but it is too late, the poem implies, and yet, the unstopping wheel may also suggest a reason for not abandoning all hope. Montale wrote to Gianfranco Contini on 1 November 1945: 'Lo spicchio indica quelle porte girevoli nelle quali uno rischia di tornare indietro se non esce in fretta: divise in quattro garitte; può darsi che tournants vada benissimo' (p. 923). [The segment points to that revolving door in which there is a risk of turning right round if you do not leave sharply: divided into four sentry-boxes; I dare say *tournants* goes very well.] Running the risk of being sent back where you came from if you do not get out quickly: this is Montale's comment on the high point of Italian fascism.

In the final lines of 'Eastbourne' another note of strange familiarity recurs:

> Nella plaga che brucia, dove sei
> scomparsa al primo tocco delle campane, solo
> rimane l'acre tizzo che già fu
> Bank Holiday. (p. 171)
>
> In the burning expanse, where you
> vanished at the bells' first strike, only
> the acrid brand remains that was once
> Bank Holiday.

Montale explains the last line to his readers. This is an Italian's idea of an English Bank Holiday. As Montale noted 'La festa non ha pietà perché non cancella il vuoto, il dolore ecc.' These are his emptiness and sadness, experienced from his way of looking at the world, a world in which the ordinary Italian word 'sei' rhymes with the foreign borrow '*Holiday*'. The poem's final line reinforces my distance from the originating occasion; it is not hard to imagine envying Montale's fortune in attributing his significances to, and finding his meanings in, a place so familiar to English eyes as Eastbourne.

Montale's 'Eastbourne' responds to an occasion; the poem finds its shape and nature through a pondered relationship with an experience. A translator's response to the source within himself, the private reason for wanting to translate, which motivates his rendering a foreign text in different terms, needs to be redirected as attention to the original whose occasion he may envy. The actions performed in translating the original are circumscribed by the foreign text. How circumscribed? According to what implicit principles? Such questions, I am arguing, bear upon the ethics and psychology of differing approaches to translation.

V

Poetry is, it has been said, what gets lost in translation.[31] Yet poems are for ever being translated. Untranslatability can itself stimulate envy; equally, as I have said, envy can show itself in damage done to the text recast in another language, for: 'Envy interferes most of all with these constructive attempts because the object which is to be restored is at the same time attacked and devalued by envy.'[32] Speaking to Frederick Seidel for the *Paris Review*, Robert Lowell said, 'I felt some sort of closeness to the Rilke and Rimbaud poems I've translated, yet they were doing things I couldn't do. They were both a continuation of my own bias and a release from myself.'[33] Lowell's tenses place him in a historical continuity of artistic careers, 'they were doing things', and also at a timeless point where all artistic productions are weighed in the same balance 'things I couldn't do'.

The secondary impulse to translate is expressed in Lowell's Introduction to *Imitations*: 'This book was written from time to time when I was unable to do anything of my own' and 'All my originals are important poems. Nothing like them exists in English'.[34] These remarks condense in the interview as 'they were doing things I couldn't do'. If Lowell had said 'Rimbaud and Rilke did things. I can't do anything at the moment', the earlier poets would not then be called 'a continuation of my own bias' because the separation of contexts between original and translation would be clear. Lowell's possibly envying and competitive rivalry motivated

---

[31] The remark is Robert Frost's, but see Donald Davie, 'The Translatability of Poetry', *The Poet in the Imaginary Museum*, ed. B. Alpert (Manchester, 1977), 153–7.

[32] Klein, *Selected Klein*, 224–5.

[33] Robert Lowell, *Collected Prose*, ed. R. Giroux (1987), 252. Lowell has expressed similar sentiments about Tristan Corbière: 'I felt with a shock all the things he could say that I couldn't.' Cited by David Kalstone, *Becoming a Poet: Elizabeth Bishop with Marianne Moore and Robert Lowell*, ed. R. Hemenway (1989), 125.

[34] Ibid. 234.

and set at risk his own work. One reviewer has called *History* an 'inflated and conflated meditation on Romantic figures of all time used as vague precursors of Lowellian angst'.[35] His 'humble megalomania'[36] could prove damaging to Lowell, his friends, his art, and scope.

Lowell's *Imitations* are adaptations of the originals, the 'things I couldn't do', for the purposes of encouraging 'my own bias'. They can sound like self-parody, for Lowell is exercising his manner by engrafting it on to a foreign original, and the projection of a manner can cause the envious damage. Lowell marks a distance from his sources, calling his pieces 'imitations', but also indicates what the originals are. 'The Coastguard House' carries the indication 'Montale: *La Casa dei doganieri*'. Lowell does not use the conventional preposition 'from' or 'after' to indicate that accuracy is not to be expected. His pieces are nearer to translation than Pound's *Homage to Sextus Propertius* or, at a further remove, Johnson's 'The Vanity of Human Wishes'.[37]

Reviewing *Imitations*, Hill noticed signs of damage. About the version of lines from Baudelaire's 'Le Cygne', he suggested that—

It is as though we are intended to recognize, in Lowell's poem, that the lyric maintains a perilous autonomy against mundane attrition. It shows itself scarred at the edge, somewhat distorted, as though from a partial melting down.[38]

Hill is concerned with lyric poetry's maintaining itself aloof from the daily grind, and with the danger in this aloofness, whereby, confusing authenticity with essence, a style may die of its own purity. Hill's work has been a long study in how, stylistically, the mundane is kept in its place, but a place where the weight of worldly existence, its grinding down, can bear significantly upon the lyric strenuously held aloof. Lowell's versions of these important poems, Hill is saying, allow us to recognize this 'perilous autonomy' because they subject the originals to attrition. Base

---

[35] Peter Dale, 'Fortuitous Form', *Agenda*, 11 (Spring–Summer 1973), 74.
[36] Ibid.
[37] Tomlinson discusses these issues of translating distance and stages of remove in *Oxford Book of Verse in English Translation*, pp. vii–xi.
[38] Hill, 'Robert Lowell: Contrasts and Repetitions', *Essays in Criticism*, 13 (April 1963), 193. See Tomlinson, *Oxford Book of Verse in English Translation*, pp. x–xi, for further comment on this translation.

metal has slipped into the recasting medium, and devaluation has occurred.

Lowell's feeling that Rimbaud and Rilke are confrères who 'were doing things I couldn't do' corresponds to Solmi's 'moto di invidia, un rimpianto d'aver perduto l'occasione lirica irritornabile, di averla lasciata a un più fortunato confratello di altra lingua'. Envy of the lost original occasion is a damaging illusion, for it can hinder the work of translation. Nevertheless, translators also need their impure motives, including envy of another's occasion, which may be purified in the ground of work—if done with a proper jealousy of the original's qualities.

To think that foreign poems are untranslatable can prompt envy of their aloofness, their unreachability. Attempts at imitations may be spoilings of what cannot be had. Yet respectful translation within real limits is possible. Through processes of work, study, and revision, envy may be converted into a desire, like jealousy, to understand the nature of the original. This will be a discovery of what is untranslatable in it, an understanding which emerges through exploration of the partial equivalences and inevitable differences between the languages from and into which the translation is being made. Knowledge of the histories both individual and cultural which have created these differences is thus enlarged. The understanding of such differences constitutes an increase in self-knowledge. The translator can feel grateful for such knowledges, and, in achieving states for which gratitude is due, can be doubly grateful that envy has been transmuted and ancillary creative work has been achieved.

VI

First and last, Sereni insisted on the positive impulse towards life in Montale's poetry. In 1940, reviewing *Le occasioni*, he noted that 'tutti—o quasi—sono d'accordo nel riconoscere un'accentuazione nettissima del lato affermativo, cordiale, di un montaliano "amor vitae", scaturito, dalla raffigurazione stessa in cui l'antico "male d'esistere" si chiude'[39] [all—or almost all—are agreed in recognizing an extremely sharp accentuation on the

[39] Sereni, *Letture preliminari*, 7.

affirmative side, of a Montalean 'love of life', released, from the representation itself in which the age-old 'evil of existence' is enclosed]. Forty-two years later, at a conference in Milan on the first anniversary of Montale's death, Sereni reaffirmed the existence of an impulse towards life in a poetry epistemologically doubtful about the life towards which it moves the reader:

ma è altrettanto chiaro che tra le suggestioni di quegli anni, in quella naturalezza di accostamento e di identificazione, andava formandosi il vero nostro debito (extraletterario, occorre dirlo?) verso la poesia di Eugenio Montale: di quella poesia che in tanto dubbio suo sull'esistenza, ci aveva appassionati in gioventù alla vita. A tutt'oggi quel debito non risulta estinto.⁴⁰

but it is equally clear that among the suggestions of those years, in that naturalness of encounter and of identification, was forming our true debt (extra-literary, need I say?) to the poetry of Eugenio Montale: that poetry which in his extensive doubt about existence, had given us a passion in youth for life. To this day that debt has not been written off.

Montale's life-affirming doubt about existence informs 'La casa dei doganieri', a poem which shows the influence of Robert Browning.⁴¹

Montale has described how 'la reputazione di Browning ha certo una doppia faccia; e in Italia addirittura una brutta faccia'.⁴² [Browning's reputation certainly has a double face; and in Italy even an ugly face.] He pictures how Browning, 'illustrato da floreali litografie, egli è stato il poeta prediletto dei vedovi inconsolabili, delle zitelle dal cuore traffitto' [illustrated with flowery lithographs, has been the preferred poet of inconsolable widowers, of spinsters with broken hearts]. Here is the poet of those wounded by life, a consolatory retreat, a companion of melancholic withdrawal, 'un poeta archeologico-sentimentale, di gusto *liberty*' [an archeologico-sentimental poet, in *liberty* style]. Montale contrasts this face with 'il vero Browning, il poeta caro agli esuli e agli imagisti di trent'anni

---

⁴⁰ Sereni, 'Il nostro debito verso Montale', *Eugenio Montale*, Atti del Convegno (Milan, 1982), 39.
⁴¹ For further work on relations between Montale and Browning, see Francesca Montesperelli, 'Montale e Browning: Poesia dell'oggetto', *Paragone*, 326 (April 1977), 55–81; 'Browning e Montale: *Love in a Life* e *Gli orecchini*', *Studi inglesi*, 5 (1978), 475–97; 'Letture parallele', *Sigma*, 13 (1980), 61–76; 'Rassegna montaliana' (1 and 2), *Il Cristallo*, 23:1 (1981), 87–108, and 23:2, 23–40.
⁴² This and the three following citations from Montale, *Sulla poesia*, 468–9. See Montale, *Second Life of Art*, 188–9.

fa' [the true Browning, the poet dear to the exiles and imagists of thirty years ago]. Here is the Victorian poet who inspired Pound and the early modernists. Montale also notes in his imaginary interview: 'Da molti anni la poesia va diventando più un mezzo di conoscenza che di rappresentazione.'[43] [For many years poetry has been becoming more a means of understanding than of representation.] This development, from poetry as a representing of what is known to a means of understanding, an exploration of understanding's limits, shows in Browning's work, and is the closest link between him and Montale.

A memory of Browning's 'Two in the Campagna' may have prompted lines from the early poem 'I limoni': 'il filo da disbrogliare che finalmente ci metta | nel mezzo di una verità' (9) [the thread to unravel which finally puts us | in the middle of a truth]:

> For me, I touched a thought, I know,
>   Has tantalized me many times,
> (Like turns of thread the spiders throw
>   Mocking across our path) for rhymes
> To catch at and let go.[44]

Browning's stanza with the 'turns of thread the spiders throw' seeks for a definitive knowledge of experience which is not forthcoming, but which in the seeking provides a vital relation to the world around. The desire to discover a flaw in nature, placing us in the middle of a truth, and its frustration in 'I limoni', make for the state of bounded attention into which the contingent, with its clear separateness, impinges and warms through the sudden reappearance of lemon trees.

'Two in the Campagna' is a love poem of recollection. In stanzas 3 and 4 the thought, the spider's thread, is followed out and reached for twice with the repetition of 'Help me to hold it!' in 'Hold it fast!' When the memory of Browning's poem recurs in Montale's work, the threads associated with thoughts hard to hold are recollections of a thoroughly lost occasion. 'La casa dei

---

[43] Ibid. 564.
[44] Browning, *The Poems*, 2 vols., ed. J. Pettigrew and T. J. Collins (Harmondsworth, 1981), i. 728. The draft of Montale's 'Due nel crepuscolo' is dated 5 Sept. 1926, though its title [Two in the twilight], 'un po' alla Browning' (p. 954) [a little after Browning], was added in 1943. 'I limoni' is from Nov. 1922. The Browningesque character of the draft of 'Due nel crepuscolo', without the title's hint, is enough to suggest that Montale was aware of Browning's poem in the mid-twenties.

doganieri' is from 1930. 'Two in the Campagna' seems to be recalled in the repeated reference to holding a thread:

> Tu non ricordi; altro tempo frastorna
> la tua memoria; un filo s'addipana.
>
> Ne tengo ancora un capo; ma s'allontana
> la casa e in cima al tetto la banderuola
> affumicata gira senza pietà.
> Ne tengo un capo; ma tu resti sola
> né qui respiri nell'oscurità.   (p. 161)
>
> You don't remember; other time impedes
> your memory; a thread is being wound.
>
> I still hold an end of it; but distant grows
> the house and on its roof-top the smoke-stained
> weathervane pitilessly turns.
> I hold an end of it; but you remain alone
> nor breathe here in the darkness.

Browning's poem ends with the poised attachment and separation of lovers encountering the limits of embodied experience:

> Only I discern—
> Infinite passion, and the pain
> Of finite hearts that yearn.[45]

The 'Only I discern' is ambiguous: it can mean 'except that I discern' or 'I am the only one who discerns'. The first of these has an optimistic slant, as it implies a further possibility, a continuing effort of attention and approach; the second cancels the hope by reiterating the isolation, the wishful thinking of the speaker. This too shapes a fundamental equivocation about the apprehension of this world. Hopes are deflected or disappointed but never obliterated; the combination of 'passion' and 'pain' allows for various emphases. In 'La casa dei doganieri' the relationship and its occasion are in the past and Montale is an 'Only I' in the second sense: 'Ne tengo un capo; ma tu resti sola | né qui respiri'.

In a letter to Alfonso Leone of 19 June 1971, Montale indicated the largely imaginary character of the 'occasion':

La casa dei doganieri fu distrutta quando avevo sei anni. La fanciulla in questione non poté mai vederla; andò . . . verso la morte, ma io lo seppi

---

[45] Browning, *Poems*, i. 730. See, for an analysis of this ambiguity, Eric Griffiths, *The Printed Voice of Victorian Poetry* (Oxford, 1989), 235.

molti anni dopo. Io restai e resto ancora. Non si sa chi abbia fatto scelta migliore. Ma verosimilmente non vi fu scelta.   (p. 917)

The customs-officers' house was destroyed when I was six. The girl in question could never have seen it; she went . . . towards death, but I found out many years later. I remained and remain still. One doesn't know who made the better choice. But in all likelihood there was no choice.

'La fanciulla in questione' is Anna degli Uberti, daughter of an admiral who was also an acquaintance of Ezra Pound.[46] Anna and Montale were holiday friends between 1920 and 1924. They never met again, she dying in Rome at the age of 55 in 1959. She appears in 'Annetta', a poem which confirms its connection with the earlier work: 'Anche i luoghi (la rupe dei doganieri . . .) | non avevano senso senza di te.' (p. 490) [Even the places (the customs-officers' cliff . . .) | had no sense without you.] Montale attempts to put the girl back into the picture.[47] His habitual 'dubbio . . . sull'esistenza' also appears in 'Annetta' when, referring to her death, he writes:

> Perdona Annetta se dove tu sei
> (non certo tra di noi, i sedicenti
> vivi) poco ti giunge il mio ricordo.   (p. 490)
>
> Forgive me Annetta if where you are
> (certainly not amongst us, the self-styled
> living) my memory barely reaches you.

He strikes the same note in the letter to Alfonso Leone: 'Io restai e resto ancora. Non si sa chi abbia fatto scelta migliore.' Two issues follow from this. The first is what Montale means or, better, implies with regard to 'La casa dei doganieri' by the word 'occasione'. The second concerns connections between vital attachment and loss, loss of memory, or death, in the poem.

Sereni gave an account of the volume's title when, reviewing *Le occasioni*, he described Montale's poetry as a 'poesia fedele alle proprie origini terrestri, alle difficoltà che l'hanno condizionata, alle *occasioni* che l'hanno favorita'.[48] [poetry faithful to its actual earthly origins, to the difficulties that have conditioned it, to the

---

[46] Montale, *Corriere della sera 1876–1986, Montale e il Corriere* (Milan, 1986), 21, and Humphrey Carpenter, *A Serious Character: The Life of Ezra Pound* (1988), 571, 599, 619, 627, 637.

[47] She occurs again in the late poem 'Ah!', Montale, *L'opera in versi*, ed. R. Bettarini and G. Contini (Turin, 1980), 708.

[48] Sereni, *Letture preliminari*, 9.

occasions that have favoured it]. Here the word means primarily 'material circumstances', but another meaning is suggested, as when the word is pasted on the windscreens of second-hand cars: 'a bargain'. These two combine in the equivocal, 'an opportunity'. The more morally valuable meaning implies a poetry faithful to the world other than itself from which it has arisen and to which it returns. Meaning 'opportunity', the word has a shadow of self-interest in it: a poetic opportunism which seizes its chances, one eye on occasions of which it can make something. 'La casa dei doganieri' appears such a piece of opportunism, later confessed by the poet; he has condensed his feelings about the girl into an occasion, the 'proprie origini terrestri' (the customs-officers' house), which she had never seen, demolished before he met her. This might lead to the conclusion, shared by Italian critics who are alluded to in 'Il tu', that the 'you' of 'Tu non ricordi' is *un istituto* (p. 275), an institution, and not a real figure, not part of the poem's actual earthly origins at all.

Such criticism of 'La casa dei doganieri' takes no account of the negation and uncertainty in the poem. Recalling Sereni's observation, an 'amor vitae' may be released from the enclosed 'male d'esistere'—the latter felt in the absence and separation which is the most evident theme of 'La casa dei doganieri':

> Tu non ricordi la casa dei doganieri
> sul rialzo a strapiombo sulla scogliera:
> desolata t'attende dalla sera
> in cui v'entrò lo sciame dei tuoi pensieri
> e vi sostò irrequieto.   (p. 161)

> You don't remember the customs-officers' house
> on the precipice over the rocky shore:
> desolate it awaits you since the evening
> when your swarming thoughts entered it
> and restlessly stopped there.

To object that the girl is not a real figure, not part of the poem's actual earthly origins, is to prevent objects in the poem from evoking something lost, something which they are not, but which they need in the circumstances to be such vivid signs of loss. The 'tu' makes the landscape's objects intensely recalled. Montale's skill involves filling the pronoun with the sense of a real person, for the moment it became no more than a device, its human occasion drawn from a description of landscape would be lost. There is this justice in Montale's lines from 'Annetta': 'Anche i luoghi . . . non avevano senso senza di te.' The vividness of the observed world in Montale's poem starts from a contradiction: she does not remember the place replete with her, yet without her the place would have no meaning, no purpose.

The poet's uncertainty contributes to this active contradiction, for the vividness and invitation in observed things depends on a perplexity about what they mean. If the poet knows what they signify, their vigour as pointers is diminished. This is how the exclamation about the petrol tanker's light and the question which follows indicate a life to be experienced as it disappears:

> Oh l'orizzonte in fuga, dove s'accende
> rara la luce della petroliera!
> Il varco è qui?   (p. 161)
>
> Oh the fleeing horizon, where the light
> of the tanker seldom flares!
> Is this the way?

The word 'petroliera' audibly recalls the first stanza's rhymes: 'scogliera' and 'sera'. It points forward to a concealed internal rhyme in the final couplet, where the poet's perplexed confrontation with experiences is definitively clinched by another rhyme:

> Tu non ricordi la casa di questa
> mia sera. Ed io non so chi va e chi resta.   (p. 161)
>
> You don't remember the house of this
> my evening. And I don't know who leaves and who stays.

Lowell writes 'All my originals are important poems. Nothing like them exists in English'; yet similar definitive uncertainties are deployed in the conclusions to poems by Browning: 'as I said before' or 'Well, I forget the rest',[49] and Barbara Everett has singled out the poet's 'peculiar truth of endings'.[50] Thomas Hardy too can end with: 'We do not know', 'And I was unaware', and 'I cannot tell!'[51]—he being another English poet with whom Montale has indicated affinities.[52]

[49] Browning, *Poems*, i. 561, 643.
[50] Barbara Everett, *Poets in Their Time* (1986), 178.
[51] Thomas Hardy, *The Variorum Edition of the Collected Poems*, ed. J. Gibson (London, 1979), 466, 150, 222.
[52] See Montale, *Sulla poesia*, 527–9; *Selected Essays*, 103–4; *L'opera in versi*, 726.

VII

Lowell's 'The Coastguard House' rivals its original, deploying unchecked aggressive impulses to give itself poetic power. His version adapts George Kay's prose crib (Lowell acknowledges this), exercising what Vendler, praising it, called 'his own irregular, idiomatic, and forceful' voice. In his Introduction, Lowell states, 'I have been reckless with literal meaning, and labored hard to get the tone. Most often this has been *a* tone, for *the* tone is something that will always more or less escape transference to another language and cultural moment.'[53] What is he saying? Lowell is not trying to translate the literal meaning; he is being reckless with it. The literal meaning, not easily separated from other meanings of a poem, has had to be sacrificed in translating the 'tone'. But it is not an attempt at Montale's tone, because this can't be translated. Instead, there is an alternative tone, something resembling a Lowell poem, though one oddly 'scarred at the edge, somewhat distorted'.

Here are the first two lines of 'La casa dei doganieri' again:

> Tu non ricordi la casa dei doganieri
> sul rialzo a strapiombo sulla scogliera . . . (p. 161)

'You don't remember the shore-watchers' house on the cliff sheer above the rocky coast'.[54] Here is the opening of 'The Coastguard House':

> A death-cell? The shack of the coastguards
> is a box over the drop to the breakers . . .[55]

Lowell's lines do have a tone, though not Montale's. He gives 'shack' for 'casa', picks it up with 'box' for which there is no original, but which supports the fabricated opening, 'A death-cell?', in that the shack is perhaps to look like a coffin. His 'breakers' translates the situation though not the Italian words. In return, Lowell's phrases have a consonantal interdependence: shack, box, breakers, which gives texture to the imitation. 'A

---

[53] Lowell, *Collected Prose*, 232.
[54] G. Kay (trans. and ed.), *The Penguin Book of Italian Verse* (Harmondsworth, 1958), 392–3.
[55] Three quotations in the following discussion from Lowell, *Imitations* (1962), 115–16.

death-cell?' is in the Lowellian manner of dramatic opening bids:
'An old dog's eye?', 'Remember?', 'Remember our lists of birds?',
'Who loved more?'[56]

Montale's tone is quieter, obscurely and remotely tender. His
poem concludes by recalling the 'Tu non ricordi' that Lowell
dispensed with in his imitation:

> Tu non ricordi la casa di questa
> mia sera. Ed io non so chi va e chi resta.   (p. 161)

Montale's conclusion rhymes a precariously passing pause on
'questa' with the final stop of the poem on 'resta', on who 'stays'.
The relationship between the fixed and the disappearing is at the
poem's heart, its feeling shaped in rhyming the fleeting against the
firm. Lowell's conclusion is different:

> You haven't taken my one night's possession to heart;
> I have no way of knowing
> who forces an entrance.

Lowell seems to have taken his original for the occasion of a one-
night stand. The girl addressed has not taken this 'to heart', which
may mean she is not hurt, or does not care, and as a result of her
indifference, the 'I' of the poem does not know who it is that insists
on having his way, or cannot know who the 'you' is that has made
such an impact on him. Lowell's occasion is more overtly fraught
than Montale's, and it is as if the 'I' of the imitation held a grudge
against the girl. 'I have no way of knowing' might be evading
blame for not knowing, where 'io non so', more like Browning or
Hardy, feels quietly in a quandary.

Lowell says: 'I have tried to keep something equivalent to the
fire and finish of my originals. This has forced me to do considerable rewriting.'[57] There is more to writing well than fire and finish,
and Lowell's forcefulness in 'The Coastguard House' is excessive.
'La casa dei doganieri' gains its vigorous attachment to life though
a paradoxical perplexity, a muted uncertainty. The poem is shaped
well, and its conclusion is definitively right, but it is neither
triumphant nor despondent. Lowell's piece gains power at the
expense of strength. Lowell 'forces an entrance' into 'La casa dei
doganieri' and perhaps his final lines are an acknowledgement of

---

[56] Lowell, *Selected Poems*, rev. edn. (New York, 1977), 48, 99, 101, 179.
[57] Lowell, *Collected Prose*, 232.

this. Envious attacks on others effect a concomitant loss of self-knowledge. By envying the gifts of others you may misjudge or denigrate your own. Lowell too has 'no way of knowing | who forces an entrance'. The imitation is neither Lowell nor Montale; or, more accurately, since a translation would never give either, the point at which considered approximation is abandoned for self-assertion leaves the piece far too near Lowell, but a Lowell self-confounded by the alien matter he has appropriated in pursuit of his own bias.[58]

A distinction between power and strength implies a criticism of what is sometimes called the 'mighty line'.[59] Montale's 'Libeccio sferza da anni le vecchie mura',[60] which Kay gives as 'South winds have lashed the old walls for years', is powerfully reimagined by Lowell: 'For years the sirocco gunned the dead stucco with sand'. The sand is Lowell's idea, as is 'gunned' to which it is an auditory

---

[58] Commenting on his version of Rimbaud's 'Memoire', Marjorie G. Perloff similarly concludes 'Lowell's imitation is neither fish nor fowl; it is at once too free a translation and not free enough', *The Poetic Art of Robert Lowell* (Ithaca, NY, and London, 1973), 70. In the course of her discussion Perloff states 'the real issue is not the morality of Lowell's verse translations, or lack of it, but their aesthetic value' (p. 57). I am arguing that aesthetic value derives from the particular character of creative work, and that such work is subject to complex ethical considerations. Though placing the composition of translations into a moral landscape, I do not want to say that Lowell was merely 'morally reprehensible', rather to define, with his example, considerations about the art that seem important. Mark Rudman, in *Robert Lowell: An Introduction to his Poetry* (New York, 1983), states that *Imitations* is 'so much the product of a driven man, a single-minded, original, often maniacal poet who described his own style as rather "grisly and mechanical" . . . I think *Imitations* was justified, not morally reprehensible, and was appropriate and necessary for Lowell at that point in his career' (p. 103). There's no arguing with the last clause. The cost of that necessity is part of what I am examining.

[59] See Davie, 'Robert Lowell', *The Poet in the Imaginary Museum*, 262: 'From that demotic idiom which has become, since Williams, ever more *de rigueur* for American poets, Lowell is excluded because of his early schooling in the drumming decasyllable, "the mighty line" '.

[60] This line has been singled out for praise in an extended justification of Lowell's methods here and in other Montale versions. See Donald Carne-Ross, 'The Two Voices of Translation', *Robert Lowell: A Collection of Essays*, Twentieth Century Views, ed. T. Parkinson (Englewood Cliffs, NJ, 1969), 166–9. My discussion of 'La casa dei doganieri' disagrees with Carne-Ross's suggestion that these are 'superb interpretations'. Speaking of a passage from 'Arsenio' he notes that 'Lowell is using the greater poetic resources of English to complete what exists *in posse* in Montale's words.' There is room for differences in ideas of translation, but I am not falling back on a desire for crude and illusory literalism if I say that this completing of Montale's poem seems presumptuous, unconvincing, and unattractive to me. For further support of Lowell's methods, see Alfredo Rizzardi, 'Appunti tra due poeti', in Lowell, *Poesie di Montale* (Bologna, 1960), 7–23.

answer; 'sirocco' is a different kind of wind, but it too makes for an echo in the line with 'stucco'. The inventiveness is striking, and as it strikes, so a status claim is made for the mind that constructed it. The phrase is histrionic in its identification of time's destructive action. Montale makes a discovery about something he has seen or imagined. Lowell's line has fire and finish, attributing value to the maker of the line. It is part of the drama in being a poet, which means possessing a verbal power that presents special insights and privileges. With the mighty line and the powerful phrase goes the large perspective and the high claim of poetry's powers. The line 'For years the sirocco gunned the dead stucco with sand', because it so captures the effects of the passage of time in its verbal vigour, seeks to rise above them, to become immune to them. It is in pursuit of autonomy from mundane attrition; but it reveals that attrition in action, being insufficiently watchful of how such autonomy is perilous to the imitation, the image of the original poem, its poet, translator, and a reader.

VIII

Highly wrought phrasing exacts costs which are perilously incurred. Yet there are more or less valuable ways of achieving it, as can be seen by comparing a sonnet of Lowell's with one by Hill. Both have Spanish originals. The last of Lowell's poems from 'The Ruins of Time' in *Near the Ocean* diverges from its original, Gongora's 'De la brevedad engañosa de la vida', in the sestet:

> ¿Confiésalo Cartago, y tú lo ignoras?
> Peligro corres, Licio, si porfías
> en seguir sombras y abrazar engaños.
>
> Mal te perdonarán a ti las horas;
> las horas que limando están los días,
> los días que royendo están los años.[61]

J. M. Cohen gives prose versions in *The Penguin Book of Spanish Verse* (the acknowledged source for both Lowell's and Hill's originals):

---

[61] J. M. Cohen (trans. and ed.), *The Penguin Book of Spanish Verse*, 3rd edn. (Harmondsworth, 1988), 278–9.

Does Carthage confess it and you not know it? You are running into danger, Licio, if you persist in following shadows and embracing deceptions.

The hours will hardly forgive you, those hours that are wearing away the days, those days that are gnawing away the years.

Lowell's sestet is writing far less fiercely gestural than 'The Coast-guard House':

> Do Rome and Carthage know what we deny?
> Death only throws fixed dice, and yet we raise
> the ante, and stake our lives on every toss.
> The hours will hardly pardon us their loss,
> those brilliant hours that wore away our days,
> our days that ate into eternity.[62]

He does without the addressee of the poem, Licio, who focuses and locates the moral warning of the original. He outdoes 'Carthage' by upping the stakes to 'Rome and Carthage'. He lifts into glamorous life the repetition of 'las horas' with 'hours' and then 'brilliant hours'. Rome is added for the good reason that even the victors must succumb to time's levelling, and Lowell explains: 'The theme that connects my translations is Rome, the greatness and horror of her Empire' and yet 'How one jumps from Rome to the America of my own poems is something of a mystery to me.'[63] The answer might be: by direct analogy ingenuously suggested. The mighty line decontextualizes and sponsors a large perspectival sweep. Lowell's poem imitates the larger processes of imperious appropriation and simultaneously comments on parodic copying. His 'brilliant' is sardonic. The individual addressee of Gongora's original offers too small a perspective for Lowell's purposes. His 'we' is all America, himself included, and her allies too. It is more, for it dismisses the European empires to which it alludes. This is why Vendler is right to speak of Lowell's versions as announcing a claim to 'possess the past in a commanding, not a subordinate manner', though the poet's contradictions enable him simultaneously to demonstrate and mock imperious grasp. Peter Dale, cited earlier, has referred to Lowell's sweeping together of a thousand experiences as 'pretentious; and the humble megalomania

---

[62] Lowell, *Near the Ocean* (1967), 55.
[63] Ibid., *Note*, n.p.

of it all is oppressive.'⁶⁴ Lowell's humility is in the ingenuousness of 'How one jumps . . . is something of a mystery to me.' His megalomania is in his outdoing Gongora, realigning the Spanish original with a far larger historical sweep by making a few great jumps in the rendering.

Geoffrey Hill in '7. Lachrimae amantis', from the 'Lachrimae' sequence in *Tenebrae*, also imitates freely from a text given in J. M. Cohen's anthology. Here is a sestet again, this time from Lope de Vega's '¿Que tengo yo que mi amistad procuras?':

> ¡Cuántas veces el ángel me decía:
> '¡Alma, asómate agora a la ventana,
> verás con cuanto amor llamar porfía!'
>
> Y cuántas hermosura soberana:
> 'Mañana te abriremos'—respondía,
> para lo mismo responder mañana!⁶⁵

J. M. Cohen has:

How many times did the angel say to me: 'Now, soul, look out of your window, and you will see how lovingly he persists in knocking!'

And how many times, oh supreme beauty, did I reply: 'I will open tomorrow', only to make the same reply upon the morrow!

Here is Hill's imitation:

> So many nights the angel of my house
> has fed such urgent comfort through a dream,
> whispered 'your lord is coming, he is close'
>
> that I have drowsed half-faithful for a time
> bathed in pure tones of promise and remorse:
> 'tomorrow I shall wake to welcome him.'⁶⁶

Hill's poem does not have the freshly direct dialogue of its original, but transposes that dialogue's feeling into its phrasing: the 'urgent comfort' or the 'pure tones of promise and remorse'. Hill gains a poised ending by taking Lope's penultimate line and making a conclusion, compressing into it the intimation of a promise emptying, explained in the original. This is laden at one and the same time with the desire to amend and recognition of backsliding. Hill

---

⁶⁴ Dale, 'Fortuitous Form', 74.
⁶⁵ Cohen, *Penguin Spanish Verse*, 302–3.
⁶⁶ Hill, *Collected Poems* (Harmondsworth, 1985), 151.

shades into his sestet the tones of a love relationship under duress. The sonnet's title, 'Lachrimae Amantis', suggests it too. His phrase 'the angel of my house' alludes to Coventry Patmore's poem 'The Angel in the House': it is as if the religiously faithful wife is reassuring her husband of his delivery from temptation, yet however much the man wishes to believe her, apologizes for previous infidelity, and promises to reform, still he cannot be confident of a change for the better.[67] Hill is committed to a poetry of highly wrought phrasing, but he is suspicious of how brilliance may menace. He is circumspect about the claim to be translating; adapts without appropriating; may improve, but does not appear to outdo. If he envied Lope de Vega, negative feelings were absorbed and transformed in the work of achieving an attuned equivalence.

In 'On Translating Homer', Matthew Arnold gives a picture of the ideal translation:

Coleridge says, in his strange language, speaking of the union of the human soul with the divine essence, that this takes place

> Whene'er the mist, which stands 'twixt God and thee,
> Defecates to a pure transparency;

and so, too, it may be said of that union of the translator with his original, which alone can produce a good translation, that it takes place when the mist which stands between them—the mist of alien modes of thinking, speaking, and feeling on the translator's part—'defecates to a pure transparency,' and disappears.[68]

Arnold, on this occasion, cannot be credited. His union of the translator with an original is a form of consummation like death, whereby the true and necessary alienness of both translator and translated is wished away. To be able to translate like this, seeing not through a glass darkly but face to face, would be making love in heaven:

> Easier than air and air, if spirits embrace,
> Total they mix, union of pure with pure
> Desiring . . .[69]

---

[67] See, for further discussion of Hill's poem in relation to Lope de Vega, Michael Edwards, *Poetry and Possibility: A Study in the Power and Mystery of Words* (Basingstoke, 1988), 170–1.

[68] Matthew Arnold, *The Portable Matthew Arnold*, ed. L. Trilling (New York, 1949; London, 1980), 211–12.

[69] John Milton, *Paradise Lost*, VIII. 626–8.

As Empson wrote in *Milton's God*: 'Raphael explains that the angelic act of love is by total interpenetration, a thing which human authors have regretted that they cannot achieve.'[70] The capacity to become transparent which is required for such ecstasies is not ours to have; we must inhabit our bodies, minds, eyes, and voices. Translation is the correlation of significant differences. We have no need to envy Milton's angels, or regret that we cannot mix totally. We have our impermanent opacities to maintain.

[70] William Empson, *Milton's God* (Cambridge, 1981), 105.

8

Ezra Pound: Translation and Betrayal

I

Writing from Rapallo on 24 May 1936 to the Japanese poet Katue Kitasono, Ezra Pound, referring to his knowledge of Chinese characters, admitted, 'the enormous gaps of my IGNOR-ANCE'. He also affirmed 'Two things I should do before I die, and they are to contrive a better understanding between the U.S.A. and Japan, and between Italy and Japan.' The products of transla-tors can help increase understanding between cultures. To achieve this involves working to discover more about the world they are translating from, more about the language and society into which they are translating, and more about where they stand in relation to both. From Siena on 13 August Pound developed the idea: 'The reasons for Italo-Japanese understanding lie deep . . . The span to America may take longer. But Italy can serve as a middle. This is what I tried to indicate in my *Jefferson and/or Mussolini*.'[1] These three statements seem blithely hopeful about the processes of cultural mediation and the mediator himself. Pound's life work is a tribute to the capacities of a man to believe that despite his ignorance he can foster international understanding. From this near contradiction arose some of Pound's finest poems and his worst mistakes.

Wyndham Lewis's remarks on Pound in *Time and Western Man* point to the poet's penchant for seeing himself and his contempor-aries through precedents in history. 'A Man in Love with the Past' discusses Pound as a translator and imitator:

By *himself* he would seem to have neither any convictions nor eyes in his head. There is nothing that he intuits well, certainly never originally. Yet

[1] *Ezra Pound and Japan: Letters and Essays*, ed. S. Kodama (Redding Ridge, Conn., 1987), 28 (twice), 32. For further material on Pound's involvement with Italian culture, see my 'Ezra Pound and Italian Art', in *Pound's Artists*, ed. R. S. Humphries (1985).

when he can get into the skin of somebody else, of power and renown, a Propertius or an Arnaut Daniel, he becomes a lion or a lynx on the spot.[2]

Making a passing allusion to Arnold's 'Dover Beach', Lewis praises what he sees as Pound's greatest strength, one hedged about with dangers:

He has really walked with Sophocles beside the Aegean; he has *seen* the Florence of Cavalcanti; there is almost nowhere in the Past that he has not visited . . . But where the present is concerned it is a different matter. He is extremely untrustworthy where that is concerned.

Danger for Pound lies in another near contradiction: if by himself he does not intuit well or originally, how can readers be sure of his intuitions about poets from past ages that he enters? If he does not have a reliable grasp on the present, how can he have one on the past?

In a famous passage on the 'historical sense',[3] T. S. Eliot stresses the need to enter into the literatures of the past so as to intuit what it means to be living and writing now. Both depend upon each other. He says that you cannot know where you are standing if you have no idea where you have come from, and that you do not know where you have come from if you do not know where you are standing. The two aspects of cultural self-knowledge grow together. If Lewis is right about Pound's unreliability regarding the present, then he cannot have properly '*seen* the Florence of Cavalcanti'. Yet Eliot is putting forward an argument about the literature of Europe; Lewis, talking about perception and knowledge of people. Does it follow that Pound is unable to fulfil Eliot's requirements as regards literature, if he is unable to meet Lewis's regarding intuitions about other people?

Pound embodies in his life and work the pun on *tradotta* meaning 'translated' and *tradita* meaning 'betrayed'. The phrase 'Italia tradita' is deployed by Pound in Canto LXXIV, the first of *The Pisan Cantos*, written during the poet's captivity in an American Army detention centre through the summer of 1945. It appears in a passage derived from the writings of Leo Frobenius, a German anthropologist whom Pound admired, and concerns the rebuilding of a city:

[2] Wyndham Lewis, *Time and Western Man* (1927), 87.
[3] T. S. Eliot, 'Tradition and the Individual Talent', in *The Sacred Wood* (1920), 49.

4 times was the city rebuilt, Hooo Fasa
   Gassir, Hooo Fasa dell' Italia tradita
now in the mind indestructible   (p. 430)[4]

Conflating the instance of rebuilding with the phrase 'of betrayed Italy', Pound insinuates a hope that the Italy of Mussolini, on which he had pinned many hopes, might be reconstructed. This is supported by an earlier passage where a similar phrase, 'Lute of Gassir. Hooo Fasa', appears at the conclusion to a series of lines recalling the sight of Lake Garda. There, at Salò between autumn 1943 and spring 1945, Mussolini 'ruled' Northern Italy as a puppet of Hitler. Pound visited the Fascist Social Republic at Salò in the hope of continuing his work on behalf of the economic ideas that he believed the Duce intended to implement. Mussolini had fallen from power in July 1943, betrayed, the propaganda ran, by the army under General Badoglio, by some of the fascist council (the Gerarchi), and by the King, Vittorio Emmanuele.[5] This is what 'tradita' means for Pound. In the passage viewing Lake Garda from Gardone, looking towards Catullus' villa at Sirmione, watching the water 'in the stillness outlasting all wars', Pound cites three lines in Italian:

> 'Cosa deve continuare?'
> 'Se casco' said Bianca Capello
> 'non casco in ginnocchion'   (p. 427)

This means: 'What ought to endure?', to which Bianca Capello replies, 'If I fall, I do not fall on my knees'. She is voicing fascist propaganda of the 1943–5 period. The 'I' is Mussolini, and he says he will fight to the last, and die like a man. When Pound included it in the first of *The Pisan Cantos* Mussolini was dead. Pound wrote 'dell' Italia tradita | now in the mind indestructible'. That second line derives from the poet's study of the 'dove sta memoria' passage in Guido Cavalcanti's canzone 'Donna mi prega'. Cavalcanti's canzone in translation forms most of Canto XXXVI. Pound's work as a textual editor, commentator, and translator of Cavalcanti is here entangled with his work as a promoter and

---

[4] Page references to the 4th collected edn. of *The Cantos of Ezra Pound* (1987) are given in parentheses. Copyright 1948 by Ezra Pound. Reproduced by permission of New Directions Publishing Corporation.
[5] Pound makes further allusion to the supposed betrayal of Mussolini by the King in *The Cantos*, 473, and see Mary de Rachewiltz, *Discretions* (1971), 184.

propagandist for an idealized Mussolini. This is the poet as a *traduttore* and a *traditore*, the second understood not in the context of 'Italia tradita', but of America and the case against Pound compiled by the FBI.

II

Reviewing Adrian Stokes's *The Quattro Cento* in *The Criterion*, Kenneth Clark notes a danger in passionate art criticism: 'but how hard it is to discriminate without seeming to condemn—no doubt because love is blind'.[6] Pound did not believe that 'love is blind'; rather that the *Amor* he tries to define in his 'Cavalcanti' essay stimulates enhanced sight. This capacity to see in an intense, visionary way derives, he claims, from a Mediterranean and non-Christian view of the body. He thought that Cavalcanti, as well as other Italian and Provençal poets 'are opposed to a form of stupidity not limited to Europe, that is, idiotic asceticism and a belief that the body is evil'. Pound thinks this is a cause of what he describes as the Christian's

invention of hells for one's enemies, and mess, confusion in sculpture . . . always symptomatic of supineness, bad hygiene, bad physique (possibly envy); even the diseases of mind, they do not try to cure as such, but devise hells to punish, not to heal, the individual sufferer.[7]

Cavalcanti (whom Dante implies may be damned as a heretic, when talking to his father in *Inferno* X[8]) had, according to Pound, a poetic vision which distinguishes itself from Christian objections to finding life's fulfilment in sexual satisfaction. Aggravating his view that the medieval poets had introduced a new philosophy of love in a theory of vision, was Pound's belief that this value—which he called *virtù*, adopting a word from 'Donna mi prega'—had been lost 'somewhere about 1527'. 'We appear to have lost', he wrote in the same essay, 'the radiant world where one thought cuts through another with a clean edge', and gave for example, 'the

---

[6] K. M. Clark, review of Adrian Stokes, *The Quattro Centro*, in *The Criterion* (Oct .1932), 148.

[7] Two references to *The Literary Essays of Ezra Pound*, ed. T. S. Eliot (1954), 150.

[8] See *Inferno* X. 52–72.

glass under water, the form that seems a form seen in a mirror'. He defines this loss by contrasting the image of the body in Botticelli, for instance, with that in Peter Paul Rubens:

The people are corpus, corpuscular, but not in the strict sense 'animate', it is no longer the body of air clothed in the body of fire; it no longer radiates, light no longer moves from the eye, there is a great deal of meat, shock absorbing, perhaps—at any rate absorbent.[9]

The other side of this argument is in Kenneth Clark's observation of nudes by Rubens and Rembrandt that 'Christian acceptance of the unfortunate body has permitted the Christian privilege of a soul'.[10] Here there is a disjunction between the body and soul. Pound is asserting that this disjunction did not exist for Cavalcanti by his phrase describing the people as 'not in the strict sense "animate"'. He finds the separation of body and soul exemplified in a contrast between intrinsic detail and extrinsic ornament in poems: 'Long before that a change had begun in poetry. The difference between Guido Cavalcanti and Petrarch is not a mere difference of degree, it is a difference in kind.' This is Pound's version of Eliot's more famous 'dissociation of sensibility'.[11]

In the Introduction to his edition of *Pound's Cavalcanti*, David Anderson notes:

Pound often avoided using the verb 'to translate,' preferring a calque such as 'to bring over' that recalls the etymology of the conventional term. When his first translation of Cavalcanti's 'Donna mi prega' appeared in *The Dial* in 1928, he called it a 'traduction,' replacing the usual word with a Latinism derived ultimately from *traductio*, 'a leading across.'[12]

When Pound brings over or leads across a poem from the Tuscan past, does he locate himself within a historical process continuous, despite vast differences, with Cavalcanti? Or does the disjunction of 'about 1527' place Pound definitively outside the world from which he is attempting to bring over Cavalcanti's poetry? Here is the Italian text that Pound had printed in 1928 and 1932:

---

[9] Two references to Pound, *Literary Essays*, 154, 153.

[10] Kenneth Clark, *The Nude* (Harmondsworth, 1960), 328.

[11] Pound, *Literary Essays*, 153. For 'the dissociation of sensibility' see T. S. Eliot, *Selected Essays*, 3rd edn. (1951), 287–8. Eric Griffiths has some instructive remarks on these historical 'falls' in 'Hill's Criticism: A Life of Form', P. Robinson (ed.), *Geoffrey Hill: Essays on his Work* (Milton Keynes, 1985), 178–9.

[12] David Anderson, *Pound's Cavalcanti* (Princeton, NJ, 1983), p. ix.

In quella parte
>   dove sta memoria
> Prende suo stato
>   si formato
>   chome
> Diafan dal lume
>   d'una schuritade
> La qual da Marte
>   viene e fá dimora
> Elgli é creato
>   e a sensato
>   nome
> D'alma chostume
>   di chor volontade
>
> Vien da veduta forma ches s'intende
>   Che'l prende
>   nel possibile intelletto
> Chome in subgetto
>   locho e dimoranza
> E in quella parte mai non a possanza
>
> Perchè da qualitatde non disciende
>   Risplende
>   in sé perpetuale effecto
> Non a diletto
>   mà consideranza
> Perche non pote laire simiglglianza[13]
>
> In that part
>   where memory is
> It [love] takes its state
>   is formed
>   as
> Transparent object from light
>   of a darkness
> The which, from Mars,
>   comes and makes [its] home
> It [love] is created
>   and has a felt
>   name

> Habit from the soul
> > volition from [the] heart
> It comes from form seen that is understood
> > That takes
> > > in the possible intellect
> As in [the] subject
> > > place and habitation
> And in that part never has power
>
> Because it does not lower in quality
> > Shines
> > > in him [a] perpetual effect
> It does not have pleasure
> > > but contemplation
> Because it cannot increase its likeness[14]

The passage is far from simple, and Italian editions contain many footnotes rephrasing it into a modern idiom. Pound's text appears corrupt in a number of places, a possible one being the repeated 'gl' in 'simiglglianza'.[15] Here is his first attempt at the passage:

> In memory's locus taketh he his state
> Formed there in manner as a mist of light
> Upon a dusk that is come from Mars and stays.
> Love is created, hath a sensate name,
> His modus takes from the soul, from heart his will;
>
> From form seen doth he start, that, understood,
> Taketh in latent intellect—
> As in a subject ready—
> > > place and abode,
>
> Yet in that place it ever is unstill,

---

[14] For a different rendering of a variant text, see J. E. Shaw, *Guido Cavalcanti's Theory of Love: The Canzone d'Amore and Other Related Problems* (Toronto, 1949), 98.

[15] Shaw notes of Pound's text and edition: 'The Laurentian X, 46 is one of the less authoritative manuscripts of our poem, and the Italian text is consequently unreliable. The translation in English verse is more obscure than the original in any version, and the "Partial Explanation" contributes no light on the meaning; nor do the desultory remarks entitled "The Vocabulary" and "Further Notes" '(ibid. 213). Attilio Bertolucci's words, reported from a conversation with Charles Tomlinson, are a reminder that Pound's was pioneering work: ' "It's all very well," he said, "for Contini to denigrate Pound's edition of Cavalcanti, but without Pound where would the revival of Cavalcanti be? What did the Italians *know* of Cavalcanti when Pound discovered him? Nothing ..." ' *Some Americans* (Berkeley, CA, and Los Angeles, 1981), 124.

Spreading its rays, it tendeth never down
By quality, but is its own effect unendingly
Not to delight, but in an ardour of thought
That the base likeness of it kindleth not.

The following is the Canto XXXVI version of Cavalcanti's lines:

Where memory liveth,
it takes its state
Formed like a diafan from light on shade
Which shadow cometh of Mars and remaineth
Created, having a name sensate,
Custom of the soul,
will from the heart;
Cometh from a seen form which being understood
Taketh locus and remaining in the intellect possible
Wherein hath he neither weight nor still-standing,
Descendeth not by quality but shineth out
Himself his own effect unendingly
Not in delight but in the being aware
Nor can he leave his true likeness otherwhere. (p. 177)

Both bring over a mysterious immaterial activity. Love is formed 'as a mist of light I Upon a dusk', or, 'a diafan from light on shade'. The use of 'dusk' in the first version is misleading, with its suggestion of an irrelevant time of day. The opting for 'diafan' adds foreign glamour to the Canto XXXVI text. What love takes from the soul begins as 'modus' and becomes 'custom'. This is an improvement. The former word is a latinism from *modus vivendi*, but sounds odd, while the later word is supported by the dictionary.

Cavalcanti's 'possibile intelletto' may suggest that love finds a place in the minds of people who are prepared to receive it, who are adepts of love.[16] Thus, the first version's 'latent intellect' is better and more accurately suggestive than 'in the intellect possible'—where the placing of the adjective after the substantive badly deforms the implication, as if love were a latency, or it were chance whether love finds a home or not. For 'Chome in subgetto', Pound's first version ('As in a subject ready') indicates a parallel construction, so that the line helps explain 'possibile intelletto'.

---

[16] For an exhaustive scholastic account of the ideas in this section of so arcane a poem, see Shaw, *Cavalcanti's Theory*, 16–51. My discussion is merely a modern reader's response to the poem and Pound's attempts to translate it.

The words may, however, refer to the person loved, so that love finds its place in both the mind of the person loving and in the person loved, an interactive process, as Pound was keen to assert in his definition of 'virtù'.[17] The Canto XXXVI version, with its peculiar line, 'Wherein hath he neither weight nor still-standing', translates a variant reading. J. E. Shaw gives 'pesanza' for 'possanza' and translates it as 'pain'; Pound's translation 'weight' is a literal rendering of 'pesanza'. Both Pound's attempts at this line are problematic. Love's lack of 'still-standing' reworks the cluttered negative 'ever is unstill'. The reading 'possanza' is a poeticism, like one of its dictionary definitions: 'puissance'. The meaning may be that in the 'possibile intelletto' and in the 'subgetto', love does not dominate or take power ('possanza') or that it is not a burden ('pesanza'). These, though, are only hints and guesses.

Pound conveys the idea that love does not lower in its quality, which is not how Shaw reads the line. Furthermore, if Giulio Cattaneo,[18] the editor of *Rime* (1967), is right, 'in se' does not mean 'in its own effect' or 'himself his own effect', where it refers to love's inherent force, but rather means 'in lui', that is to say, within the person in whose possible intellect love has taken up residence. Similarly, Cattaneo's note encourages a likelihood that Pound's 'delight' in both texts for the Italian 'diletto' does not convey the correct implication. 'Delight' in English has spiritual uplift in its associations, so it is odd to read that love does not have its effect in delight. If, however, it means 'piacere', pleasure or enjoyment, then the suggestion is that love does not live in sensual indulgence but in intellectual contemplation. Pound's original 'ardour of thought' is evocative in the right way, where 'being aware' sounds a bit flat.

Pound's final line in both versions has weaknesses. Gianfranco Contini[19] thinks that 'simiglianza' means 'the image which mediates consciousness', or, the presence which makes us aware of love's acting upon us. The odd verb 'laire' is 'largir' in Contini's text, and it may mean that in appearance and in quality love stays

---

[17] See Pound, *Literary Essays*, 151–2; Donald Davie, *Ezra Pound: Poet as Sculptor* (1965), 109, 131, and Nicole Ward Jouve's generous remarks on Pound translating Cavalcanti in *Baudelaire: A Fire to Conquer Darkness* (1980), 204.
[18] See Cavalcanti, *Rime*, ed. G. Cattaneo (Turin, 1967), 47–9.
[19] Ibid. 48.

the same. The poetic attraction of Cavalcanti's text lies partly in its closely interwoven rhymes which delineate contrapuntal cadences within the lines. Pound makes emblematic attempts at these, but cannot, understandably, sustain the effect throughout.

III

Being within 'the process by which our knowledge is developed'[20] means listening well to what other people say. Pound wrote to Eliot about Lewis's criticism of him in *Time and Western Man*, '& apart from 3 dead & one aged arcivescovo who gave me 3 useful hints, ole W. is my only critic—you have eulogized and some minor have analysis'd or dissected—all of which please tell the old ruffian if you can unearth him.'[21] Pound, however, had many critics, the majority of whom were not his friends. On 16 June 1912, an anonymous reviewer in the *Observer* wrote of the recently published *Sonnets and Ballate of Guido Cavalcanti*, 'Pound has taste in ejaculations, as is proved by his staccato preface and his heading of one sonnet, doubtless with authority, "Hoot Zah!!!"; but he has small taste in words and a dull ear for rhythm.'[22] The reviewer prefers Rossetti's versions, which Pound honourably mentions in his introduction. His comparison of lines by Rossetti with those by Pound indicates the smoothness and consistency of diction in the earlier poet's work:

> With other women I beheld my love—
> Not that the rest were women to mine eyes,
> Who only as her shadows seem to move.

This is Rossetti's rendering of the first three lines from 'Ballata II'.[23] Here is Pound's version of 1912:

---

[20] Part of a phrase of T. H. Green's cited by Geoffrey Hill in *The Lords of Limit: Essays on Literature and Ideas* (1984), 149; and see Griffiths, in Robinson (ed.), *Geoffrey Hill: Essays on his Work*, 178–80.

[21] Pound, *Pound/Lewis: The Letters of Ezra Pound and Wyndham Lewis*, ed. T. Materer (1985), 225.

[22] Four citations from the *Observer*, 16 June 1912, review printed in Ezra Pound and Dorothy Shakespear, *Their Letters*, ed. O. Pound and A. Walton Litz (1985), 116–17.

[23] This Ballata is not in Cattaneo's edition of the *Rime*, and may be regarded by scholars, since Gianfranco Contini's edn., as not by Guido.

Ladies I saw a-passing where she passed;
Not that they seemed as ladies to my vision,
Who were like nothing save her shadow cast.

When these lines were republished in *Umbra* (1920) they had been improved by the removal of the poeticism 'a-passing'; the period polite form 'ladies', which makes the girls seem lower class in line 2, has made way for the more literal 'women':

Fair women I saw passing where she passed;
And none among them woman, to my vision;
But were like nothing save her shadow cast.[24]

Rossetti's lines are better poetry as it was conventionally defined in that year. Yet Rossetti's 'Who only as her shadows seem to move' does not arrest the attention: it mellifluously lulls. Pound's 'Who were like nothing save her shadow cast' has much to recommend it. The 'nothing' is more of a shock; 'save' may be an archaism, but it compacts and turns the line's meaning sharply; while 'her shadow cast' is more active and consonantal.

The *Observer* reviewer ends with a nationalistic swipe: 'Some folk who have intelligence will, however, be content with Rossetti's translations, incomplete as they are, and will suppose that Mr. Pound's work must be meant for those Americans who find Rossetti's English distasteful to them.' Worse was to follow. Faber and Gwyer published Pound's *Selected Poems* in 1928 when Eliot joined the firm, and a new edition of the Cavalcanti translations was discussed. Pound failed to get the contract, but in the following year signed one with the Aquila Press. The firm had begun printing a lavish Complete Works when it went bankrupt. The finished pages were sent to Pound in Rapallo. He managed in 1932 to publish a *Rime* with Edizioni Marsano of Genoa, which was subtitled *Edizione rappezzata fra le rovine* [Edition pieced together amid the ruins]. David Anderson notes: 'Essentially a critical edition of the Italian texts addressed to an Italian audience, the book ends with a series of essays in English and the first few pages of a bilingual edition.'[25]

Pound might have been advised to wait until a more propitious moment; he was never good at this, writing one of his best pieces

---

[24] Pound, *The Translations of Ezra Pound*, 101.
[25] Anderson, *Pound's Cavalcanti*, p. xxii.

of self-criticism to James Joyce in a letter of 7–8 June 1920: 'The
curse of me & my nation is that we always think things can be
bettered by immediate action of some sort, any sort rather than no
sort.'[26] Reviewing Pound's *Rime* in 1932, Mario Praz was more
devastating than the anonymous critic of 1912:

Paleographic pastimes alternate with anecdotes of an exotic flavor, with
allusions of greater topical interest (Gandhi, Marx, 'the Hebrew disease,'
'the hindoo disease'), with vague citations, dropped with the gesture of a
great lord who slips a twenty lire piece into the hand of a beggar . . .[27]

He adds: 'Over all of this there hovers an infectious atmosphere of
errors' and then 'The rest , . . is the work neither of a critic nor of
a poet; it is an amusing but rather exquisitely Poundian bric à-
brac, sprinkled with curiosities'. Praz's review takes Pound to task
for the critical prose, over which he had perfect control, and the
state of the text over which he had far less.

Pound was not always good at bringing the force of a criticism
home to his own person or action, tending rather to throw it back
aggressively on to some external cause. Mario Praz was Senior
Lecturer in Italian at the University of Liverpool between 1924 and
1932. It is depressing to read in two letters of Pound to Wyndham
Lewis dated 13 and 15 December 1936:

Why dont you keep your eye on Mario Praz? Why do you allow that
semitic coxcomb to infect a Fascist State & misinform the Wops re. British
Litterchur! Fie!

And then:

What am I expected to do about one frousty li'l purrferrer in Liverpool/
[Mario Praz] asphixiated by Herb Read and Baby/crumby [Lascelles
Abercrombie] and the rest of yr/ Island singbirds? Blighter dont do it HERE.[28]

To be within 'the process by which our knowledge is developed'
involves hearing with more candour than this the point that others
are trying to make about one's work, even if they are doing it with
malice. A further problem of Pound's *Rime* is that the edition
straddles two or more contexts unclearly and uneasily. Cultural

---

[26] Pound, *Pound/Joyce: The Letters of Ezra Pound and James Joyce*, ed. F. Read
(New York, 1967), 176.
[27] Three citations from Mario Praz, 'Two Notes on Ezra Pound', in A. Jung and
G. Palandri (eds.), *Italian Images of Ezra Pound* (Taipei, 1979), 106 (twice), 106–7.
[28] Two citations from *Pound/Lewis*, 191.

mediation involves an attempt at reliably locating, however broadly or narrowly depending on cases, both from where and to where the mediation is moving.

Pound's embroilment with Mussolini's Fascist State shows a similar loss of contexts. Not only does Pound seem out of touch with the America and Britain to which he might have been mediating the virtues of the Duce in his book *Jefferson and/or Mussolini*, but also with the Italy, and the Italian government, whom he made numerous attempts to influence and guide during the 1930s. Pound failed to take the force of what critics said. He also failed to interpret the implications for himself of the Italian Government's reluctance, bemusement, and silence.

V

Pound began attempts to make contact with Mussolini on 23 April 1932, and was finally granted an audience on 30 January 1933. He had sent Mussolini a copy of *The Cantos*. Of this audience, there is only what Pound recorded in Canto XLI:

'MA QVESTO,'
    said the Boss, 'è divertente.'
catching the point before the aesthetes had got there;
Having drained off the muck by Vada
From the marshes   (p. 202)

What Mussolini said is something like: 'But this [*The Cantos*] is a. amusing, or b. entertaining, or c. funny.' It is not clear from the context what the point that the Duce is catching might have been, or what point the poet assumes he might be catching. Perhaps Pound thought Mussolini was using the word 'divertente' to mean 'diverting', in the sense of making someone go somewhere unexpected. The sneer at 'aesthetes' suggests Pound's wish to believe that he had made contact with a man of action, who could also read his poem better than specialists because he knew what it was for, the practical, political, and economic reforms it advocated. It seems unlikely that Mussolini had read *The Cantos* Pound sent him, or that if he had he would have understood them. Above all, Pound is not even considering for a moment that the phrase 'Ma qvesto è divertente' is an empty compliment, made by someone who merely needs something flattering to say to a stranger who wants to speak to him for a few minutes: not that it definitely is, but merely that it might be, and the lack of doubt about the phrase opening Canto XLI indicates Pound's culpable innocence.

Niccolò Zapponi, in *L'Italia di Ezra Pound*, records how, late in 1939, Pound made contact with the *Istituto relazioni culturali con l'estero*. He made a number of proposals: to publish a series of articles studying the relation of past American politicians to the ideas of Fascism; to publish an English-language literary magazine for discussion of Italian culture, politics, economics, and American life; and to produce a summary of the articles published in Italian daily papers. Each of these projects would have been intended to increase what Pound considered to be knowledge about Italy in America and America in Italy. It is his belief that he could achieve this which led to his activities on Rome Radio in the years 1941–3, and his attempts to continue such work in the Civil War period of 1943–5. The proposals Pound made in 1939 were passed to Luigi Villari, an expert on relations with the United States. Not only did he think that Pound's proposals were 'assai inopportuno' [extremely untimely], he also had the following substantial reservations about Pound's character:

> Il Sig. Pound è un poeta americano residente a Rapallo, assai affezionato all'Italia e in forte simpatia col Fascismo (. . .) È un uomo di ingegno e cultura e ispirato da ottimi sentimenti nei nostri riguardi, ma è un confusionario e vuole anche occuparsi di questioni economiche finanziarie sulle quali ha idee alquanto fantastiche.
>
> Negli Stati Uniti il Pound è apprezzato come poeta ma come scrittore politico ed economico non è preso sul serio, onde un'iniziativa originata da lui non avrebbe molto peso.[29]

Mr Pound is an American poet living in Rapallo, fond of Italy and highly sympathetic to Fascism . . . He is a clever and cultured man full of fine feelings towards us, but he is muddle-headed and wants to deal with economic and financial matters about which he has somewhat fantastical notions. In the United States Pound is appreciated as a poet but is not taken seriously as a writer on politics and economics, so any project devised by him would not have any great weight.

Here is the sad spectacle of a man who has not gained or sustained sufficient contact with two contexts attempting to persuade others that he is able to mediate between these societies.

---

[29] Niccolò Zapponi, *L'Italia di Ezra Pound* (Rome, 1976), 60.

Pound's view of Mussolini did not correspond in many details to the historical personage who bore the name. The poet was at pains to indicate that the key to Mussolini was not merely what he had achieved, but trust in what he might yet do. In *Jefferson and/or Mussolini* he wrote that 'Any thorough judgment of MUSSOLINI will be in measure an act of faith, it will depend on what you *believe* the man means, what you believe that he wants to accomplish.'[30] Pound persuaded himself that Mussolini wanted to accomplish a radical reform of the economic system of Italy in opposition to the international banking system which Pound called the 'usurocracy'. On 22 December 1936, he sent a letter to Mussolini which began:

DUCE! DUCE!
Molti nemici molto onore.
Voglio vedere tutti gli USURAI fra i nemici d'Italia.[31]

DUCE! DUCE!
Many enemies much honour.
I want to see all the USURERS among the enemies of Italy.

Niccolò Zapponi comments, after quoting this letter in full, 'Come è facilmente immaginabile, Mussolini non rispose alla lettera.' [As is not difficult to imagine, Mussolini did not reply to the letter.] Pound could have drawn conclusions from this and other silences, and there is little evidence to suggest that the Duce had any intentions of implementing the range of economic reforms that might have satisfied the poet.[32] Furthermore, it is an indication of the political and propagandistic desperation of the Fascist regime in 1941 that they allowed Pound to broadcast from Rome.

Pasolini, writing of the lyrical style which informs what many believe are the best passages in *The Cantos*, has an acute point about Pound's politics in this period:

What launches him into his enchanting repetitions is a trauma that leaves him completely unadapted to the world. His subsequent choice of Fascism

---

[30] Pound, *Jefferson and/or Mussolini* (1935), 33.
[31] Two citations from Zapponi, *L'Italia di Ezra Pound*, 51, 52.
[32] See David Trotter, *The Making of the Reader* (1984), 98–103, and Earle Davis, *Vision Fugitive: Ezra Pound and Economics* (Lawrence, Kans., and London, 1968), 176–80.

was at once a way to mask his unadaptability and an alibi that allowed him to pretend to himself that he was present here.[33]

In addition, Pound's conspiracy theory of history served to defend him against the threat to his self-esteem attendant on information or arguments that might challenge his political analysis. In a letter to John Drummond of 18 February 1932 he stated: 'I believe that anything human will and understanding of contemporary Italy cd. accomplish, he [Mussolini] has done and will continue to do. Details later. Don't be blinded by theorists and a lying press.'[34] Thus is avoided the attrition of comparison. Pound's attempts to see through a usurocratic conspiracy served to conceal from him complexities and conflicts in the world he claimed to render transparent.

Pasolini is, in effect, aligning Pound with the 'aesthetes' of the opening to Canto XLI who had not 'got there'. The poet's illusions about Fascism allow him to pretend to himself that he is not an aesthete, and that he is not detached from the world of politics and the processes by which some political knowledge is acquired, of which a questioning scepticism combined with an ability to weigh conflicting interests will play at least some part. Pound seems to have had little skill in such activities. What Pasolini says accords with much of the evidence, and yet it is only half the case, for, in a literal sense, Pound was 'present here', in front of the microphone at Rome, or at the Salò Republic on Lake Garda.[35]

Because of his illusions about Mussolini and his government Pound supported the Fascist State in Italy. Individuals support governments for various reasons. It does not follow that since you do not agree to the letter with all of a regime's policies you can expect immunity from criticism or judgements for your acts which are then claimed by others to constitute support for it. Luigi Villari

[33] Pier Paolo Pasolini cited by Anderson, 'Breaking the Silence', in *Paideuma*, 10 (1981), 345, translating Pasolini, *Descrizioni di descrizioni* (Turin, 1979), 295–6; and for another translation see 'On Pound', trans. R. M. Clarke, *PN Review* 46, 12 (1985), 63.

[34] Pound, *The Selected Letters of Ezra Pound 1907–1941*, ed. D. D. Paige (1950), 239.

[35] See Humphrey Carpenter, *A Serious Character: The Life of Ezra Pound* (1988), 621, and Julian Cornell, *The Trial of Ezra Pound: A Documented Account of the Treason Case by the Defendant's Lawyer* (1966), for the legal problem of witnesses to the acts of treason.

described Pound as a *confusionario*, and the poet was culpably muddle-headed on this point. He imagined that he could act independently of country or context, and also that he could situate himself in certain contexts so as to exploit them for what he thought were the best interests of his economic programme, and so of the entire world.

Two instances come from the years 1944–5. The first is cited by Noel Stock:

in *Il Nazionale* of 4 September 1955 a writer by the name of Damaso Riccioni said that he had met the poet at Lake Garda in 1944 with Serafino Mazzolini, Foreign Minister of the Salò Republic. Pound had defended himself against accusations that the broadcasts were wrong and according to Riccioni spoke of being guided by an interior light and claimed that his ideas were above warring factions . . .[36]

Pound is attempting, by the phrases 'an interior light' and 'above warring factions', to spirit himself out of having to be responsible for his being 'present here', while manifestly being so. The second comes from his interrogation by Acting Major Amprim at Genoa in the spring of 1945. Pound stated that 'I have at all times opposed certain grey zones of the Fascist opportunism by defining fascism in a way to make it fit my own views.'[37] A writer may work 'within the process' by a relation to words. The 'process' here means the many ways in which words come to have senses and to be understandable and usable by people of various and multiple persuasions, how words grow and change in relation not only to the speech of 'the same people living in the same place',[38] but also, with an international language such as English, to the diverse social and political circumstances within which they live.

Yet in Pound's statement the word 'fascism' is not being understood as others may hear and use it, whether Italians, or Americans, or anyone for that matter. It is being used only as Pound understood it. The word was not his private property, and the FBI understood 'fascism' to mean, roughly, 'the enemy', and, as such, constructed a case of treason against Pound. They took it for granted that Pound was 'present here', was within the historical

---

[36] Noel Stock, *The Life of Ezra Pound* (Harmondsworth, 1985), 519.

[37] Pound, 'Pound's Interrogation at Genoa', *Helix* (Australia), 13 and 14 (1983), 131.

[38] James Joyce, *Ulysses*, ed. H. W. Gabler, W. Steppe, and C. Melchior (Harmondsworth, 1986), 272.

process, not outside it and insisting on personally intuited occult facts to an uncomprehending world. The FBI assumed that Pound was in the process, and, as a result, arranged a *processo* for him: that is to say, in English, a trial.

VI

Pound's equivocation about the word 'fascism' may have been calculatedly evasive. The publication of a fourth collected edition of *The Cantos* in 1987, containing for the first time Cantos LXXII and LXXIII, has made available two of the poet's least attractive works. These two cantos were written in Italian during 1944 and printed in a Salò journal, *Marina Repubblicana*, in January 1945. They appear in the Faber edition untranslated, out of chronological sequence, at the back. The second is subtitled *Cavalcanti/Corrispondenza Repubblicana*, and constructed upon another broad analogy. 'Cavalcanti' narrates a war story to the American whom he singles out because his translator loves the Italian 'pel mio spirito altiero I E la chiarezza del mio intendimento.' (p. 811) [for my lofty spirit and the clarity of my understanding.]

Pound's Italian echoes phrases from 'Donna mi prega'. His 'spirit altiero' combines 'Ed é si altero I ch'é chiamato amore' [because it is so lofty that it is called love] from the opening, with 'merto I spirito' [wounded spirit], towards the conclusion; his 'intendimento' recalls Cavalcanti's envoi, urging his poem to stay with those 'ch anno intendimento' [who have understanding].[39] Thus the canto draws authority from a poem about a theory of love on to a speaker who also utters such lines as 'Roosevelt, Churchill ed Eden I bastardi ed ebreucci I Lurchi e bugiardi tutti' (p. 811) [Roosevelt, Churchill, and Eden I bastards and jews I All of them gluttons and liars]. Here then, for convenience, is Humphrey Carpenter's summary of the events. Passing through Rimini, this 'Cavalcanti' met the ghost of a peasant girl only just killed:

She was singing because of the way in which she had met her death. Cavalcanti explains that some Canadian troops had been on their way to rout the German occupying forces in Rimini, and to destroy what still

---

[39] Pound, *The Translations of Ezra Pound*, 132, 140 (twice). Pound translates 'merto' as first 'noble', then 'deserving'.

stood of the town. Some of them raped the girl. Four or five of them, guarding German prisoners, then told her to direct them to the Via Emilia. The girl answered that she would lead them there herself, and she set off, deliberately taking them through a field which she knew her brother had laid with mines.[40]

Twenty of the Canadian soldiers were killed, as was the violated girl. The German prisoners were rescued. The canto provides a repellent picture of the twisted emotions engaged in Pound by the civil war at this time in Italy in its closing months. The account of rape, revenge, and self-destruction is rendered more sordid by the interweaving of a propagandistic thread: the implication is that Allied troops have a monopoly on raping girls and that the girl's revenge is an act of fascist patriotism. The question of who the Italian patriots were, at that moment, is exactly what was being violently contested as Pound composed the poem.

Here is Pound's deployment of the 'voice' of Cavalcanti, in a loose imitation of the internally rhymed form of 'Donna mi prega', and aligning the Tuscan poet with the Axis forces:

Domandarono la strada
    per la Via Emilia
       a una ragazza,
      una ragazza stuprata
Po' prima da lor canaglia.
 —Be'! Be'! soldati!
      Quest'è la strada.
  Andiamo, andiamo
      a Via Emilia!—
Con loro proseguiva.
     Il suo fratello aveva scavato
I buchi per le mine,
    là verso il mare.
Verso il mare la ragazza,
     un po' tozza ma bella,

---

[40] Carpenter, *Serious Character*, 639; see also Barbara Eastman, 'The Gap in *The Cantos*: 72 and 73', *Agenda*, 17–18 (Autumn–Winter–Spring 1979–80): 'With the plot mechanism of the rape, then, Pound supplies a realistic justification for the slaughter of the enemy celebrated in Canto 73, if not for its celebration. It is war, we might infer, *ergo* this is a justice beyond ethics which he praises once, and once only, in his poetry' (p. 153); and Richard Reid, 'Determined Cones of Shadow', *Helix* (Australia), 13 and 14, (1983), 114: 'Pound attempted his most violent act of translation . . . The poem presents less a poetic persona than an impersonation.'

Condusse la truppa.
                        Che brava pupa! che brava pupetta!   (pp. 812–13)
They asked the way
                    for the Via Emilia
                                    of a girl,
                        a girl who had been raped
By them just before, vermin.
        —Here! Here! soldiers!
                                    This is the way.
        Let's go, let's go
                        to Via Emilia!—
She went on with them.
                        Her brother had dug
The holes for the mines,
                        there towards the sea.
Towards the sea the girl,
                        a bit dumpy but pretty,
Led the troop.
            What a good girl! What a good little girl!

That this is in any creative sense 'by' Cavalcanti cannot be sustained. The manner in which the 'ragazza stuprata' is described has nothing in common with the *dolce stil nuovo*: 'un po' tozza ma bella' means 'a bit dumpy but pretty'; my dictionary gives a variation of it as a set phrase to exemplify 'tozzo': '*È bella, ma un po' tozza*, she is beautiful, but a little squat'. Another word which characterizes the view of the girl is the word 'pupa' and its familiar diminutive 'pupetta', which means 'little girl' or 'baby girl' in dialect, and can also mean 'doll'. It could be used by boys of their girlfriends. The Milanese poet Antonia Pozzi used it about herself in poems written during the 1930s, where she is referring equivocally to being called this before they were obliged to separate.[41] It sounds affectionate but patronizing. Pound's poem attempts even greater heights of exclamatory, vicarious 'patriotic' fervour, concluding:

[41] See Antonia Pozzi, *La vita sognata*, ed. A. Cenni and O. Dino (Milan, 1986), 107, 109. Mary de Rachewiltz recalls the word being used about her in 1945: 'An Italian voice that sounded drunk: "*Vieni pupa.*" A shrill female voice cursed him. This looked bad indeed.' (*Discretions*, 248).

                    Nel settentrion rinasce la patria,
Ma che ragazza!
            che ragazze,
                    che ragazzi,
                            portan' il nero!'   (p. 814)
        In the north the fatherland is reborn,
    What a girl!
        what girls,
                what young men,
                        wear the black!

It is inviting fascist youth to sacrifice itself for an expiring illusion of which, within months, Pound would say he had adapted the name to fit his own views.

What is betrayed here, furthermore, is Pound's love for the Cavalcanti whom he had worked to present to English and Italian readers. The tone of voice with which the raped girl is addressed and described does not correspond with the tone in Cavalcanti's verse and in Pound's translation of the lines which include 'dove sta memoria'. Lewis had said in 'A Man in Love with the Past':

I like, respect, and, in a sense, reverence Ezra Pound; I have found him a true, disinterested and unspoilt individual. He has not effected this intimate entrance into everything that is noble and enchanting for nothing.[42]

Admirers of Pound can find many instances where his 'intimate entrance' can be felt to have resulted in an ennobling of the poet. What is objectionable in Canto LXXIII is that, far from ennobling him, Pound degrades his noble ancestor. The poem instances what Cavalcanti says does not happen to love in 'Donna mi prega':

                In quella parte mai non ha possanza
                    perché da qualitate non descende:
                    risplende—in sé perpetual effetto . . .[43]

Canto LXXIII descends to lust and revenge where people, whether they be a Tuscan poet or a girl from Rimini, or the soldiers, are exploited as if they were puppets. A respect for the otherness of people and things is not present in the ventriloquistic appropriation of Cavalcanti or 'his' view of the 'ragazza stuprata'.

---

[42] Lewis, *Time and Western Man*, 87.
[43] Cavalcanti, *Rime*, 48.

VII

When Pound stated 'I have at all times opposed certain grey zones of the Fascist opportunism by defining fascism in a way to make it fit my own views',[44] his use of the word 'fascism' does not exemplify a 'precise definition', nor an understanding of the word within the multiple contexts of those who have different reasons to speak it; rather, it is an unmitigated instance of an artist who projects a preconception on to his material. While *The Pisan Cantos*, which were the next part of his poem to be composed, may, to some extent, be appreciated as a work of reparation and renewal, there are passages in it, and elsewhere throughout his work, which instance the poet having his own way with words.

Pound also told Amprim in Genoa that he had written to Alessandro Pavolini in autumn 1943 and gone to Salò where he saw Fernando Mezzasoma. They are hailed towards the end of Canto LXXXIV: 'Xaire Alessandro ǀ Xaire Fernando, e il Capo' (p. 539). Denis Mack Smith, in his *Mussolini*, remarks of Pavolini at Salò that he 'believed in terrorism as a policy and liked to repeat conventional fascist remarks about the purifying effects of a blood-bath'.[45] The appearance of that word 'blood-bath' almost immediately after their names in the last Pisan canto indicates, I hope, Pound's anxiety about the terroristic activities of his heroes from Lake Garda. In Canto LXXX he suggests such qualms by writing, 'Your gunmen tread on my dreams' and 'the problem after any revolution is what to do with ǀ your gunmen' (p. 496). The lines may refer to the activities of the black-shirt gangs in Mussolini's first years of power. Their judiciously speculative tone is disturbing, because not deeply or extensively exercised by the 'problem'. Moreover, by considering it a problem of 'emphasis ǀ error or excess of ǀ emphasis' (p. 496) Pound makes it seem an aesthetic matter like expressing an idea in a balanced way. A 1910 *Manchester Guardian* review of *The Spirit of Romance* had noted: 'Mr Pound, for all his excess of emphasis, never aims at forcing his judgement on the reader'.[46] With terrorism, however, there are no opportunities to revise a mistaken decision.

---

[44] Pound, 'Pound's Interrogation at Genoa', 131.
[45] Denis Mack Smith, *Mussolini* (1983), 306.
[46] Stock, *Life of Ezra Pound*, 114.

The 'mastery', the technical 'control' in Pound's analogy is illusory for both politics and art. By associating a political problem with a compositional one, and so reiterating implicitly his analogy of Mussolini as artist, Pound lifts the political issue out of its context in specific instances of extra-legal violence. By doing so within his poem and its technical context, he fails to respond fully to the demands of either political or compositional problems. Pound does see, however, that there is a 'problem'. The rhythmic delicacy and overall design of Canto LXXX can reaffirm a belief in Pound as 'il miglior fabbro'; but it is chilling and instructive to remember that the better craftsman, who so effectively helped Eliot revise *The Waste Land*, on this occasion conceived of a writer's technique as analogous to handling a rule of terror.

In her Notebook for 4 and 5 November 1909, Dorothy Shake-spear copied out a remark made about her future husband by Fredric Manning: ' "He (Ezra) is not as other men are—He has seen the Beatific Vision Which is an extenuating circumstance." '[47] Yet Pound's differences from other men were contained within a continuum of similarity; if not, Dorothy would not have been able to recognize him as a man. It is this continuum of similarity with which I want to conclude. Its existence is a reason for rejecting the assertion that his difference, having 'seen the Beatific Vision', is in fact an 'extenuating circumstance'.

Daniel Pearlman has observed that 'distrust of introspection and its consequence, a naive lack of psychological and moral self-awareness, is the great weakness in Pound that his friend Eliot hits on in *After Strange Gods*';[48] Eliot, commenting on Pound's Hell Cantos XIV–XV, wrote:

If you do not distinguish between individual responsibility and circum-stances in Hell, between essential Evil and social accidents, then the Heaven (if any) implied will be equally trivial and accidental. Mr. Pound's Hell, for all its horrors, is a perfectly comfortable one for the modern mind to contemplate, and disturbing to no one's complacency: it is a Hell for the *other people*, the people we read about in the newspapers, not for oneself and one's friends.[49]

---

[47] Pound and Shakespear, *Their Letters*, 9.
[48] Daniel Pearlman, 'Ezra Pound: America's Wandering Jew', *Paideuma*, 9 (Winter 1980), 471.
[49] T. S. Eliot, *After Strange Gods* (1934), 43.

Canto LXXIII is 'dross', is not 'What thou lovest well' (p. 521) because the raped girl's suicide and killing of the soldiers in the minefield is 'comfortable . . . to contemplate, and disturbing of no one's complacency'; that is to say, the events do not disturb Pound's fictional 'Cavalcanti' or Pound himself. Just as for culture and history, so too for Hell. It is not a set of facts for the contemplation of the like-minded. It too, in so far as it exists in life and art, is a 'process by which our knowledge is developed'. This is what Eliot is saying about literary and lived hells.

Pound's idea of evil—'Time is the evil' (p. 147), 'The Evil is Usury' (p. 798)—is not internalized. What is evil in the world is experienced because imposed from without, not recognized as corresponding with something in himself. If you believe in the unPoundian idea that evil may be discovered within yourself, the resulting recognitions of complicity, guilt, and shame make it conceivable for you to find yourself in the place of the guilty. This being the case, I cannot finally judge and condemn Pound; there is so much in his poetry, and in his literary and cultural conduct, to admire. William Empson almost balances his strengths and weaknesses:

> he is such a clever man, and has such natural good feelings, that he actually hasn't had to do any conscious thinking for fifty years or so. The way his mind decides for him is rather too much above his own head; he is inspired, and hardly to blame when he is mistaken. What his feelings consider good are homely and practical things, and this has to be recognised as more important for a judgement on him than his views.[50]

Pound's 'natural good feelings' were his desires to make fine art, help other writers and artists, improve the quality of poetry in English, increase the understanding between cultures and nations, alleviate poverty and death caused by unnecessary economic hardship, and prevent wars that breed more wars. These should always be remembered and valued.

However, Empson repeats Frederic Manning's indulgence when he writes 'he is inspired, and hardly to blame when he is mistaken'. The second does not follow from the first. The burden of responsibility for the disaster that befell him, his poem, and what remained of his consciously propagated values, in and before 1945, lies

---

[50] William Empson, 'Rhythm and Imagery in English Poetry', *Argufying: Essays on Literature and Culture*, ed. J. Haffenden (1987), 161.

principally with Pound himself. Though 'the halls of hell' (p. 521) at Pisa were imposed on him from without, *The Pisan Cantos* are his long poem's real hell. Yet of that hell's depths passages in those cantos remain grimly unaware. The section as a whole approaches the conditions of a hell in Eliot's terms because, in *The Pisan Cantos*, Ezra Pound, at that time barely known to himself, became one of the other people, the people we read about in newspapers; he became as other men are; he became for a time one of us.

9
Robert Browning's Grasp

I

On 15 January 1845, in the second letter to her future husband, Elizabeth Barrett wrote:

You have in your vision two worlds—or to use the language of the schools of the day, you are both subjective & objective in the habits of your mind. You can deal both with abstract thought & with human passion in the most passionate sense. Thus, you have an immense grasp in Art . . .[1]

Paying a compliment, she prefigures the terms of Browning's 'Essay on Shelley' (1852), and shows how to apply to her future husband his distinction between subjective and objective poet. For Browning, as for the objective poet, 'the world is not to be learned and thrown aside, but reverted to and relearned'(i. 1003);[2] yet equally, Browning and the subjective poet are to intuit 'Not what man sees, but what God sees—the *Ideas* of Plato, seeds of creation lying burningly on the Divine Hand—' (i. 1002), and 'it is towards these that he struggles'. Elizabeth's effusion was a response to the praise in Browning's letter of two days earlier, where he affirms that she was the truly subjective poet, the Shelleyan visionary, while he was merely and exclusively objective: 'You speak out, *you*, I only make men & women speak—give you truth broken into prismatic hues, and fear the pure white light'.[3] While each of the lovers-in-potential is writing to idealize and worship the poetry of the other, Elizabeth Barrett's literary foresight and criticism seem, more than Browning's: 'shadows which futurity casts on the present'.[4]

Browning was casting shadows too, for ten years later his *Men*

[1] Robert Browning, *The Letters of Robert Browning and Elizabeth Barrett Barrett, 1845–1846*, 2 vols., ed. E. Kintner (Cambridge, Mass., 1969), i. 9.

[2] Browning, *The Poems*, 2 vols., ed. J. Pettigrew and T. J. Collins (Harmondsworth, 1981); references in parentheses give the vol. and page nos.

[3] Browning, *The Letters*, i. 7.

[4] Percy Bysshe Shelley, 'A Defence of Poetry', in *The Complete Works*, 10 vols., ed. R. Ingpen and W. E. Peck (1926; New York, 1965), vii. 140.

and Women appeared. In 'Andrea del Sarto' he might be qualifying Elizabeth's praise of a decade before: 'Ah, but a man's reach should exceed his grasp, | Or what's a heaven for?' (i. 646) Stretching out a hand as far as it will go and opening the palm, you reach slightly further than if you make a fist to grasp something. A poet's reach is thus a little longer than a boxer's. But reaching with an open hand, you cannot keep hold of things or loved ones. Daniel Karlin writes that 'As always, in Browning, the sense of touch is primary'.[5] Perhaps a reaching to touch, a stretching towards someone else is nearer his poetry's heart. When Elizabeth Barrett writes that Browning has 'an immense grasp in Art', she is correct—though not because he is all-encompassing, but because he does not grasp things. He has an immense grasp, meaning a large but incomplete practical apprehension, of why not grasping is the finer thing.

In Andrea's 'a man's reach should exceed his grasp,' his 'should' can be understood in two related ways. First, it means a moral obligation: a man's reach ought to exceed his grasp, and heaven is there to orientate and reward the striving. Secondly, it speculates about how all things may have been ordained: a man's reach probably does exceed his grasp because he has been placed at that point in a created order between the concrete and the sky. In the opening of *The Ring and the Book* Browning states that man is 'Formed to rise, reach at, if not grasp and gain | The good beyond him,—which attempt is growth,—' (p. 42).[6] When Elizabeth wrote that Browning had an 'immense grasp' she was referring to his 'mental hold' or 'comprehensiveness of mind'. Yet that meaning connects with the physical sense—a 'hold' or 'grip' of the hand. Andrea must be aware of the physical meaning even if his primary sense is the mental one: with a painter the two are inextricable.

My physical reach does exceed my grasp, and the mere fact of it supports Andrea's second meaning: we have been placed between the concrete and the sky, and it is our nature to strive upwards. This is a recipe for complacency. At the same time, that a man's reach ought to exceed his grasp implies that it need not: it is our nature to grasp and be grasping, to sink downwards, but we must strive not to succumb to this temptation. This is a call to personal

---

[5] Daniel Karlin, *The Courtship of Robert Browning and Elizabeth Barrett* (Oxford, 1985), 111.
[6] Browning, *The Ring and the Book*, ed. R. D. Altick (Harmondsworth, 1981); references in parentheses with a page no. only refer to this volume.

vigilance. Here is a moral stance which, if taken for granted, I fail to live by, and, if inhabited with a continuous knowledge of my failure to live up to its requirements of me, I may perhaps fulfil.

The coexistence of a bracing and a complacent view of humanity's place regarding the finite and the infinite was observed by Thomas Hardy when he remarked in a letter to Edmund Gosse of 3 March 1899:

The longer I live the more does B.'s character seem *the* literary puzzle of the 19th century. How could smug Christian optimism worthy of a dissenting grocer find a place inside a man who was so vast a seer & feeler when on neutral ground?[7]

The line and a half from 'Andrea del Sarto' contains that gap between what can be conceived and what achieved on earth. It allows for a 'smug Christian optimism' in the acceptance that we have been made like this, and occasions a depression deriving from perpetual failure to measure up. This failure galvanizes the continuing struggle of the Browning who is 'so vast a seer and feeler'.

Hardy's 'so vast a seer' recalls the subjective poet of the 'Essay on Shelley' who reaches after 'seeds of creation lying burningly on the Divine Hand' (i. 1002); but Browning, to use Hardy's unappealing but apt word, is also a 'feeler'. In his poems, seeds of creation are also lying burningly on the human hand, as it reaches towards an object of love. 'Inapprehensiveness', from *Asolando: Facts and Fancies* (1889), shows the survival into his last work of mental habits traceable throughout. The *Oxford English Dictionary* gives for *inapprehensive*, something 'that does not grasp mentally, or perceive by sense' and something 'that does not apprehend danger'. Browning and Mrs Arthur Bronson[8] are standing 'simply friend-like' in the twilight looking at the view about which the lady has grown lyrical. The poet cannot respond to her speculations because absorbed by 'Something that I could not say at all', which he then writes in the poem:

> [']By you stands, and may
> So stand unnoticed till the Judgement Day,
> One who, if once aware that your regard

---

[7] Thomas Hardy, *The Collected Letters*, 7 vols., ed. R. Purdy and M. Millgate (Oxford, 1978–87), ii. 216.

[8] See Browning, *More than Friend: The Letters of Robert Browning to Katharine de Kay Bronson*, ed. M. Meredith (Waco, Tex., 1985), pp. lviii–lx.

Claimed what his heart holds,—woke, as from its sward
The flower, the dormant passion, so to speak—
Then what a rush of life would startling wreak
Revenge on your inapprehensive stare
While, from the ruin and the West's faint flare,
You let your eyes meet mine, touch what you term
Quietude—that's an universe in germ—
The dormant passion needing but a look
To burst into immense life!'
                     'No, the book
Which noticed how the wall-growths wave' said she
'Was not by Ruskin.'
             I said 'Vernon Lee?'   (ii. 887)

Browning's unsayable speech self-mockingly criticizes the lady for
failing to look his way. It hankers after an instant when their eyes
might touch 'Quietude'—a 'universe in germ' or those 'seeds of
creation' lying burningly on a hand that no one reached towards.
There's a fondly comic acceptance of the imaginary situation in
the poem's concluding lines, the words they did say. Browning,
at this late date keen as ever to remain faithful to Elizabeth's
memory, is glad to note he has his dormant passion still, and not
a little relieved that Mrs Bronson did not take her eyes from the
view.

Browning's poem honours his friend by imagining that they
could have played the roles of lovers in one of his famous lyrics.
'Inapprehensiveness' affectionately repeats many of those poems'
characteristics. There is a division between the apprehensible and
the apprehended. The lady wonders whether 'Ruskin noticed here
at Asolo | That certain weed-growths on the ravaged wall | Seem'
(ii. 887)—at which point the syntax gives out, and it probably was
not Ruskin after all. The separation between seeing and knowing
in situations with married people, possible couples, or lovers is
another place where 'a man's reach should exceed his grasp'
(i. 646).

Andrea del Sarto does not grasp his wife Lucrezia: 'Let us but
love each other. Must you go?' (i. 648). Is Andrea a constant lover?
He has a dignity similar to that achieved by Leopold Bloom in
catching on to his wife's infidelity and letting her go. Writing about
'Two in the Campagna', Ian Jack suggests that 'The secret of
constancy in love . . . the speaker seems to regard as an intellectual

thing that he is always on the point of grasping'.⁹ Constancy in love is not shown by grasping at a loved one, but by reaching from a distance. Browning had an 'immense grasp in Art' exactly because he refuses to grasp; his poems show that the 'secret of constancy in love' lies not so much in 'having and holding' as in reaching for, catching at, and letting go. This is what happened when Browning and Elizabeth were married on 12 September 1846:

after the wedding she drove to the house of the old friend whom she was supposed to have been visiting, was collected from there in another carriage by her two sisters, and taken for a drive to Hampstead Heath, pretending all the while that nothing unusual had happened. As for the bridegroom, he too, at the age of thirty-four, lived with his parents, in suburban New Cross; he drove there straight after the wedding, and wrote his wife the two-hundred-and-eightieth letter which he had written to her since they had first begun to correspond, twenty months earlier. . . . For a week after the marriage, the couple remained apart; at the end of that week, they left England as stealthily as they had married.¹⁰

II

Browning writes about the relations between artist and work, perceiver and perceived, women and men, earth and heaven, as a drama of reaching to touch, of being on the point of grasping, of holding and understanding, or holding and believing. His work is a constant struggle to set in tenuous harmony the purposes and aims of a secular and divine love. These dramas take place in his poems' rhythms and forms.

Ezra Pound in 'Mesmerism', a youthful parodic homage to Browning, raises his glass: 'Here's to you, Old Hippety-Hop o' the accents'.¹¹ It is a line which itself displays the *sprezzatura* and *gusto* of Browning's verse. *Sprezzatura* is not in English dictionaries; it is an Italian word which has been used to describe the style of Byron's *Don Juan* and means 'studied carelessness; nonchalance'. The poet appears to play fast and loose with his chosen form and metre, but, since his carelessness is 'studied', the nonchalance has significance. *Gusto* is in English dictionaries; it means 'Taste, liking', or

⁹ Ian Jack, *Browning's Major Poetry* (Oxford, 1973), 142–3.
¹⁰ Karlin, *Courtship*, 16.
¹¹ Ezra Pound, *Collected Shorter Poems* (1952), 27.

'enthusiastic and vigorous enjoyment or appreciation', or less often 'over-abundant vitality'. In Hazlitt's essay 'On Gusto' it describes a painterly vision and method of depiction where the flesh 'seems sensitive and alive all over'.[12]

Pound has affirmed that 'The real life in regular verse is an irregular movement underlying.'[13] The rhythm, while in touch with and shaped by the metre, moves independently of it. A line of verse gains rhythmic vitality by being studiedly careless of the metrical norm, which readers remain conscious of because the carelessness is studied. Here is the second stanza of 'Two in the Campagna':

> For me, I touched a thought, I know,
>   Has tantalized me many times,
> (Like turns of thread the spiders throw
>   Mocking across our path) for rhymes
> To catch at and let go.   (i. 728)

Isobel Armstrong says of 'The Lost Mistress', 'There is a tight, tense economy about this poem, as with all the poems in attenuated stanzaic forms'.[14] What is the relation between 'tight, tense' and 'attenuated'? The 'tense' and the 'intense', the 'attenuated', 'tenuous', and 'tender' all derive from the Latin verb *tenere* (to hold) and Middle French *tendre* (to stretch). The poetic and passionate drama of Browning's stanza depends upon stretching towards a thought he has 'touched', has momentarily apprehended and lost. His next stanza begins by asking the woman 'Help me to hold it!' 'It' is a spider's thread, and the idea contains its impossibility; and his thought, like a spider's thread, is 'tender'—'having a soft and yielding texture: easily broken, cut, or damaged'.

Browning's stanza delicately plays off the components of the verse against each other to be intense, tenuous, attenuated, and tender. The firm and ever-present metrical pattern would be like a grasp if it held throughout: four octosyllabic iambic tetrameters followed by a six-syllable iambic trimeter. Yet the *sprezzatura* of Browning's voice speaks across the expected requirements of a metre with varying degrees of emphasis. The first person pronouns

---

[12] William Hazlitt, 'On Gusto', in *The Complete Works*, 21 vols., ed. P. P. Howe (London, 1930–4) iv. 77.

[13] Pound, *Jefferson and/or Mussolini* (1935), 94.

[14] Isobel Armstrong, 'Browning and Victorian Poetry of Sexual Love', in Armstrong (ed.), *Writers and their Background: Robert Browning* (1974), 283.

in 'I touched a thought, I know' do not settle clearly as weak stresses; in 'Has tantalized'—the 'Has' rises against its expected position; while, in 'Mocking across our path', 'Mocking' is pointedly trochaic; and, finally, in 'To catch at and let go' the metre's three iambs are given the rhythmic figure of an iamb, pyrrhic foot, and spondee.

The syntax also displays a *sprezzatura*. The parenthesis within this stanza attenuates to breaking point the grammar of the sentence it interrupts: how does 'for rhymes | To catch at and let go' attach to 'I touched a thought'? I touched a thought for rhymes? The preposition sounds odd. This attenuation finely represents the fleeting thought, which is nevertheless contained, a statement about its own fleeting and tantalizing nature, within the rhyme scheme. The poet who catches at rhymes as if by chance and casually lets them go is displaying a studied carelessness, disguised as an incapacity, which he earnestly stretches to overcome. There is a moving contradiction in the rhymes on 'know', 'throw', and 'let go', because the rhyming keeps hold of what the sentence claims is being released. This paradox touches again on 'the secret of constancy in love' by which lovers keep their proximity. Browning recognizes the difficult prerequisites for independent existence and mutually supporting passionate loyalty. He identifies in the division between reaching and grasping—enacted by the separate but dependent life of the formal elements—the necessities of allowing desires a life and expression, and of a self-denial which makes possible a respect for the life of others.

A toccata is a 'kind of rapid brilliant composition for piano, organ etc.' and its name comes from the Italian verb *toccare*: to touch. The *sprezzatura* in 'A Toccata of Galuppi's' turns a studiedly nonchalant treatment of metre and rhythm to sardonic purposes. The metrical pattern (fifteen-syllable lines, seven trochees, and a terminal stressed syllable, would be one description) mimics rapidly played musical phrases to enact the inevitable in human life, while the lighter touches of rhythmic freedom perform the participants' vain hopes that the doom of man will be reversed for them:

'Were you happy?'—'Yes.'—'And are you still as happy?'—
   'Yes. And you?'
—'Then, more kisses!'—'Did *I* stop them, when a million
   seemed so few?'
Hark, the dominant's persistence till it must be answered to!   (i. 551)

The rhythm rises to resist the pattern most assertively in the second line where 'more', '*I*', and 'so' ask to be stressed against expectations; then in the third line, reinforcing the sense, the metrical pattern reasserts its shape like fate. The closer the speech rhythm is to the metre, the more inexorable the hold that it and what it analogically represents has over a reader.

Browning is wary of grasp in the music of poetry, and can use metrical dominance satirically. There is a chilling lack of rhythmical resistance in the metre and rhyme of this enchanting passage from 'The Pied Piper of Hamelin':

> All the little boys and girls,
> With rosy cheeks and flaxen curls,
> And sparkling eyes and teeth like pearls,
> Tripping and skipping, ran merrily after
> The wonderful music with shouting and laughter.   (i. 388)

The piper must be answered to, and it is because no reaching across distance appears between metre and rhythm that he has the children in his grasp. Freedom and responsibility are held in a tensed relation with the poem's final couplet—its stress marks on 'from' attempting in vain to alter the speech rhythm: 'And, whether they pipe us free fróm rats or fróm mice, | If we've promised them aught, let us keep our promise!' (i. 391) The comedy is in rhyming ambivalently on weak and strong syllables.

A similar rhyming occurs at the end of 'Love in a Life', and there a lover's 'answering to' his love is benign because the reaching distance between metrical expectation and rhythm is alive:

> Yet the day wears,
> And door succeeds door;
> I try the fresh fortune—
> Range the wide house from the wing to the centre.
> Still the same chance! she goes out as I enter.
> Spend my whole day in the quest,—who cares?
> But 'tis twilight, you see,—with such suites to explore,
> Such closets to search, such alcoves to importune!   (i. 604)

On 5 April 1846 Browning wrote to Elizabeth: 'In this House of Life—where I go, you go,—where I ascend you run before,—where I descend, it is after you.'[15] In the first stanza, setting up an

---

[15] Browning, *The Letters*, 591.

expectation, the terminal word 'feather' has the same stress pattern as its rhyme-word's last two syllables 'together'; in the second stanza a quickening distance is performed by the rhyme of 'fortune' with 'importune'—an unstressed terminal syllable rhymed with a stressed one.[16] About 'Love in a Life', Isobel Armstrong writes, 'Rooms enclose space and only seem to define the emptiness more, and the search is a repeated greeting of emptiness, of contentless experience.'[17] This account misses the peculiar gusto, the 'over-abundant vitality', which invigorates 'Love in a Life'. It is so good-humoured about its failure to grasp content or contentment; and its unresigned comic buoyancy derives from an underlying assumption that the world is more present in the movement towards experience than in the finite and restrictively circumstanced condition of possession.

III

In his essay 'On Gusto', which appeared in *The Examiner* on 26 May 1816, William Hazlitt wrote:

There is a gusto in the colouring of Titian. Not only do his heads seem to think—his bodies seem to feel. This is what the Italians mean by the *morbidezza* of his flesh-colour. It seems sensitive and alive all over; not merely to have the look and texture of flesh, but the feeling in itself. For example, the limbs of his female figures have a luxurious softness and delicacy, which appears conscious of the pleasure of the beholder.[18]

Later Hazlitt notes: 'Rembrandt has it in everything; everything in his pictures has a tangible character.' Go to the National Gallery, appear to be about to touch a Rembrandt or Titian, and one of the guards will request you to keep your distance; the painters themselves may only have touched the painted flesh with the aid of a brush held at arm's length. The act of painting can be a remote touching by proxy. The good painting with gusto is an invitation to reach towards the world and inhabit experience; the distance

---

[16] *OED* gives both 'im*por*tune' and 'import*une*'; the dilemma would be enough to produce a suitably equivocal ending, though I am happier with the second form in this poem.

[17] Armstrong, 'Browning and Victorian Poetry', 290.

[18] Two references to Hazlitt, 'On Gusto', 77, 78.

implies respect for the integrity of other beings and things. Browning's poems, and particularly those about painters and painting, are alive with these ambivalent implications.

In 'Pictor Ignotus', the Quattrocento Florentine painter, comparing himself with a young and fashionable artist, sees how he might have responded to the demands of a secular vigour in art:

> And, like that youth ye praise so, all I saw,
>   Over the canvas could my hand have flung,
> Each face obedient to its passion's law,
>   Each passion clear proclaimed without a tongue;
> Whether Hope rose at once in all the blood,
>   A-tiptoe for the blessing of embrace . . .   (i. 397)

He thinks he could have painted human beings with gusto. Why didn't he? The conflict between secular and religious patronage during this period and in this painter's career is startlingly represented as a fear that purity will be raped by grossness:

> . . . Who summoned those cold faces that begun
> To press on me and judge me? Though I stooped
>   Shrinking, as from the soldiery a nun,
> They drew me forth, and spite of me . . . enough!   (i. 398)

This is hauntingly obscure. The painter opts for religious patronage, a withdrawal from life into boredom and neglect because he does not paint with gusto, but does 'the same series, Virgin, Babe and Saint, I With the same cold beautiful regard' (i. 398). He can console himself with 'At least no merchant traffics in my heart' (i. 398), but the future will be with secular patronage and a more earthly style which he can no longer even reach to embrace.

Reaching to embrace is what Fra Lippo' Lippi is interested in, caught 'past midnight' and 'at an alley's end I Where sportive ladies leave their doors ajar' (i. 540). Brother Lippo is in a dilemma similar to that of the artist in 'Pictor Ignotus', between the demands of the secular and the religious; his method of coping with the problem displays, like his art, plenty of gusto. Fra Lippo Lippi wants, in Hazlitt's terms, to make his religious personages 'sensitive and alive all over', and it leads him into temptation, trouble in both art and life. The Prior comments on his work: ' "Oh, that white smallish female with the breasts, I She's just my niece . . ." ' (i. 545) He wants to put a stop to Lippi's representation from the life, to the preparatory nude studies which his pictures suggest must have preceded them.

The purpose of Fra Lippo's monologue is to explain himself out of the grasp of the night-watch, and he does so by arguing that to paint with gusto he needs to do research:

> This world's not blot for us,
>   Nor blank; it means intensely, and means good:
>   To find its meaning is my meat and drink.   (i. 548)

He describes a picture he has in mind which, amongst a formal array of religious figures, shows the painter appearing as if by accident. 'Back I shrink', he says, 'in this presence, this pure company!' (i. 549) He is about to be judged and found wanting— 'Then steps a sweet angelic slip of a thing I Forward, puts out a soft palm—"Not so fast!"' (i. 549) The reaching hand signals an intercession, here and elsewhere in Browning's work. Fra Lippo is using gusto in his monologue to talk himself out of trouble, he pictures himself in the painting able to escape 'not letting her go I The palm of her, the little lily thing I That spoke the good word for me' (i. 549). Why is Browning interested in artists who are members of religious orders? The intense distance between reaching and touching, his moral preference for reaching over grasping are occasioned by a religious painter with gusto, with a desire for the world.

Brother Lippo is a romantic and sensual comedian in his monologue. Yet these same dynamics turn tragic in the relations between Pompilia and Caponsacchi from *The Ring and the Book*. A priest accused of having an affair with Guido Franceschini's wife, whom he has assisted in a flight from her husband, Giuseppe Caponsacchi ends his monologue arguing that 'priests I Should study passion; how else cure mankind, I Who come for help in passionate extremes?' (p. 321) Priests should reach, the poet implies, but they were better not to try to grasp.

IV

Browning and Elizabeth had a long-running disagreement about spiritualism. She believed in it, and he did not. As 'Mr Sludge, "The Medium"' extendedly demonstrates, he found himself repelled by the business. Reasons for this emerge from a seance they attended in Ealing on the night of 23 July 1855. Daniel Home, an American medium and a model for Mr Sludge, was presiding. 'In preparation for the poets, Home and Miss Rymer, also a medium, had woven a wreath of clematis and placed it in the room'; during the proceedings the following is reported to have happened:

A hand, 'clothed in white loose folds, like muslin,' appeared from the edge of the table opposite the Brownings. Both saw the hand as coming from under the table . . . Presently a larger hand appeared, pushed the wreath off the table, picked it up from the floor, carried it toward Elizabeth— now seated next to Home at his desire—and placed it on her head. The hand bearing the wreath was, as she saw it, 'of the largest human size, as white as snow, and very beautiful.' At her request, it now carried the wreath under the table and gave it to Robert. He was touched several times on the knees and hands—'a kind of soft & fleshy pat,' he told Mrs. Kinny, 'but not so that I could myself touch the object. I desired leave to hold the spirit-hand in mine, and was promised that favour—a promise not kept.'[19]

Browning's poetry has many hands that reach to touch in it. In 'A Light Woman' the speaker condemns himself by latching on to the poet's thematic resource: 'And, Robert Browning, you writer of plays, | Here's a subject made to your hand!' (i. 595) Browning's poetry sponsors the hands of the living in reaching out towards love and life. On 23 July 1855, he and his wife were subjected to a parody of a necessary imaginative dynamic in his poems—except that the 'hand' was supposed to have been that of a visitor from the dead called Wat. This occasion represents a 'tug of love' between the medium Daniel Home and the poet Browning for the spiritual and emotional orientation of Elizabeth Barrett.

Betty Miller, who finds 'an element of self-recognition in Browning's recoil from Home',[20] argues that, for Elizabeth, spiritualism offered an alternative to melancholy. It gave her an assurance, reinforcing faith, that she had not killed her brother. He had been drowned in a sudden squall while sailing in Babbacombe Bay, on 11 July 1840. However, Bro, as he was called in the family, had

---

[19] William Irvine and Park Honan, *The Book, the Ring, and the Poet* (1975), 332.

[20] Betty Miller, *Robert Browning: A Portrait* (1952), 186.

stayed in Torquay at her insistence, and they had parted after a quarrel on the day he died. Miller puts Elizabeth's collapse down to sibling rivalry. She was still in a state of part physical, part psychosomatic invalidism when the poets began their correspondence five years later. A decade after that, when they had been married for nearly nine years, Browning's revulsion at Home seems a recognition that mediums who feign possession by the dead could grasp hold of the weaker side of his wife's mind by stimulating feelings of remorse, which the seances would partially appease, and draw her out of life towards her own dead whom she would soon join.

As Hazlitt says of painting in his essay 'The Dulwich Gallery', 'the dead re-appear, by means of this "so potent art!"' [21] Here is Browning on his art of poetry from the opening of *The Ring and the Book*:

> . . . although nothing which had never life
> Shall get life from him, be, not having been,
> Yet, something dead may get to live again,
> Something with too much life or not enough,
> Which, either way imperfect, ended once:
> An end whereat man's impulse intervenes,
> Makes new beginning, starts the dead alive . . .   (p. 42)

Though in this respect the artist might see 'an element of self-recognition' in his view of the medium—yet his recoil is justified because the purpose of his potency, this gusto, is to orientate his readers into, not out of life. Elizabeth thought this when on 26 June 1846 she wrote to Browning: 'There is hope & help for the world in you—& if for the world, why for me indeed much more.' [22] Karlin sees Browning as 'willing (if not compelling) her, in the division of her feelings between the desire for life and the desire for death, to choose life.' [23] Browning might naturally be jealous of the power that mediums could exert over Elizabeth, because they appeared to oppose the direction in which he believed hands should healthily reach. *The Ring and the Book*, in its obsessive returning to images of hands, plays out, as a drama of absolutes in conflict,

[21] Hazlitt, 'The Dulwich Gallery' in *The Complete Works*, 19.
[22] Browning, *The Letters*, ii. 817–18.
[23] Karlin, *Courtship*, 139.

this tug between those that might snatch us towards death and those which would invite us towards life and vitality.

Hands appear to reach towards Giuseppe Caponsacchi in Book I, expressing the priest's dilemma: 'Now Heaven, now earth, now heaven and earth at once, I Had plucked at and perplexed their puppet here' (p. 50). In Book IV, Pompilia's danger and her salvation also imply reaching hands: 'Where stood one saviour like a piece of heaven, I Hell's arms would strain round but for this blue gap.' (p. 180) This gap recurs in Caponsacchi's own monologue when he starts to muse over his studies:

> thinking how my life
> Had shaken under me,—broken short indeed
> And showed the gap 'twixt what is, what should be ... (p. 278)

On 2 January 1698, Guido Franceschini and his accomplices gained access to where Pompilia and her parents were living in Rome by giving Caponsacchi's name at the door—to prove once more that the pair were lovers, Guido explains. The stabbing is described thus in Book IV, where Guido:

> lifts her by the long dishevelled hair,
> Holds her away at arms' length with one hand,
> While the other tries if life come from the mouth ... (p. 196)

Here, from the image of a grim efficiency, comes the worst of possessing an immense grasp in life.

The speaker in Book II, who represents the opinion of 'Half-Rome', has, like Andrea del Sarto, a problem with amorous cousins, and he is passing on a warning. He sides with Guido in the view that husbands have the right to punish infidelity in their wives. The court of Justice might have criticized Guido for not killing his wife immediately he had apprehended the fleeing couple, but bringing them to Rome for judgement and a suit of divorce:

> What you touched with so light a finger-tip,
> You whose concern it was to grasp the thing,
> Why must law gird herself and grapple with? (p. 106)

Such killing would not be crime but punishment, the voice argues; Browning's word 'grasp' signals a counter interpretation. 'The Other Half-Rome' is for Pompilia, and quotes her to explain why she fled towards the city with Caponsacchi's aid:

> Earth was made hell to me who did no harm:
> I only could emerge one way from hell
> By catching at the one hand held me, so
> I caught at it and thereby stepped to heaven . . .   (p. 147)

Browning says in Book I that this speaker is right, but only for fanciful and sentimental reasons; yet his preference for this version of the story is in the memory of 'Two in the Campagna' here: 'for rhymes I To catch at and let go' (i. 728). Pompilia's 'stepped to heaven' is ambiguous with dramatic irony, as is the word 'heaven' in those lines from 'Andrea del Sarto'. In 'stepped to heaven', given the hell on earth of her marriage, the word could mean the arms of Caponsacchi. This sentimental speaker coyly suggests sexual fulfilment for the pair:

> Ever the courtly Canon: see in such
> A star shall climb apace and culminate,
> Have its due handbreadth of the heaven at Rome . . .   (p. 134)

As he speaks, Pompilia is dying of stab wounds and about to step out of life to heaven, which she does at the end of her monologue: 'God stooping shows sufficient of His light I For us i' the dark to rise by. And I rise.' (p. 375) While the protagonists are caught up in a physical, ethical, and spiritual drama of grasping and reaching, the reader is invited to stretch in the direction of what the poem presents as the truth. Yet since there is never much doubt what Browning thinks of the story in outline, what is the truth to be discovered? And in what sense of the word 'grasp' is it to be apprehended?

Robert Langbaum thinks it is grasped fully and firmly. His chapter on the poem in *The Poetry of Experience* concludes:

Judgment goes on, in other words, below the level of argument and hence the dramatic monologue, which makes it possible for us to apprehend the speaker totally, to subordinate what he says to what we know of him through sympathy.[24]

Langbaum thinks *The Ring and the Book* a relativist poem, not because its truth is '*indefinite* or a *matter of opinion*', but because the conditions for apprehending the truth are of this world, refracted through the limitations of who is speaking and dependent

---

[24] This and the two following citations are from Robert Langbaum, *The Poetry of Experience* (Harmondsworth, 1971), 110, 107, 110.

upon judgement of a character's intentions from his or her words.
Yet readers are, for Langbaum, in an ideal and unworldly position
because, with sympathy, they can 'apprehend the speaker totally'.
Such total apprehension is grasp not reach, a critical fantasy
fulfilment, as unsatisfactory as that achieved by Porphyria's lover.
Browning cannot have assumed that his reader would be able to
hold in mind everything said by everyone in *The Ring and the
Book*. He must have thought we ought to try. Leigh Hunt,
reviewing *Paracelsus* in 1835, observed that 'The reader of such a
work has his effort to make, as well as the writer has had his—his
powers of apprehension, as the other has had his powers of
production, to keep on the stretch.'[25]

Langbaum's view is like reading the poem without the poetry,
because the speakers in *The Ring and the Book* do not exist as
independent entities from which language is spontaneously gener-
ated. Yet Browning's Italians all speak the Browningese dialect of
English. John Killham, criticizing Langbaum's view, states that 'it
is a quality of all fiction to deal with individual persons and events,
and ... we must always be guided by the author's revelations
concerning his characters'. But Killham draws, from Browning's
insistence in Book I on where the truth lies, the sad conclusion that
it need not be reached towards. It is put into readers' closed hands:
'Browning has worked exceedingly hard, but his reader has nothing
to do save watch a demonstration.' Killham calls the poem 'an
elaborate Victorian monument to the faith that truth does not
depend upon human testimony, but is absolute.'[26] His word 'watch'
is misjudged though, because a reader has to work at the poem,
and what is demonstrated through a reading is not who is guilty
and who innocent.

'Chesterton described *The Ring and the Book* as "essentially a
detective story"', Jack observes, but concludes 'if the essential
thing about a detective story is that the reader is kept guessing to
the end about the identity of the criminal then Browning's poem
has nothing in common with a detective story.'[27] If you have been

---

[25] B. Litzinger and D. Smalley (eds.), *Robert Browning: The Critical Heritage*,
(1970), 44.

[26] Three references to John Killham, 'Browning's "Modernity": *The Ring and
the Book*, and Relativism', in I. Armstrong (ed.), *The Major Victorian Poets:
Reconsiderations* (1969), 159–60 and 172 (twice).

[27] Jack, *Browning's Major Poetry*, 294–5.

the victim of a crime of violence and survived, as Pompilia did for four days, you may know who did it and your concern (as for readers of detective stories which are not whodunnits) is whether the known criminal will be brought to justice. You might also want to understand how and why the criminal could have done such a thing, what states of mind are thus revealed, and what relation exists between the contemplation of such human capacities and the vulnerability of human judgement and justice in the face of them.

Questions of motive are at the heart of Browning's concern: did Caponsacchi help Pompilia escape from Guido because they were lovers, or were intending to be lovers, or because he wished to perform an altruistic act however attracted to the girl? The educated but cynically worldly speaker of Book IV describes Caponsacchi's intervention using Browning's recurrent terms:

> ['] Here my hand holds you life out!' Whereupon
> She clasped the hand, which closed on hers and drew
> Pompilia out o' the circle now complete.   (p. 182)

The 'clasped' and 'closed' might imply sexual conspiracy between the pair; this monologuist thinks it is the old story of an aged husband and a young wife: 'Whose fault or shame but Guido's?' (p. 182) Pompilia uses the same image of hands to refer to the priest's role, but in overtly spiritual terms:

> So, what I hold by, are my prayer to God,
> My hope, that came in answer to the prayer,
> Some hand would interpose and save me—hand
> Which proved to be my friend's hand . . .   (pp. 341–2)

Later, expressing their relationship as a divine quest, she speaks of Caponsacchi's 'hand | Holding my hand across the world' (p. 366), the poet linking and separating those hands over his line-ending. Bottinius, the lawyer writing a defence of Pompilia in Book IX, describes the moment when, stopping on their flight to Rome, Caponsacchi carried the exhausted Pompilia to the Inn. There, the following morning, they were overtaken by Guido, who claims to have caught them with every evidence of having consummated their passion. Bottinius suggests:

> And his good hand whose stalwart arms have borne
> The sweet and senseless burthen like a babe
> From coach to couch . . .   (p. 451)

His task is to vindicate Pompilia's innocence, and he does so by reminding his reader that she was asleep when Caponsacchi had 'the pale beauty prisoned in embrace' (ibid.).

Bottinius also thinks that Caponsacchi would have been tempted by the occasion, 'And why curb ardour here?'(ibid.) His analogy with the death of Archimedes—'absorbed by thought' he was 'ignorant of the imminence o' the point' (ibid.) which stabbed him—implies Caponsacchi probably did make love to her, but while he is guilty of sin, she is not, because unaware. Thomas Carlyle too thought that in reality 'the girl and the handsome young priest were lovers'.[28] In Browning's poem, Caponsacchi denies it, describing the moment at the Inn:

> I never touched her with my finger-tip
> Except to carry her to the couch, that eve,
> Against my heart, beneath my head, bowed low,
> As we priests carry a paten . . .   (p. 309)

'Against my heart, beneath my head, bowed low' expresses the desire to possess her which he assures his listeners he resisted. The Pope, in Book X, finds much 'amiss, | Blameworthy, punishable' (p. 507) in the manner of their flight, but of the priest he says that 'thou wast pure, | I find it easy to believe' (p. 508). The Pope also assumes that Caponsacchi would have wanted to make love: 'was the trial sore? | Temptation sharp? Thank God a second time!' (p. 509) This moment lies at the heart of Browning's work because, when the world thinks they must have been lovers it has some truth on its side. They might have been, and Caponsacchi at least felt the possibility; but the poem believes that they were not, and the much-reiterated images of hands, like the moments of approach to experience in Browning's best love lyrics, suggest that he reached but, unlike Guido, did not grasp.

Towards the end of his work on *The Ring and the Book*, in a letter of 22 February 1869, Browning wrote to Julia Wedgwood, responding to her criticism of Guido's presentation as a bestial villain:

We differ apparently in our conception of what gross wickedness can be effected by cultivated minds—I believe the gross*est*—all the more, by way

---

[28] Irvine and Honan, *Book, Ring, Poet*, 428, citing W. Allingham, *A Diary*, ed. H. Allingham and D. Radford (1907), 207.

of reaction from the enforced habit of self denial which is the condition of men's receiving culture.[29]

Browning's Caponsacchi outstrips both Fra Lippo Lippi, and the inactive Duke Ferdinand of 'The Statue and the Bust', because, within painful impossibilities, he performs two of Browning's moral ideals: the recognition of passion contained within self denial, and the enacting of a desire to behave in accordance with what is felt to be right. Barbara Melchiori's essay 'Browning in Italy' concludes with this speculation:

An Italian mistress would have changed a great deal more for Browning than his attitude to Italian politics—almost certainly much of the contorted puritanism which so complicates his poetry would have disappeared.[30]

Yet his poetry draws readers towards the far-reaching significance of just those complications.

V

Apparent failure—is that what Browning's work has proved to be? Leo Salingar, though acknowledging the debts of later poets to Browning's experiments, thought so:

Once Browning's opinions had fallen out of date, the muddle and patchwork of his art were clearly to be seen. He failed to revive the poetic drama or create a satisfying novel in verse; he failed to reach a stable compromise between the visionary and the realist.[31]

An initial defensive response to this summary would point out that of the first two failures—to revive the poetic drama, and create a satisfying novel in verse—Browning failed in a context where no one else unquestionably succeeded. Of the third, his failure 'to reach a stable compromise between the visionary and the realist', it might be suggested that human beings do not often, if indeed ever, achieve it. What is more, a compromise between the visionary

---

[29] Browning, *Robert Browning and Julia Wedgwood: A Broken Friendship as Revealed in their Letters*, ed. R. Curle (1937), 188.

[30] Barbara Melchiori, 'Browning in Italy', in Armstrong (ed.), *Writers and their Background: Robert Browning*, 170.

[31] Leo Salingar, 'Robert Browning', in B. Ford (ed.), *New Pelican Guide to English Literature*, vi. *From Dickens to Hardy* (Harmondsworth, 1958, rev. edn. 1982), 246.

and the realist might only too easily produce neither. Browning noted as much himself in the 'Essay on Shelley' when he criticized 'poetry, false under whatever form, which shows a thing not as it is to mankind generally, nor as it is to the particular describer, but as it is supposed to be for some unreal neutral mood, midway between both and of value to neither' (i. 1005). To make these mitigating pleas does not remove the force of Salingar's observations, for he is judging Browning on the poet's terms. Still, if Browning failed by his own lights, he achieved more than most poets manage in succeeding.

However intriguing *The Ring and the Book* may be to committed readers, many of the poet's most loyal and hard-working editors and critics believe Browning's masterwork to be a tiresome diversion. Jack writes that 'it is difficult to see it as other than a dead end in the history of English poetry',[32] while, as noted above, Killham persuasively argues that *The Ring and the Book* is 'an elaborate Victorian monument to the faith that truth does not depend upon human testimony, but is absolute' and its moral explicitness 'intensifies the pessimism the poem finally displays'.[33] Eugenio Montale catches at the gloomy fate of Browning's epic when in 'Dopo una fuga' he mentions Giuseppe Caponsacchi as among 'spettri . . . di illeggibili poemi' [phantoms . . . of unreadable poems].[34] Nowadays shorter pieces are mostly preferred. Poets who harbour yearnings to write works the size of *The Ring and the Book* might look at the problems of Browning's masterpiece and *The Cantos of Ezra Pound* to find ample reason for discouragement. The moral explicitness and critical vulnerability of *The Ring and the Book* involve Browning's relations to his sources, his treatment of the facts of the Roman Murder Case. Jack writes that 'it would be better, subtler, more interesting, if what we guess to have been the historical truth were (in any event) presented as the imaginative truth of the poem'.[35] This is not the case, and what would be produced according to such a formula of making the historical truth and the imaginative truth coincide would not be Victorian, or for that matter, modern poetry. It would not, in Sir

[32] Jack, *Browning's Major Poetry*, 299.
[33] Killham, 'Browning's "Modernity" ', 172.
[34] Eugenio Montale, *L'opera in versi*, ed. R. Bettarini and G. Contini (Turin, 1980), 388.
[35] Jack, *Browning's Major Poetry*, 296.

Philip Sidney's eyes, be poetry at all: 'the historian, wanting the precept, is so tied, not to what should be but to what is, to the particular truth of things and not to the general reason of things, that his example draweth no necessary consequence, and therefore a less fruitful doctrine'.[36] Are modern critics in a better position to guess than Browning? Why did not the poet, like Carlyle when he read the poem, think that in reality 'the girl and the handsome young priest were lovers'? Why do the truth of the imagination and historical truth diverge in this case? And is it only in this case? Is Browning's failure to be attributed to him alone? A better poet could have succeeded? Or is Browning's apparent failure an instance of a more general failure of imaginative truth in its dealings with history? Or is it readers who are failing? By accepting Browning's poem as a failure, read or unreadable, do his readers surrender ground on the place of imagination in understanding the world, or, even more crucially, give up the place of imagination in attributing value to the world?

VI

Commenting on his translation of the *Old Yellow Book*, Browning's main source for the poem, J. M. Gest wrote in 1927 that the poem is 'not the pure gold of truth but the gilded ring of his imagination'. Gest, an American lawyer, outlines what are Browning's creative divergences from the facts as given in the source. Of Caponsacchi, for instance, who was relegated for 'complicity in the elopement or flight, and for the seduction of Francesca Comparini and for carnal knowledge of her', Gest considers Browning's 'adulation of him . . . nauseating to anyone who takes the trouble to read the cold facts of the story'. Gest is particularly incensed by Browning's treatment of the legal profession in Books VIII and IX: 'Browning had no acquaintance whatever with the law of the Old Yellow Book, and apparently had no desire to acquire it.' This led him to conclude that 'it is a dangerous thing for any one, no matter how brilliant he may be, to meddle with what he does not

---

[36] Sir Philip Sidney, *Miscellaneous Prose*, ed. K. Duncan-Jones and J. Van Dorsten (Oxford, 1973), 85.

understand, and it is a foolish thing to ridicule it'.[37] Gest's second charge of foolishness seems irrefutable, and his entire attack is hard to deflect.

Browning had been warned. In 1833 John Stuart Mill wrote two reviews of *Pauline*, neither of which was published. Mill's marginal notes, however, found their way to the poet. They conclude prophetically, given Browning's later involvement with the invalid Elizabeth Barrett:

He feels not remorse, but only disappointment; a mind in that state can only be regenerated by some new passion, and I know not what to wish for him but that he may meet with a *real* Pauline.

Meanwhile he should not attempt to show how a person may be *recovered* from this morbid state,—for *he* is hardly convalescent, and 'what should we speak of but that which we know?'[38]

This is good advice to a young author, but, sticking to the letter of 'what should we speak of but that which we know?', a severe and perennial problem appears. How does a writer know when he or she knows enough to begin to speak? Gest begs the questions when he maintains 'that whenever any writer, poet or not, selects a subject, he should before he writes about it, take some pains to acquire sufficient knowledge of it'.[39] What are the criteria for deciding on the sufficiency of knowledge for poetry? When does historical rigour become imaginative rigor mortis? Browning worked hard reading the sources, finding additional material, visiting the places where the principal events occurred. However, this is not the problem, for, as Donald Smalley observes, Browning 'recast the facts of the Old Yellow Book to fit a largely subjective and preconceived view of the case'.[40] The continuity of Browning's thinking about human relations, even to the images of hands in the poem, suggests that he had the preconceptions long before. Yet, here are two kinds of knowing: knowing the facts, and knowing a pattern of meaning. The second of these is elsewhere called imaginative truth, but the problems of those words 'imaginative'

---

[37] Five references to J. M. Gest, *Old Yellow Book* (Boston, 1925), 623, 11, 9, 625, 626. For further discussion of Caponsacchi's culpabilities, see Beatrice Corrigan, *Curious Annals* (Toronto, 1956), pp. xliii–xlv.

[38] John Stuart Mill, 'Browning's *Pauline*', in *Literary Essays*, ed. E. Alexander (Indianapolis, New York, Kansas City, 1967), 48.

[39] Gest, *Old Yellow Book*, 16.

[40] Browning, *Essay on Chatterton* (1842), ed. D. Smalley (Harvard, 1948), 13.

and 'truth' when put together and the status they have in the world
are indicated by Gest when he notes that the Pope did not in fact
review the whole of Guido Franceschini's case: 'The tenth book of
The Ring and the Book is purely imaginary, though it contains
some of Browning's finest poetry.'[41]

Perhaps this is true, but it is distinctly galling, for the expressions
'purely imaginary' and 'finest poetry' add up to saying that
Browning has produced some attractive moonshine. We may, if so
inclined, enjoy the poem, but as a contribution to the study of
experience it is better understood as wishful thinking. Not only has
Browning's view of the case been made to appear mistaken in the
light of a better judged view, Carlyle's for example, but Browning's
method of demonstrating a stretch towards full comprehension of
experience through work and intuition has been resoundingly
defeated, and then indulged or flatteringly tolerated, by a sense of
truth susceptible to historical analysis. The study of what *was* has
made the creation of what *should have been* seem a fine but
unreliable entertainment. The inescapable predicament of Browning's poem is that its author 'managed so effectively to fuse factual
detail with ideal conception that his handiwork has the air and
substance of reality'.[42] This is an overstatement, but there is a
predicament because the poem has been shown to be airy and
insubstantial in its view of the case, thus discrediting the process of
conceiving, of poetically imagining, experience in such a light and
in such a long poem.

VII

Attacking Chesterton's *Robert Browning*, W. Hall Griffin on 5
March 1904 questioned the extent of the poet's involvement with
the Risorgimento:

On p. 90 one reads:—
'When Browning was first living in Italy, a telegram which had been
sent to him was stopped on the frontier and suppressed on account of his
known sympathy with the Italian Liberals.'
Upon this statement is based over a page of reflections upon the origin of

---

[41] Gest, *Old Yellow Book*, 17.
[42] Browning, *Chatterton*, ed. Smalley, 52.

Browning's 'hatred of the Imperial and Ducal and Papal systems of Italy.'
Browning went to Italy in 1846. He was then practically unknown in
England; he was utterly unknown in Italy, and his Liberal sympathies still
more unknown. Fourteen years later, in 1860, during the last year of his
life in Italy, and after his wife's poems had stirred Italian hearts, a
telegram, not to, but from him, was stopped, not at the frontier, but in
Rome.[43]

As Griffin adds, the poetry of the Brownings which championed
the cause of Italian unity is in Elizabeth Barrett Browning's *Casa
Guidi Windows* (1851) and her *Poems before Congress* (1860).
G. M. Trevelyan's *English Songs of Italian Freedom* (1911) devotes
only ten of its 210 pages to Robert Browning's poems—antholog-
izing 'The Italian in England', the last five stanzas of 'Old Pictures
in Florence', and ' "De Gustibus—" '.[44]

Nevertheless, Browning's interest in, and attachment to the fate
of the Risorgimento should not be underestimated. Chesterton's
blunders may come of a real confusion. During 1844, at the time
of Browning's second visit to Italy, it became public knowledge
that Mazzini, who was an exile in England, was having his mail
intercepted and opened by the British Government. The capture
and execution of the Bandiera brothers after their abortive 'invasion' of Calabria in 1844 brought this to public notice. Browning's
poem, 'The Italian in England', dramatizes the fate of a betrayed,
temporarily defeated patriot in the North of Italy dominated by
Metternich from Vienna:

> However, if I pleased to spend
> Real wishes on myself—say, three—
> I know at least what one would be.
> I would grasp Metternich until
> I felt his red wet throat distil
> In blood through these two hands . . .   (i. 401–2)

This was a poem Mazzini knew, read to his supporters, and
translated into Italian.

The final five stanzas of 'Old Pictures in Florence' criticize the
impracticality of the Florentines after the suddenly won freedoms

---

[43] W. Hall Griffin, in *The Athenaeum*, 3984 (5 March 1904), 307.
[44] William Clyde De Vane, *A Browning Handbook* (New York, 1955), 157,
describes 'The Italian in England' as 'one of the few expressions of Browning's
intense sympathy with the cause of Italian freedom'.

of 1848, an impracticality which led to their almost immediate loss in 1849, during the aftermath of the Piedmontese army's defeat by Austria's 80-year-old General Radetzky at Custoza. In stanza 32 of 'Old Pictures in Florence', the 'certain dotard' is Radetzky, and a synecdoche for the Austrian Empire:

> When the hour grows ripe, and a certain dotard
>   Is pitched, no parcel that needs invoicing,
> To the worse side of Mont Saint Gothard,
>   We shall begin by way of rejoicing;
> None of that shooting the sky (blank cartridge),
>   Nor a civic guard, all plumes and lacquer,
> Hunting Radetzky's soul like a partridge
>   Over Morello with squib and cracker.   (i. 663)

' "De Gustibus—" ' sides with those in opposition to Bourbon rule in the kingdom of the Two Sicilies, Sicily itself and the Neapolitan South of Italy:

> A girl bare-footed brings, and tumbles
> Down on the pavement, green-fresh melons,
> And says there's news today—the king
> Was shot at, touched in the liver-wing,
> Goes with his Bourbon arm in a sling:
> —She hopes they have not caught the felons.
> Italy, my Italy!   (i. 701–2)

All three instances express, indirectly, loyalty to a cause that is, at the time of speaking, in defeat. Browning's poems support the progress towards Italian unity by insinuating a confidence of success in a context of historical set-back, exile, military catastrophe, and miscarried assassination.

'Apparent Failure' is a poem whose ambiguous title suggests that the failure is either evident or merely a superficial appearance. It is set in the French capital during 1856 when the Congress of Paris was negotiating an end to the Crimean War. Browning's first stanza contains an apt allusion to the diplomacy of Cavour in Paris, where, as Sir J. A. R. Marriott points out, he 'was recognized as among the ablest of European diplomatists'.[45]

---

[45] Sir J. A. R. Marriott, *The Makers of Modern Italy: Napoleon–Mussolini* (Oxford, 1931), 99. See also De Vane, *Browning Handbook*, 312–13.

Walking the heat and headache off,
 I took the Seine-side, you surmise,
Thought of the Congress, Gortschakoff,
   Cavour's appeal and Buol's replies . . .   (i. 860)

The importance of the peace conference for the cause of Italian
unity lies in Piedmont's being part of the Alliance against Russia.
At the Congress, thanks to the insistence of Great Britain and
despite Austria's protests, Cavour was present. Buol was the
Austrian delegate and, because of Austria's role as defender of the
status quo in Italy, Cavour's opponent. The aptness of these events
to Browning's title and the theme of 'Apparent Failure' becomes
evident from Marriott's brief account:

> The Treaty was actually signed, the Congress on the point of adjourn-
> ment, before Cavour got his chance. It came at an extraordinary sitting of
> 8 April, when Lord Clarendon flung a bombshell into the Conference by
> denouncing, with a vehemence which Mr. Gladstone might have envied,
> the deplorable condition of Naples and the Papal States. Cavour wisely
> contented himself with a modestly and moderately worded speech in
> support of Clarendon.[46]

Without directly confronting Austria, the power which maintained
Papal and Bourbon authority, Italian independence was reintro-
duced as an issue for the powers of Europe. Browning's message in
the poem, after he has mused upon the bodies of three suicides in
the Paris morgue, is never to imagine that failure is complete, as
Cavour's patience and determination show. The poet's notorious
optimism speaks through in the final stanza:

My own hope is, a sun will pierce
 The thickest cloud earth ever stretched;
   That, after Last, returns the First,
Though a wide compass round be fetched;
   That what began best, can't end worst,
Nor what God blessed once, prove accurst.   (i. 862)

Browning's gusto, his apparent confidence of ultimate vindication
expressed through a vigorously buoyant verse, has proved unpal-
atable to T. S. Eliot, who in 1931 observed that Browning's
'knowledge of the particular human heart is adulterated by an

---

[46] Ibid. 101.

optimism which has proved offensive to our time, though a later age may succeed in ignoring it'.[47]

Yet Browning's optimism for Italian unity, though undeniable, is hedged round by instances of failure, never directly called for by the poet. In stanza 31 of 'Old Pictures in Florence' he asks 'What if I take up my hope and prophesy?' (i. 663) Though he expresses the desire for Italian unity, his mediating it through the hope to see Giotto's Campanile completed, his poem's comic rhymes, its long question in the final stanza function to diffuse any prophetic or polemical engagement. That final stanza is interrogatively expectant, not presagefully sure:

> Shall I be alive that morning the scaffold
>   Is broken away, and the long-pent fire,
> Like the golden hope of the world, unbaffled
>   Springs from its sleep, and up goes the spire
> While 'God and the People' plain for its motto,
>   Thence the new tricolour flaps at the sky?
> At least to foresee that glory Giotto
>   And Florence together, the first am I!   (i. 664)

Despite hoping for the best in that final exclamation mark, the parallel of Giotto's Campanile and Italian unity, seen too in Browning's searchings for neglected past glory in paintings, suggest that these acts of building completion are unlikely in the foreseeable future. Browning's 'foresee' means something nearer to 'hope for the best', than 'visualize what will be the case'. That Italian unity was achieved by 1870 is hardly proof of Browning's prophetic foresight.

VIII

The poet's tactical equivocation, created within a cheerful obliquity of style, can be felt by reading through G. M. Trevelyan's *English Songs of Italian Freedom*, where most of the poems are enthusiastic invocations to Italian leaders and movements, direct calls for perseverance where the writer's voice is aligned with the general aspirations of revolt against tyranny. Here is part of Strophe 2

[47] T. S. Eliot, 'Donne in Our Time', in *A Garland for John Donne 1631–1931*, ed. T. Spencer (Cambridge, Mass., 1931), 15.

from Shelley's 'Ode to Naples', inspired by the Carbonari revolution of July 1820:

> Arrayed in Wisdom's mail,
> Wave thy lightning-lance in mirth!
> Nor let thy high heart fail,
> Though from their hundred gates the leagued Oppressors
> With hurried legions move!
> Hail, hail, all hail![48]

Metternich's Protocol of Troppau promulgated on 19 November 1820 ensured the ultimate defeat of the Neapolitan liberals whom Shelley had supported in this poem with thirty-two exclamation marks. Elizabeth Barrett Browning is an heir to the Shelleyan poetry of political enthusiasm. In *Casa Guidi Windows* and *Poems before Congress*, she sticks her neck out in an impressively uncircumspect manner. The former charts her hopes for Pope Pius IX, Pio Nono, as a reformer and supporter of the liberals, a hope which proved false, while in the latter her belief in Napoleon III as a liberator of Italy, first displayed in 'Napoleon III. in Italy' is called into question with 'First News from Villafranca'. In 1859, after the horrible battle of Solferino, the French Emperor suddenly negotiated a peace with the Austrians, leaving the Veneto still in their hands:

> No, not Napoleon!—he who mused
>   At Paris, and at Milan spake,
>   And at Solferino led the fight:
> Not he we trusted, honoured, used
>   Our hopes and hearts for . . . till they break
>   Even so, you tell us . . . in his sight.[49]

The honesty and bravery of Elizabeth Barrett Browning—who, on her death-bed, was trying to discuss the relative strengths of Ricasoli and Cavour with Isa Blagden—cannot be overestimated.[50] Yet the Risorgimento poetry of Shelley and Elizabeth demonstrates

---

[48] See G. M. Trevelyan (ed.), *English Songs of Italian Freedom* (1911), 31, and Shelley, *Complete Works*, 53.

[49] Elizabeth Barrett Browning, *The Poetical Works*, 3 vols. (1907), iii. 14 and, for 'Napoleon III. in Italy', ii. 171–89.

[50] 'she whispered "Did you say Ricasoli said his politics were identical with those of Cavour, only they took different views of the best way of carrying them out?"— yes—"Ah, so I thought." ' Browning, *Letters of Robert Browning: Collected by T. J. Wise*, ed. T. L. Hood (1933), 61.

a problem for poets addressing the future, those who would, in the terms of Shelley's 'Defence of Poetry', be 'the mirrors of the gigantic shadows which futurity casts upon the present':[51] events can prove mistaken the conviction of their own raised voices. In detail and in specific historical hopes they may be sadly misled. Their mirrors, if vaguely reflecting the course which events in Italy were to take, are too unevenly polished to give any close accuracy to their picture of what they believe *must be*. Far from reinforcing the prophetic claim of the poet, examples from Shelley's and E. B. Browning's work indicate how insubstantial such a claim, and the poetry it issues forth, *must*, by its own nature, *be*. This, Robert Browning knew.

In 'The Poet as Hero. Dante; Shakespeare' (1841), Carlyle expresses the highest hopes for the poet, who 'is a man sent hither to make . . . more impressively known to us'

—that sacred mystery which he more than others lives ever present with. While others forget it, he knows it;—and I might say, he has been driven to know it; without consent asked of *him*, he finds himself living in it, bound to live in it. Once more, here is no Hearsay, but a direct Insight and Belief; this man too could not help being a sincere man![52]

No living poet could live up to this job description. These highest claims being made for poetic authority, acted on, would result in the embarrassment of poems and poets. Browning, eleven years later in his 'Essay on Shelley', has to put the issue more temperately and pragmatically: 'I would rather consider Shelley's poetry as a sublime fragmentary essay towards a presentment of the correspondency of the universe to Deity, of the natural to the spiritual, and of the actual to the ideal' (i. 1012). That phrase, 'a sublime fragmentary essay', equivocates between the absolute knowledge of a sacred mystery effused via a poet—a 'sublime . . . essay'—and a more humanly flawed production, a 'fragmentary essay'—where the pun on 'essay' as 'a piece of writing' or 'an attempt' leans the phrase towards the latter of these meanings. John Stuart Mill's criticism of *Pauline* ('and "what should we speak of but that which we know?"') bears fruit in Browning's tactical scepticism about a poetic knowledge which has no substantiation in the actual, which is all for a *must be* and only when in disappointment an *is*.

---

[51] Shelley, *Complete Works*, vii. 140.
[52] Thomas Carlyle, *The Works*, 30 vols. (1904), v. 81.

In stanza 21 of 'Old Pictures in Florence', Browning projects a vision of the after-life:

> There's a fancy some lean to and others hate—
>   That, when this life's ended, begins
> New work for the soul in another state,
>   Where it strives and gets weary, loses and wins . . .   (i. 661)

His familiarly styled 'There's a fancy' casts this might-be visionary passage in the form of chat, or what Carlyle could call 'Hearsay'. Sure enough, the next stanza of 'Old Pictures in Florence' begins 'Yet I hardly know' (i. 661). Poets may choose between 'hardly' and 'barely' partly on the associations of the adjectives from which the adverbs derive. Such associations in this case allow for a faint ambiguity in 'I hardly know' which hovers between: 'I can scarcely be expected to know' and 'I know with difficulty'. This sense of difficulty and work required lead back into the obdurate actual from the exultant and enthusiastic ethereal of a prophetic voice.

Browning's use of Giotto's unfinished Campanile functions in Florentine history as an ideal in the trammels of the actual, and as a figure for the poet's moral aesthetic theory. In stanza 17 he refers to the anecdote in Vasari which tells of Giotto describing a perfect circle with one movement of the hand:

> Giotto!
> Thy one work, not to decrease or diminish,
> Done at a stroke, was just (was it not?) 'O!'
> Thy great Campanile is still to finish.   (i. 660)

The image of a perfect circle in an incomplete state recurs through Browning's work. It corresponds to the remark in 'Old Pictures in Florence' that Man 'receives life in parts to live in a whole' (i. 659). It is in the conclusion to 'Apparent Failure' where he hopes, 'That, after Last, returns the First, | Though a wide compass round be fetched' (i. 862). Browning returns to the image in the letter he wrote on 10 December 1855, replying to Ruskin's criticism of syntactic obscurity in *Men and Women*:

In *prose* you may criticize so—because that is the absolute representation of portions of truth, what chronicling is to history—but in asking for more *ultimates* you must accept less *mediates*, nor expect that a Druid stone-circle will be traced for you with as few breaks to the eye as the

North Crescent and South Crescent that go together so cleverly in many a suburb.[53]

Browning is fending off the accusation that his poetry lacks enough '*ultimates*' and that his meaning is obscured, by arguing that his absolute is there, but concealed in an oblique syntax interrupted by asides (an indirection necessitated by the wish to embed his aspirations in the perceptible), and that these obliquities produce a circle but with the stages of articulation missing. The defence is not wholly convincing because no reason is given why if you want more ultimates you must accept less mediates. What it betrays is an equivocation about the connection between the perceptible and the significant: Browning's poetry displays an uncertainty about whether the absolute values it promulgates are derivable from the actual, or whether what *should be* cannot be perceived in what *is*.

The distinction between poetry and prose which the letter implies lays emphasis on an intuition of absolutes, of ultimates which may be received through a poetic rendering of the actual. Prose is an 'absolute representation of portions of truth, what chronicling is to history'. Prose, by this account, gives you less truth—but what you receive is fully articulated for you; poetry gives you more truth, but it has to be derived from language which includes the experience of truth's occultation and discovery. Browning implies this, urging Ruskin to read more athletically:

I *know* that I don't make out my conception by my language; all poetry being a putting the infinite within the finite. You would have me paint it all plain out, which can't be; but by various artifices I try to make shift with touches and bits of outlines which *succeed* if they bear the conception from me to you. You ought, I think, to keep pace with the thought tripping from ledge to ledge of my 'glaciers', as you call them; not standing poking your alpenstock into the holes, and demonstrating that no foot could have stood there; suppose it sprang over there?

Yet Browning calls the ultimates, the moral absolutes which give truth to his poems, *his* conception. Here again is the equivocation about perception of the actual and perception of absolute value. Does value derive from experience of the world, poetry then demonstrating a process which happens in perception, or is value brought to bear upon the world, but conceived elsewhere?

[53] Two references to Browning, *Poetry and Prose*, sel. S. Nowell-Smith (1950), 752, 751–3.

IX

Killham writes that, in *The Ring and the Book*, Browning 'illustrates in a very obvious way the old parallel between an artist and God: both are creators and lawgivers in their created worlds'.[54] This sees through and discounts the poet's reiterated disclaimers to absolute insight and access to truth. Browning, in his own voice, describes a moment in the process of the murder trial:

> In due time like reply
> Came from the so-styled Patron of the Poor,
> Official mouthpiece of the five accused
> Too poor to fee a better,—Guido's luck
> Or else his fellows', which, I hardly know . . . (pp. 27–8)

There is Browning's 'hardly' again. Killham knows about the poet's equivocations and interprets his theory of partial insight as a veil:

Browning's denial is an attempt to conceal his true estimate of his rôle: and there is something embarrassing in having the Pope in the poem shown to come right in his judgment of Guido by courtesy not of God but an intuition like that Browning himself claims.[55]

Browning's intuition is even more 'embarrassing', to use Killham's word, because it corresponds with God's view, even derives from God. In Book I, after describing Pompilia's death-bed monologue, Browning introduces the Trial, which will

> teach our common sense its helplessness.
> For why deal simply with divining-rod,
> Scrape where we fancy secret sources flow,
> And ignore law, the recognized machine[?] (pp. 52–3)

Browning's collocation of 'common sense', 'divining-rod', and 'secret sources' implies that ethical intuitions, intuitions of absolute truth, may be gained through common sense, but common sense must then suffer the subtle distortions of secondary moral colouring—hearsay and legal sophistry, for example. Browning's great attempt in *The Ring and the Book* is to demonstrate and lead a reader to the conclusion that dreadful human events can be

---

[54] Killham, 'Browning's "Modernity"', 170.
[55] Ibid.

experienced as ethical intuitions of the truth of things *through* an experience of moral colouring. He would like his readers to feel that the most reliable instrument for making these intuitions is 'common sense'—a pre-existing pattern of normative assumptions about right action. Henry James implies this, and situates the poet's subterfuges. Browning is

with all his Italianisms and cosmopolitanisms, all his victimisation by societies organised to talk about him, a magnificent example of the best and least dilettantish English spirit.[56]

When Killham writes that 'Browning's denial is an attempt to conceal his true estimate of his rôle' he hints at two important readjustments. First, Browning must lessen the overt claim of the poet to receive truth, to know as others do not, because the claim is felt by 'common sense' to be spurious, and plays into the hands of those who wish to discount or ignore the poetic imagination, and further it disinclines readers to respond directly to what poets can legitimately do. Secondly, as James shows, Browning's denial serves to bring the imaginative faculties of the poet into potential accord with the unthreatening 'common sense' of his readers' sensibilities. James refers to 'Italianisms and cosmopolitanisms' and 'victimization by societies organised to talk about him': the former phrase sides a little with an English suspicion of foreigners while the latter keeps an identifying reader aloof from a different misreception: the mentality of the fan club. Browning must negotiate his way between, by negotiating with the neglect of the antipathetic as with the adulation of the unquestioningly converted.

Though Killham is out to show *The Ring and the Book* to be 'an elaborate Victorian monument', with justice, he suggests by his remarking on 'Browning's denial' a modern feature of the poet's work. Browning was among the first poets to act upon a feeling of obligation to reduce the overt claim of the poet to the grasping of absolute knowledge, gaining thus compensatory possibilities (those outlined for the Objective Poet in the 'Essay on Shelley'); at the same time, he tacitly refuses to surrender the Subjective Poet's potential access, be it partial, be it fragmentary, to absolute value. Thus he seeks to sustain a relationship with readers, though he feels no longer able to assume to teach, or expect to be listened to,

[56] Henry James, *English Hours*, ed. A. L. Lowe (1960), 35–6.

on his own terms. Browning's great hope, his sense of the circle coming round, is achieved if he has carried the reader with him to a truth with which the reader happily concurs. He suggests as much describing the Pope's monologue: 'Then comes the all but end, the ultimate I Judgment save yours.' (p. 55) Yet the problem, readers and critics have felt, lies just here. Some can enjoy the prolixity of evoked actuality, the plenitude of realized assumption in the poem, and can hardly fail to receive Browning's version of the events, but may also feel strongly tempted to withhold full concurrence. It seems impossible finally to accept Browning's re-creation of what *was* as embodying, as being in effect the same as, what *should have been*.

Pompilia's illiteracy is important as far as the murder case is concerned in the degree of justification it provides Guido for claiming a smear to his honour, and so for taking the law into his own hands. Did Pompilia and Caponsacchi, like Robert and Elizabeth, exchange letters in which they grew intimate and then planned to escape together? Book II, the opinion that favours Guido's side of the case, has: 'Last come the letters' bundled beastliness'. The speaker believes it clinches the case, evidencing conspiracy to commit adultery, but:

> The accused, both in a tale, protest, disclaim,
> Abominate the horror: 'Not my hand'
> Asserts the friend—'Nor mine' chimes in the wife,
> 'Seeing I have no hand, nor write at all.'
> Illiterate . . .   (p. 95)

The accusation then turns to Guido: he forged the evidence of conspiracy. In Book III, the other extreme of opinion, the speaker concentrates on Caponsacchi's saying that he did not initiate the correspondence, and the letters he received were so overwhelmingly passionate and false-sounding, 'over-luscious honey-clot', that he grew suspicious of Pompilia's motives—until, that is, the pair met and spoke. The monologuist of Book III is uncertain and confused about the issue: 'but the tale here frankly outsoars faith: I There must be falsehood somewhere.' (p. 135) Yet he believes, or appears to, from the sudden ease and smoothness in his voice, that Pompilia could not have conspired because of her illiteracy:

> Pompilia quietly constantly avers
> She never penned a letter in her life

> Nor to the Canon nor any other man,
>> Being incompetent to write and read ...   (p. 135)

After wondering why Caponsacchi was so earnest to tell that he had not initiated the correspondence, since 'graceful lying meets such ready shift', this speaker conjures up the forgery theory:

> Or what do you say to a touch of the devil's worst?
> Can it be that the husband, he who wrote
> The letter to his brother I told you of,
> I' the name of her it meant to criminate,—
> What if he wrote those letters to the priest?   (p. 136)

Caponsacchi contemptuously denies that Pompilia could have written the letters he received:

>> Then your clerk produced
> Papers, a pack of stupid and impure
> Banalities called letters about love—
> Love, indeed,—I could teach who styled them so ...   (p. 310)

He also insinuates thus the forgery counter-accusation, and makes it explicitly when challenged that the letters were found at the inn where Guido apprehended the couple on their flight to Rome:

> '—How came it, then, the documents were found
> At the inn on your departure?'—'I opine,
> Because there were no documents to find
> In my presence,—you must hide before you find ...   (p. 310)

Pompilia relates how her maid brought a letter from Caponsacchi:

>> This is what he wrote.
> I know you cannot read,—therefore, let me!
> "*My idol!*" ' ...
>> But I took it from her hand
> And tore it into shreds.   (pp. 355–6)

The weight of words in the different books of Browning's poem tends to lead a reader into assuming that Pompilia was illiterate and, therefore, that the forgery charges are likely to have been correct.

This is not what J. M. Gest believes. The stories that Pompilia and Caponsacchi gave of their relationship were inconsistent and contradictory regarding their meetings and their letters. Pompilia could write. Guido most probably did no forging. Pompilia said she did not lie down in the inn at Castelnuovo; Caponsacchi said she did. Gest concludes that 'Browning has failed also to reproduce their characters as they really were.'[57] In his opening, the poet voices Gest's conclusion, one which coincides with that supposed of the 'British Public, ye who like me not' (p. 60): 'And don't you deal in poetry, make-believe, I And the white lies it sounds like?' (p. 35) Browning appears to have achieved the opposite of what he intended. Under the guise of maintaining the high claims of poets and poetic imagination by denying any overt claim to absolute truth, has he not provided material for those who would wish to see an unbridgeable discrepancy between empirical fact and imagination, allowing the former to render the latter entertaining but irrelevant?

X

What if ethical values cannot be derived from experience, if the process of life involves a continuous application and adjustment of learnt values often to unforeseen circumstances? What if no access to divinely ratified moral absolutes, or even any correlation of assumed moral values with those of a divinity can be realized? This would leave readers in a position like Caponsacchi's when, early in his monologue, he describes himself:

> thinking how my life
> Had shaken under me,—broke short indeed
> And showed the gap 'twixt what is, what should be,—
> And into what abysm the soul may slip,
> Leave aspiration here, achievement there,
> Lacking omnipotence to connect extremes ...   (p. 278)

Whereas Caponsacchi has the extremes of earth and heaven, now 'what should be' has no sure source beyond the need to project it and live by its constraints. Yet this need is not fully answered by the conscious operation of projecting a meaning. It also requires an apprehension of events as containing in their circumstances and consequences moral significance. As well as needing to live by moral codes, it is necessary to feel that these codes correspond to

---

[57] Gest, *Old Yellow Book*, 623. For Pompilia's ability to write see Corrigan, *Curious Annals*, p. xlv.

how the world is, and that they may be apprehended as if intuitions from experience. If these are the conditions, it is as important in poetry to sustain the feeling of value inhering in experience as to accept that this feeling may be an illusion necessary to benevolence and good conduct.

In 'The Tense of Poetry' from *The World's Body*, John Crowe Ransom explores the predicament of poems in a world of prose analysis, of scientific and historical fact and explanation. He reaches a position that situates any poem, any work of art during and since the nineteenth century, in a quandary similar to that of *The Ring and the Book*, a state like Giuseppe Caponsacchi's, or with Ruskin's alpenstock making the ground shake under it, likely to fall into the abyss between *what is* and *what should be*. Ransom says:

> Our arts, certainly our poems, should fill us with pride because they furnish our perfect experiences. But they fill us also with mortification because they are not actual experiences. If we regard them in a certain mood, say when the heat of action is upon us, they look like the exercises of children, showing what might have been.[58]

This is how *The Ring and the Book* appears, with the added sharpness provided by awareness throughout that behind the poem's 'perfect experiences' there lie the half-concealed and half-revealed 'actual experiences' of the historical persons and their irreparable events. Having a real documented source for the poem's evidently fictive narrations and shows of actuality chills readers beyond any precise representation the poem could furnish, by inviting remembrance of it as happening in the lives of living persons. Here's Half-Rome describing the murdered parents of Pompilia lying in the church of St Lorenzo in Lucina:

> In trying to count the stabs,
> People supposed Violante showed the most,
> Till somebody explained us that mistake;
> His wounds had been dealt out indifferent where,
> But she took all her stabbings in the face,
> Since punished thus solely for honour's sake . . .   (p. 65)

The speaker, intending to intimidate someone he believes to be dallying with his wife, harps on the facial wounds, saying that

---

[58] John Crowe Ransom, *The World's Body* (London and New York, 1938), 249.

'when you avenge your honour and only then' do you 'disfigure the subject, fray the face' (p. 66). That expression, 'fray the face', economically invites participation in the poem's re-creation of how events were, picturing the horror, and asks consideration of how one should behave—since both the action of stabbing and the action of reporting it are endowed with motivations to be contemplated.

Yet at the same instant as the horror is conjured, a 'mortification' arises in knowing that, however perfect the reading experience, this participation is not real experience of a remote actuality. Just as this is comfortingly true for the occasions of terror and pain in a poem, so is it disconcerting for the apprehension of value. When, in Book X, the Pope pronounces Pompilia 'Perfect in whiteness' (p. 504), or Caponsacchi 'surely not so very much apart' (p. 506), he reinforces the poem's moral schema, Browning's conception, and gives an absolute to hold fast to if desired. Nevertheless, the form of his poetic endeavour, its repetition of convictions shifted through shades of moral colouring, registers the imaginative projection involved even in being, according to Browning's schema, right in judgement. However much Browning might have wished to avoid it, the poetic absolutes are dissociated from the actual, which further recedes the more it is evoked in the poem.

Contrary to the apparent (in the sense of 'evident') failure which this might display to those who expect 'a stable compromise between the visionary and the realist' or who wish that 'the historical truth were ... presented as the imaginative truth',[59] the apprehended disjunction between what *was* and what *might have been* is the context for that experience of pride and mortification involved in the fostering of a benevolent inner moral life. *The Ring and the Book* is an enduring testimony and a practical help to the effort required to maintain and cherish a sense of the world as ultimately benign. There are many reasons why we should want to do this, and why, in order to do it well, a full sense of what has been called the 'fragility of goodness' is needed.[60] Browning wrote that he was a liberal because

[59] Salingar, in *New Pelican Guide*, iv. 246; Jack, *Browning's Major Poetry*, 296.
[60] See Martha C. Nussbaum, *The Fragility of Goodness: Luck and Ethics in Greek Tragedy and Philosophy* (Cambridge, 1986). Ch. 1, 'Luck and Ethics', touches some of the matters discussed here.

> All that I am now, all I hope to be,—
>   Whence comes it save from fortune setting free
> Body and soul the purpose to pursue . . .   (ii. 966)

He lent this hope to the cause of Italian unification and liberty. *The Ring and the Book* is an emblem sustaining a sense of the world's benignity, which also dramatizes the enormous obstacles to its realization, Browning's conviction, for example, of the grossest wickedness which he believed could be the result of 'reaction from the enforced habit of self denial which is the condition of men's receiving culture'.[61] Among many obstacles for sustaining a belief in the world's benignity, Browning recognized and confronted the disappearance of grounds in readers' minds for attention to the poetic imagination's working.

Browning laboured hard in the opening and close of his poem to convince readers that his imaginative activity would bring the truth of the case to life. He had good reason for wanting to do so, and reclaim a belief in poetry as a means of truth-telling. It was an impossible task, not least because the terminology he employed— 'fact' and 'fancy' for example—reinforced the division he sought to overcome. The grounds for a resolution of these terms did not, and probably do not, exist. What he did achieve is more important. He demonstrated the necessity of the imagination in restoratively attributing value to life; he showed it to be necessary precisely because history and the actual do not in themselves appear to bear value. As Ransom says:

Participating in the show which is poetry, we expel the taint of original sin and restore to our minds freedom and integrity. Very good. But we are forced to note presently . . . that it was only make-believe . . . that we are again the heirs of history . . .[62]

My only difference from Ransom is that whereas for him 'the taint of original sin' provides a religious frame in which to situate and give meaning to 'history', occasioning movement between poetry and history within the terms of a Christian outlook, the absence of this guarantee presents, and has presented since Browning's time, a universal blank against which the assertion of various human frames has merely reiterated the attempt to attribute our meanings

---

[61] Browning, *Robert Browning and Julia Wedgwood*, 188.
[62] Ransom, *World's Body*, 249–50.

to a process which we did not initiate. The great strength of *The Ring and the Book* is that it projects a vision of how life should be led, 'expels the taint', but in a context which enforces contemplation of the discrepancy between this vision and its vivid picture of just how badly lives can be led. This is its moral explicitness, its 'optimism which has proved offensive'[63] to T. S. Eliot, and also, in John Killham's words, 'the pessimism the poem displays'.[64]

Browning was convinced that partiality of knowledge and the limitations of the best art serve as guides to the intuition of humanly unattainable perfection. He thought that in art the unknowable circle could be inferred from the perceptible arc. Historical and legal commentary which discredits Browning's version of the Roman Murder Case in *The Ring and the Book* reveals the crucial doubleness in the poem's relations with sponsoring circumstances in public and personal history. A disjunction between what *is* or *has been*, and what *ought to be* or *ought to have been* might at first seem to trouble and confuse the truths of history and those of poetry. Yet this disjunction shows the necessity of the imagination's power to find axiomatic meanings in events—meanings which feel inherent though, in fact, they are not.

Modern poetry's inheritance from Browning can be found in his attempts to splice together the incompatible *is* and the *ought* in an imaginative 'as if'. A reader is made aware of the necessity both of what was, and of how it ought to have been. It is 'as if' the one inhered in the other; yet, by means of this conjoining phrase which recognizes the wish in the imaginative deed, the ethical is detached from, does not inhere in, material existence, in the world of history. Wittgenstein, imagining an omniscient person writing 'a big book' which 'would contain the whole description of the world' states:

If for instance in our world-book we read the description of a murder with all its details physical and psychological, the mere description of these facts will contain nothing which we could call an *ethical* proposition. The murder will be on exactly the same level as any other event, for instance the falling of a stone. Certainly the reading of this description might cause us pain or rage or any other emotion, or we might read about the pain and rage caused by this murder in other people when they heard of it, but there will simply be facts, facts, and facts but no Ethics.[65]

---

[63] Eliot, in *Garland for Donne*, 15.
[64] Killham, 'Browning's "Modernity"', 172.
[65] 'Wittgenstein's Lecture on Ethics', in *Philosophical Review*, 74 (1965), 6–7.

The poet's 'as if'[66] performs a fundamental imaginative leap. It helps to support the means by which what are felt to be intuitions about experience survive as other than mere make-believe, as other than wishful thinking. This shows in the difference between an imaginative 'as if' and a fanciful 'if only'. Poems may render the world the service of taking it for what it is, and of entrusting it with a needful purpose—as if that purpose were an inherent meaning.

Robert Browning's ending to his great poem invokes his wife's memory, her poetry and its place in the cause of Italian unity. It alludes to the poet Nicolò Tommasei's inscription for the tablet on Casa Guidi, which says that Elizabeth Barrett Browning *'fece del suo verso aureo anello fra Italia e Inghilterra'* (p. 707) [made of her verse a gold ring between Italy and England]. Browning had high hopes for his poem, but he was not a poet to take the wish for the deed. The final sentence of *The Ring and the Book* is a conditional:

> And save the soul! If this intent save mine,—
> If the rough ore be rounded to a ring,
> Render all duty which good ring should do,
> And, failing grace, succeed in guardianship,—
> Might mine but lie outside thine, Lyric Love,
> Thy rare gold ring of verse (the poet praised)
> Linking our England to his Italy! (p. 628)

The lecture was composed sometime between Sept. 1929 and Dec. 1930, and suggests affinities with the position arrived at with the closing propositions of *Tractatus Logico-Philosophicus*, trans. D. F. Pears and B. F. McGuinness (1961), 6.41–6.421, for example. See also Wittgenstein, *Culture and Value*, ed. G. H. von Wright and H. Nyman, trans. P. Winch (Oxford, 1980), p.3e: 'You cannot lead people to what is good; you can only lead them to some place or other. The good is outside the space of facts.' Though later Wittgenstein allows room for ethics in language games, he remains firm in the belief, I think, that value cannot be derived from fact: see, e.g., *On Certainty*, ed. G. E. M. Anscombe and G. H. von Wright, trans. D. Paul and G. E. M. Anscombe (Oxford, 1977), entries 130, 131, 166, the last of which reads: 'The difficulty is to realize the groundlessness of our believing.'

[66] See, for an exhaustive systematizing of this locution and its roles, H. Vaihinger, *The Philosophy of 'As If'*, trans. C. K. Ogden (1924).

Bibliography

Place of publication is London unless otherwise stated.

ALIGHIERI, DANTE, *The Divine Comedy*, 6 vols., trans. C. S. Singleton (Princeton, NJ, 1970–5).

ALLINGHAM, W., *A Diary*, ed. H. Allingham and D. Radford (1907).

ALLOTT, KENNETH (ed.), *The Penguin Book of Contemporary Verse*, 2nd. edn. (Harmondsworth, 1962).

ANDERSON, DAVID, 'Breaking the Silence', *Paideuma*, 10 (1981).

—— *Pound's Cavalcanti* (Princeton, NJ, 1983).

ARMSTRONG, ISOBEL (ed.), *Writers and their Background: Robert Browning* (1974).

ARNOLD, MATTHEW, *The Portable Matthew Arnold*, ed. L. Trilling (New York, 1948; London, 1980).

AUDEN, W. H., *Look, Stranger!* (1936).

—— *Spain* (1937).

—— *Collected Shorter Poems 1930–1944* (1950).

—— *The Dyer's Hand* (1963).

—— *Collected Shorter Poems 1927–1957* (1966).

—— *Forewords and Afterwords* (1973).

—— *The Collected Poems*, ed. E. Mendelson (1976).

—— *The English Auden*, ed. E. Mendelson (1977).

AXELROD, S. G., and DEESE, H. (eds.), *Robert Lowell: Essays on the Poetry* (Cambridge, 1986).

BACON, FRANCIS, *Essays*, ed. M. J. Hawkins (1972).

BAILEY, J. O., *The Poetry of Thomas Hardy: A Handbook and Commentary* (Chapel Hill, NC, 1970).

BARRELL, JOHN, *Poetry, Language and Politics* (Manchester, 1988).

BEACH, JOSEPH WARREN, *The Making of the Auden Canon* (Minneapolis, 1957).

BERGONZI, BERNARD, *Exploding English: Criticism, Theory, Culture* (Oxford, 1990).

BIGUENET, J., and SCHULTE, R. (eds.), *The Craft of Translation* (Chicago, 1989).

BISHOP, ELIZABETH, *The Complete Poems 1927–1979* (1983).

—— *The Collected Prose*, ed. R. Giroux (1984).

BRODSKY, JOSEPH, *Less Than One* (Harmondsworth, 1986).

BROWN, CLARENCE, *Mandelstam* (Cambridge, 1973).

BROWNING, ELIZABETH BARRETT, *The Poetical Works*, 3 vols. (1907).

BROWNING, ROBERT, *Letters of Robert Browning: Collected by T. J. Wise*, ed. T. L. Hood (1933).

—— *Robert Browning and Julia Wedgwood: A Broken Friendship as Revealed in their Letters*, ed. R. Curle (1937).

—— *Essay on Chatterton* (1842), ed. D. Smalley (Harvard, 1948).

—— *Letters of Robert Browning and Elizabeth Barrett Barrett 1845–1846*, 2 vols., ed. E. Kintner (Cambridge, Mass., 1969).

—— *Poetry and Prose*, sel. S. Nowell-Smith (1950).

—— *The Poems*, 2 vols., ed. J. Pettigrew and T. J. Collins (Harmondsworth, 1981).

—— *The Ring and the Book*, ed. R. D. Altick (Harmondsworth, 1981).

—— *More Than Friend: The Letters of Robert Browning to Katharine de Kay Bronson*, ed. M. Meredith (Waco, Tex. 1985).

CARLYLE, THOMAS, *The Works*, 30 vols. (1904).

CARNE-ROSS, DONALD, 'The Two Voices of Translation', *Robert Lowell: A Collection of Essays* (Twentieth Century Views), ed. T. Parkinson (Englewood Cliffs, NJ, 1968).

CARPENTER, HUMPHREY, *W. H. Auden: A Biography* (1981).

—— *A Serious Character: The Life of Ezra Pound* (1988).

CAVALCANTI, GUIDO, *Rime*, ed. G. Cattaneo (Turin, 1967).

CHAR, RENÉ, *Fureur et mystère* (Paris, 1962).

CHURCHILL, WINSTON S., *The Second World War*, 6 vols., new, rev., and reset edn. (1949).

CLARK, KENNETH (as K. M. Clark), review of Adrian Stokes, *The Quattro Cento*, in *The Criterion* (Oct. 1932).

—— *The Nude* (Harmondsworth, 1960).

COHEN, J. M., (ed. and trans.), *The Penguin Book of Spanish Verse*, 3rd edn. (Harmondsworth, 1988).

COLERIDGE, S. T., *The Complete Poetical Works of Samuel Taylor Coleridge*, 2 vols., ed. E. H. Coleridge (Oxford, 1912).

—— *Biographia Literaria*, ed. J. Engell and W. Jackson Bate (Princeton NJ, 1983).

—— *Coleridge's Dejection: The Earliest Manuscripts and the Earliest Printings*, ed. S. M. Parrish (Ithaca, NY, and London, 1988).

CONAN DOYLE, Sir ARTHUR, *The Complete Sherlock Holmes Long Stories* (1929).

COOPER, PHILIP, *The Autobiographical Myth of Robert Lowell* (Chapel Hill, NC, 1970).

CORNELL, JULIEN, *The Trial of Ezra Pound: A Documented Account of the Treason Case by the Defendant's Lawyer* (1966).

CORRIGAN, BEATRICE, *Curious Annals* (Toronto, 1956).

COX, R. G. (ed.), *Thomas Hardy: The Critical Heritage* (1970).

DALE, PETER, 'Fortuitous Form', *Agenda*, 11 (Spring–Summer 1973).

DAVIE, DONALD, *Purity of Diction in English Verse* (1952).

—— *Articulate Energy: An Inquiry into the Syntax of English Poetry* (1955).

—— 'Adrian Stokes and Pound's "Cantos"', *The Twentieth Century*, 160 (Nov. 1956).

—— *Ezra Pound: Poet as Sculptor* (1965).

—— (guest ed.), *Agenda*, Thomas Hardy Special Issue, 10 (Spring–Summer 1972).

—— *Thomas Hardy and British Poetry* (1973).

—— 'Eliot in One Poet's Life', *The Waste Land in Different Voices*, ed. A. D. Moody (1974).

—— *Pound* (1975).

—— *The Poet in the Imaginary Museum*, ed. B. Alpert (Manchester, 1977).

—— 'From the Manifest to the Therapeutic', *TLS* 4126 (30 Apr. 1982).

—— 'Adrian Stokes Revisited', *Paideuma* (Autumn, Winter 1983).

—— *Collected Poems* (Manchester, 1990).

DAVIES, EARLE, *Vision Fugitive: Ezra Pound and Economics* (Lawrence, Kans., and London, 1968).

DE RACHEWILTZ, MARY, *Discretions* (1971).

DE VANE, WILLIAM CLYDE, *A Browning Handbook* (New York, 1955).

DONNE, JOHN, *Poetical Works*, ed. H. J. C. Grierson (1933).

DRYDEN, JOHN, (trans.), *The Aeneid of Virgil*, ed. R. Fitzgerald (New York, 1965).

EASTMAN, BARBARA, 'The Gap in *The Cantos*: 72 and 73', *Agenda*, 17–18 (Autumn–Winter–Spring 1979–80).

EDWARDS, MICHAEL, *Poetry and Possibility: A Study in the Power and Mystery of Words* (Basingstoke,1988).

ELIOT, T. S., *The Sacred Wood* (1920).

—— 'Preface to the 1928 Edition', *The Sacred Wood* (1928).

—— 'Donne in Our Time', *A Garland for John Donne, 1631–1931*, ed. T. Spencer (Cambridge, Mass., 1931).

—— *The Use of Poetry and the Use of Criticism* (1933).

—— *After Strange Gods* (1934).

—— *Selected Essays*, 3rd edn. (1951).

—— *On Poetry and Poets* (1957).

—— *Collected Poems 1909–1962* (1963).

—— *To Criticize the Critic* (1965).

EMPSON, WILLIAM, *Collected Poems* (1955).

—— *Milton's God* (Cambridge, 1981).

—— *Argufying: Essays on Literature and Culture*, ed. J. Haffenden (1987).

ERLICH, VICTOR, *Russian Formalism* (The Hague, 1955).

EVERETT, BARBARA, *Auden* (1964).

—— *Poets in Their Time* (1986).

FORTINI, FRANCO, *I cani del Sinai* (Turin, 1979).

—— *Saggi italiani*, 2 vols. (Milan, 1987).

FREUD, SIGMUND, *The Standard Edition of the Complete Psychological Works*, 24 vols., trans. and ed. J. Strachey (1953–66).

GARDNER, HELEN, *The Composition of Four Quartets* (1978).

GARDNER, PHILIP and AVERIL, *The God Approached: A Commentary on the Poems of William Empson* (1978).

GEST, J. M., *Old Yellow Book* (Boston, 1925).

GITTINGS, ROBERT, *The Older Hardy* (1978).

GLOVER, JON, 'The Poet in Plato's Cave: A Theme in the Work of Geoffrey Hill', *Poetry Review*, 69 (March 1980).

GOODBODY, JOHN, and SILVER, ROBERT, 'Politicians and Other Artists: An Interview with Enoch Powell', *Trinity Review* (Summer 1977).

GOODMAN, ALICE, 'Wordsworth and the Sucking Babe', *Essays in Criticism*, 33 (April 1983).

GRIFFITHS, ERIC, 'Standing in the Shadows', *Perfect Bound*, (Cambridge), (Autumn 1978).

—— *The Printed Voice of Victorian Poetry* (Oxford, 1989).

GROSSKURTH, PHYLLIS, *Melanie Klein: Her World and her Work* (1986).

HAFFENDEN, JOHN (ed.), *Viewpoints: Poets in Conversation with John Haffenden* (1981).

HALL GRIFFIN, W., review of G. K. Chesterton, *Robert Browning* in *Athenaeum*, 3984 (5 Mar. 1904).

HAMILTON, IAN, *Robert Lowell: A Biography* (1983).

HAMPSHIRE, STUART (ed.), *Public and Private Morality* (Cambridge, 1978).

HARDY, EMMA, *Some Recollections*, ed. E. Hardy and R. Gittings (1961), 2nd edn. (1979).

HARDY, F. E., *The Early Life of Thomas Hardy* (1928).

—— *The Later Years of Thomas Hardy* (1930).

HARDY, THOMAS, *The Variorum Edition of the Collected Poems*, ed. J. Gibson (1979).

—— *The Collected Letters*, 7 vols., ed. R. L. Purdy and M. Millgate (Oxford, 1978–87).

HAZLITT, WILLIAM, *The Complete Works*, 21 vols., ed. P. P. Howe (1930–4).

HEANEY, SEAMUS, *Preoccupations* (1980).

—— *The Government of the Tongue* (1988).

HILL, GEOFFREY, 'Letter from Oxford', *London Magazine*, I (May 1954).

—— 'The Poetry of Allen Tate', *Geste* (Leeds), 3 (Nov. 1958).

—— *For the Unfallen: Poems 1952–1958* (1959).

—— 'The World's Proportion: Jonson's Dramatic Poetry in "Sejanus" and "Catiline"', *Jacobean Theatre*, ed. J. Russell Brown and B. Harris (1960).

—— 'Robert Lowell: Contrasts and Repetitions', *Essays in Criticism*, 13 (April 1963).

—— *King Log* (1968).

—— *Mercian Hymns* (1971).

—— '"The Conscious Mind's Intelligible Structure": A Debate', *Agenda*, 9–10 (Autumn–Winter 1971–2).

—— 'Three Mystical Songs', *Agenda*, 11–12 (Autumn–Winter 1973–4).

—— *Tenebrae* (1978).

—— *The Mystery of the Charity of Charles Péguy* (1983).

—— *The Lords of Limit: Essays on Literature and Ideas* (1984).

—— 'Gurney's Hobby', *Essays in Criticism*, 34 (April 1984).

—— 'Lives of the Poets', *Essays in Criticism*, 34 (July 1984).

—— *Collected Poems* (Harmondsworth, 1985).

HOMBERGER, ERIC (ed.), *Ezra Pound: The Critical Heritage* (1972).

HONDERICH, T., and BURNYEAT, M. (eds.), *Philosophy As It Is* (Harmondsworth, 1979).

IRVINE, WILLIAM, and HONAN, PARK, *The Book, the Ring, and the Poet* (1975).

JACK, IAN, *Browning's Major Poetry* (Oxford, 1973).

JAMES, HENRY, *English Hours*, ed. A. L. Lowe (1960).

JARRELL, RANDALL, *The Complete Poems* (1981).

JOHNSON, SAMUEL, *The Poems of Samuel Johnson*, ed. D. N. Smith and E. L. McAdam, 2nd edn. (Oxford, 1974).

JONSON, BEN, *Ben Jonson*, 11 vols., ed. C. H. Herford, P. and E. Simpson (Oxford, 1925–52).

JOYCE, JAMES, *Finnegans Wake* (1939).

—— *Selected Letters*, ed. R. Ellmann (1975).

—— *Ulysses*, ed. H. W. Gabler, W. Steppe, and C. Melchior (Harmondsworth, 1986).

JUNG, A., and PALANDRI, G. (eds.), *Italian Images of Ezra Pound* (Taipei, 1979).

KALSTONE, DAVID, *Five Temperaments* (New York, 1977).

—— *Becoming a Poet: Elizabeth Bishop with Marianne Moore and Robert Lowell*, ed. R. Hemenway (1989).

KARLIN, DANIEL, *The Courtship of Robert Browning and Elizabeth Barrett* (Oxford, 1985).

KEATS, JOHN, *The Poems of John Keats*, ed. M. Allott (1970).

KERMODE, FRANK, *History and Value* (Oxford, 1988).

KILLHAM, JOHN, 'Browning's "Modernity": *The Ring and the Book*, and

Relativism', *The Major Victorian Poets: Reconsiderations*, ed. I. Armstrong (1969).

KLEIN, MELANIE, *Envy and Gratitude and Other Works 1946–1963* (1975).

—— *Love, Guilt and Reparation* (1975).

—— *The Selected Melanie Klein*, ed. J. Mitchell (Harmondsworth, 1986).

KODAMA, SANEHIDE, *American Poetry and Japanese Culture* (Hamden, Conn., 1984).

KOKOSCHKA, OSKAR, *My Life* (1974).

KORBEL, JÓSEF, *Poland Between East and West: Soviet and German Diplomacy towards Poland, 1919–1933* (Princeton, NJ, 1963).

LANGBAUM, ROBERT, *The Poetry of Experience* (Harmondsworth, 1971).

LEGOUIS, ÉMILE, *William Wordsworth and Annette Vallon* (London and Toronto, 1922).

LEWIS, ALUN, *Selected Poems*, ed. J. Hooker and G. Lewis (1981).

LEWIS, WYNDHAM, *Time and Western Man* (1927).

LIPSKI, JOZEF, *Diplomat in Berlin 1933–1939*, ed. W. Jędrzejewicz (New York and London, 1968).

LITZINGER, B., and SMALLEY, D., *Robert Browning: The Critical Heritage* (1970).

LOWELL, ROBERT, *Life Studies* (New York, 1958).

—— *Poesie di Montale*, intro. A. Rizzardi (Bologna, 1960).

—— *Imitations* (1962).

—— *For the Union Dead* (1965).

—— *Near the Ocean* (1967).

—— *Notebook*, 3rd edn., rev. and expanded (New York, 1970).

—— *For Harriet and Lizzie* (1973).

—— *The Dolphin* (1973).

—— *Selected Poems*, ed. J. Raban (1975).

—— *Selected Poems*, rev. edn. (New York, 1977).

—— *Day by Day* (1978).

—— *Collected Prose*, ed. R. Giroux (1987).

LUCIE-SMITH, EDWARD (ed.), *British Poetry Since 1945* (Harmondsworth, 1970).

MACK SMITH, DENIS, *Mussolini* (1983).

MACNEICE, LOUIS, *Modern Poetry: A Personal Essay* (Oxford, 1938).

—— *The Poetry of W. B. Yeats* (Oxford, 1941).

MANDELSTAM, NADEZHDA, *Hope Against Hope*, trans. M. Hayward (1971).

—— *Hope Abandoned*, trans. M. Hayward (1974).

MANDELSTAM, OSIP, *Selected Poems*, trans. C. Brown and W. S. Merwin (1973).

—— *Selected Essays*, trans. S. Monas (Austin, Tex., and London, 1977).

MARRIOTT, Sir J. A. R., *The Makers of Modern Italy: Napoleon–Mussolini* (Oxford, 1931).

MENDELSON, EDWARD, *Early Auden* (1981).

MEYER, BRUCE, 'A Human Balance: An Interview with Charles Tomlinson', *Hudson Review*, 43 (Autumn 1990).

MILL, JOHN STUART, *Literary Essays*, ed. E. Alexander (Indianapolis, New York, and Kansas City, 1967).

MILLER, BETTY, *Robert Browning: A Portrait* (1952).

MILLER, KARL, *Doubles: Studies in Literary History*, rev. paper edn. (Oxford, 1987).

MILLGATE, MICHAEL, *Thomas Hardy: A Biography* (Oxford, 1982; corr. repr. 1987).

MILTON, JOHN, *Paradise Lost*, ed. A. Fowler (1971).

MONTALE, EUGENIO, *Selected Poems* (New York, 1965).

—— 'Twenty Seven Poems', trans. K. Bosley, G. Singh, and B. Wall, *Agenda*, 9–10 (Autumn–Winter 1971–2).

—— *Sulla poesia*, ed. G. Zampa (Milan, 1976).

—— *Selected Essays*, trans. G. Singh (Manchester, 1978).

—— *L'opera in versi*, ed. R. Bettarini and G. Contini (Turin, 1980).

—— *The Second Life of Art: Selected Essays of Eugenio Montale*, ed. and trans. J. Galassi (New York, 1982).

—— *Corriere della sera 1876–1986, Montale e il Corriere* (Milan, 1986).

MONTESPERELLI, FRANCESCA, 'Montale e Browning: Poesia dell'oggetto', *Paragone*, 326 (April 1977).

—— 'Browning e Montale: *Love in a Life* e *Gli orecchini*', *Studi inglesi*, 5 (1978).

—— 'Letture parallele', *Sigma*, 13 (1980).

—— 'Rassegna montaliana' (1 and 2), *Il Cristallo*, 23:1 and 2 (1981).

MORGAN, EDWIN, *Rites of Passage: Selected Translations* (Manchester, 1976).

NABOKOV, VLADIMIR, *Strong Opinions* (New York, 1973).

—— *Selected Letters 1940–1977*, ed. D. Nabokov and M. J. Bruccoli (San Diego, New York, London, 1989).

NAGEL, THOMAS, *The Possibility of Altruism* (Princeton, NJ, 1970).

—— *Mortal Questions* (Cambridge, 1979).

—— *The View from Nowhere* (New York, 1986).

NUSSBAUM, MARTHA, C., *The Fragility of Goodness: Luck and Ethics in Greek Tragedy and Philosophy* (Cambridge, 1986).

ORWELL, GEORGE, *The Collected Essays, Journalism and Letters*, 4 vols., ed. S. Orwell and I. Angus (1968).

OWEN, WILFRED, *The Complete Poems and Fragments*, 2 vols., ed. J. Stallworthy (1983).

PASOLINI, PIER PAOLO, *Descrizioni di descrizioni* (Turin, 1979).

—— 'On Pound', trans. R. M. Clarke, *PN Review* 46, 12 (1985).

PAULIN, TOM, *Thomas Hardy: The Poetry of Perception* (1975).

PEARLMAN, DANIEL, 'Ezra Pound: America's Wandering Jew', *Paideuma*, 9 (Winter 1980).

PEARSON, GABRIEL, 'Lowell's Marble Meanings', *The Survival of Poetry*, ed. M. Dodsworth (1970).

PÉGUY, CHARLES, *Basic Verities*, trans. A. and J. Green (1943).

PERLOFF, MARJORIE, G., *The Poetic Art of Robert Lowell* (Ithaca, NY, and London, 1973).

POLONSKY, ANTONY, *Politics in Independent Poland 1921–1939* (Oxford, 1972).

POUND, EZRA, *Jefferson and/or Mussolini* (1935).

—— *ABC of Reading* (1951).

—— *Collected Shorter Poems* (1952).

—— *The Translations of Ezra Pound* (1953).

—— *The Literary Essays of Ezra Pound*, ed. T. S. Eliot (1954).

—— *The Selected Letters of Ezra Pound 1907–1941*, ed. D. D. Paige (1950).

—— *Pound/Joyce: The Letters of Ezra Pound and James Joyce*, ed. F. Read (New York, 1967).

—— 'Pound's Interrogation at Genoa', *Helix* (Australia), 13 and 14 (1983).

—— *Pound's Cavalcanti*, ed. D. Anderson (Princeton, NJ, 1983).

—— *Pound/Lewis: The Letters of Ezra Pound and Wyndham Lewis*, ed. T. Materer (1985).

—— *Ezra Pound and Japan: Letters and Essays*, ed. S. Kodama (Redding Ridge, Conn., 1987).

—— *The Cantos of Ezra Pound*, 4th collected edn. (1987).

POUND, EZRA, and SHAKESPEAR, DOROTHY, *Their Letters*, ed. O. Pound and A. Walton Litz (1985).

POZZI, ANTONIA, *La vita sognata*, ed. A. Cenni and O. Dino (Milan, 1986).

PURKIS, JOHN, *Donald Davie, Charles Tomlinson, Geoffrey Hill*, A306 Twentieth Century Poetry, Open University (Milton Keynes, 1976).

RANSOM, JOHN CROWE, *The World's Body* (London and New York, 1938).

REED, JEREMY, *Selected Poems* (Harmondsworth, 1987).

REID, RICHARD, 'Determined Cones of Shadow', *Helix (Australia)*, 13 and 14 (1983).

RICHARDS, I. A., *Selected letters of I. A. Richards*, ed. J. Constable (Oxford, 1990).

RICKS, CHRISTOPHER, 'Cliché as "Responsible Speech": Geoffrey Hill', *London Magazine*, 4 (Nov. 1964).

—— *The Force of Poetry* (Oxford, 1984).

—— *T. S. Eliot and Prejudice* (1988).

RILKE, RAINER MARIA, *Gesammelte Werke*, 7 vols. (Leipzig, 1927).

ROBERTS, DAVID, *Jean Stafford: A Biography* (1988).

ROBINSON, PETER, 'On an Unpublished Poem by Adrian Stokes', *Adrian Stokes 1902–1972: A Supplement*, ed. S. Bann, *PN Review 15*, 7 (1980).

—— (ed.), *Geoffrey Hill: Essays on his Work* (Milton Keynes, 1985).

—— 'Ezra Pound and Italian Art', *Pound's Artists*, ed. R. S. Humphries (1985).

RUDMAN, MARK, *Robert Lowell: An Introduction to His Poetry* (New York, 1983).

RUSKIN, JOHN, *Works*, library edn., 39 vols., ed. E. T. Cook and A. Wedderburn (1903–12).

SALINGAR, LEO, 'Robert Browning', in B. Ford (ed.), *New Pelican Guide to English Literature*, vi. *From Dickens to Hardy* (Harmondsworth, 1958; rev. edn., 1982).

SCOVELL, E. J., 'In Conversation with Jem Poster', *PN Review 74*, 16 (1990).

SEGAL, HANNA, *Klein* (1979).

SERENI, VITTORIO, *Letture preliminari* (Padua, 1973).

—— 'Il nostro debito verso Montale', *Eugenio Montale*, Atti del Convegno (Milan, 1982).

—— *Tutte le poesie*, ed. M. T. Sereni (Milan, 1986).

—— *Selected Poems of Vittorio Sereni*, trans. M. Perryman and P. Robinson (1990).

SHAKESPEARE, WILLIAM, *The Complete Works*, Original Spelling Edition, ed. S. Wells, G. Taylor, *et al.* (Oxford, 1986).

—— *Shakespeare's Sonnets*, ed. S. Booth (New Haven, Conn., and London, 1977).

SHAW, J. E., *Guido Cavalcanti's Theory of Love: The Canzone d'Amore and Other Related Problems* (Toronto, 1949).

SHELLEY, PERCY BYSSHE, *The Complete Works*, 10 vols., ed. R. Ingpen and W. E. Peck (1926; New York, 1965).

SIDNEY, Sir PHILIP, *The Poems*, ed. W. A. Ringler (Oxford, 1962).

—— *Miscellaneous Prose*, ed. K. Duncan-Jones and J. Van Dorsten (Oxford, 1973).

SMITH, STAN, *W. H. Auden* (Oxford, 1985).

SMITHIES, B., and FIDDICK, P., *Enoch Powell on Immigration* (1969).

STEVENS, WALLACE, *The Necessary Angel* (1960).

—— *The Palm at the End of the Mind: Selected Poems and a Play* ed. H. Stevens (New York, 1971).

STOCK, NOEL, *The Life of Ezra Pound* (Harmondsworth, 1985).

STOKES, ADRIAN, *The Image in Form*, ed. R. Wollheim (Harmondsworth, 1972).

—— *A Game that Must Be Lost: Collected Papers*, ed. E. Rhodes (Cheadle, 1973).

—— *The Critical Writings*, 3 vols., ed. L. Gowing (1978).

—— *With All the Views: Collected Poems of Adrian Stokes*, ed. P. Robinson (Manchester, 1981).

SWAAB, PETER ALEXANDER, 'Wordsworth and Patriotism', Ph.D. thesis (Cambridge, 1989).

TANSILL, CHARLES CALLAN, *Back Door to War: The Roosevelt Foreign Policy 1933–1941* (Chicago, 1952).

TENNYSON, ALFRED LORD, *The Poems of Tennyson* , 3 vols., ed. C. Ricks (1987).

TOMLINSON, CHARLES (ed.), *The Oxford Book of Verse in English Translation* (Oxford, 1980).

—— *Some Americans* (Berkeley, Calif., and Los Angeles, 1981).

TREVELYAN, G. M. (ed.), *English Songs of Italian Freedom* (1911).

TROTTER, DAVID, *The Making of the Reader* (1984).

UTLEY, T. E., *Enoch Powell* (1968).

VAIHINGER, H., *The Philosophy of 'As If'*, trans. C. K. Ogden (1924).

VENDLER, HELEN, *Part of Nature, Part of Us: Modern American Poets* (Cambridge, Mass., 1980).

—— *The Harvard Book of Contemporary American Poetry* (Cambridge, Mass., 1985).

—— *The Music of What Happens: Poems, Poets, Critics* (Cambridge, Mass., 1988).

WAINWRIGHT, JEFFREY, 'Geoffrey Hill's "Lachrimae"', *Agenda*, 13 (Autumn 1975).

WARD JOUVE, NICOLE, *Baudelaire: A Fire to Conquer Darkness* (1980).

WEBER, CARL J., *'Dearest Emmie'* (1963).

WEISSBORT, D. (ed.), *Translating Poetry: The Double Labyrinth* (1989).

WESTLUND, JOSEPH, *Shakespeare's Reparative Comedies: A Psychoanalytical View of the Middle Plays* (Chicago, 1984).

WHITMAN, WALT, *Leaves of Grass*, ed. H. W. Blodgett and S. Bradley (1965).

WILLIAMS, BERNARD, *Morality: An Introduction to Ethics* (Cambridge, 1972).

—— *Problems of the Self* (Cambridge, 1973).

—— *Moral Luck: Philosophical Papers 1973–1980* (Cambridge, 1981).

—— *Ethics and the Limits of Philosophy* (1985).

WILLIAMSON, ALAN, 'The Reshaping of "Waking Early Sunday Morning"', *Agenda*, 18 (Autumn 1980).

WINTERS, YVOR, *In Defence of Reason* (Denver, 1956).

—— *Forms of Discovery* (Chicago, 1967).

WITTGENSTEIN, LUDWIG, *Tractatus Logico-Philosophicus*, trans. D. F. Pears and B. F. McGuinness (1961).

—— 'Wittgenstein's Lecture on Ethics', *Philosophical Review*, 74 (1965).

—— *On Certainty*, ed. G. E. M. Anscombe and G. H. von Wright, trans. D. Paul and G. E. M. Anscombe (Oxford, 1977).

—— *Culture and Value*, ed. G. H. von Wright and H. Nyman, trans. P. Winch (Oxford, 1980).

WOLLHEIM, RICHARD, *On Art and the Mind* (Cambridge, Mass., 1974).

—— *Art and its Objects*, 2nd edn. (Cambridge, 1980).

—— *The Thread of Life* (Cambridge, 1984).

—— 'Objects of Love', *TLS* 4547, 25–31 May 1990.

WORDSWORTH, DOROTHY, *Journals of Dorothy Wordsworth*, 2 vols., ed. E. de Selincourt (1941).

WORDSWORTH, WILLIAM, *The Letters of William and Dorothy Wordsworth, The Early Years 1787–1805*, ed. E. de Selincourt, 2nd edn., rev. C. L. Shaver (Oxford, 1967).

—— *The Poems*, 2 vols., ed. J. O. Hayden (Harmondsworth, 1977).

—— *Poems, in Two Volumes*, and Other Poems, 1800–1807, ed. J. Curtis (Ithaca, NY, 1983).

YEATS, W. B., *Selected Criticism and Prose*, ed. N. Jeffares (1980).

ZAPPONI, NICCOLÒ, *L'Italia di Ezra Pound* (Rome, 1976).

Index

Abercrombie, Lascelles 184
Adams, T. 2
addressee 89
Aeneas 75, 76, 134
Alberti, Rafael 83
  'Retornos del amor en los vividos
    paisajes' 83 n.
Alighieri, Dante 176
  Inferno X 176
Allott, Kenneth 108–9
allusion 49, 50, 69, 135
altruism 99, 106, 214
ambiguity 110, 117
amends 1, 88, 99, 115, 120, 170–1
Amprim, Frank L. 189, 194
Anderson, David 177, 183
another voice 70; and putting words
    into the mouth 71; ventriloquistic
    appropriation 193; ventriloquized
    70
Arbuthnot, John 2
Archimedes 215
Armstrong, Isobel 203, 206
Arnold, Matthew 105, 111, 171, 174
  'Dover Beach' 174
Arrurruz, Sebastian 117–20
art: and moral engagement 44; and
    social usefulness 44
Ashbery, John 148
atonement 131, 139; and history 132
attrition 124, 157, 168
Auden, W. H. 24–46, 100–1, 103
  'A Communist to Others' 31
  'A Summer Night' 25, 29, 30 n., 31,
    33, 35, 36, 37, 40, 41, 42, 45
  'A Summer Night 1933' 31 n.
  Collected Poems 29, 30 n.
  Collected Shorter Poems 1930–1944
    31 n.
  Collected Shorter Poems 1927–1957
    42, 43
  Forewords and Afterwords 46,
    101 n.
  'In Memory of W. B. Yeats' 29
  Look, Stranger! 29, 31 n.
  'Out on the lawn I lie in bed' 29–45
  'September 1, 1939' 33, 41, 42
  Spain 28 n.
  'Spain 1937' 42
  'Stop the clocks, cut off the
    telephone' 43 n.
  'Summer Night' 31
  The Dyer's Hand 24–6
  The English Auden 28 n., 30 n.,
    31 n., 43 n.
  'The Poet & The City' 25–8
  'The Vision of Agape' 39–40
auditory intelligence 46; 'imagined
    auditors' 137
Augustus 114
autobiography 94, 100

Bacon, Francis 144, 146, 147
Badoglio, Pietro 175
Bailey, J. O. 69, 70
barbarism 37, 52
Barrell, John 144 n.
Barrett, Edward ('Bro') 209–10
Baudelaire, Charles 157
  'Le Cygne' 157
Beach, Joseph Warren 31, 32
Bergonzi, Bernard 142
Bertgang, Zoe 3
Bertolucci, Attilio 179 n.
Bible, the 48, 122, 123
Bishop, Elizabeth 83, 84, 87, 90 n.,
    103, 104
  'North Haven' 104
Blagden, Isa 225
Bloom, Leopold 58, 201
Blunden, Edmund 91
blunders 220–1
Boethius 133
Bogan, Louise 30–1
Bolingbroke, Henry St John 108
Botticelli, Sandro 177
Bottinius, Johannes-Baptista 214–15
Brideshead, Sue 69
Brodsky, Joseph 41 n.

Bronson, Katharine de Kay 200–1
Brown, Clarence 113 n., 121
Browning, Elizabeth Barrett 92, 144,
  198–9, 201, 202, 205, 208–10,
  219, 221, 225–6, 231, 238
  Casa Guidi Windows 221
  'Napoleon III. in Italy' 225
  Poems before Congress 221
Browning, Robert 92, 144, 153,
  159–61, 164, 166, 198–238
  'A Light Woman' 209
  'Andrea del Sarto' 199–200, 201,
    211, 212
  'Apparent Failure' 222–4, 227
  Asolando: Facts and Fancies 200
  'A Toccata of Galuppi's' 204–5
  'By the Fire-Side' 164
  '"De Gustibus—"' 221, 222
  'Essay on Shelley' 198, 200, 217,
    226, 230
  'Fra Lippo Lippi' 207–8, 216
  'Inapprehensiveness' 200–1
  'Love in a Life' 205–6
  'Memorabilia' 164
  Men and Women 198–9, 227
  'Mr Sludge, "The Medium"' 208,
    209
  'Old Pictures in Florence' 221–2,
    224, 227
  Paracelsus 213
  Pauline 219, 226
  'Pictor Ignotus' 207
  'Porphyria's Lover' 213
  'The Italian in England' 221
  'The Lost Mistress' 203
  'The Pied Piper of Hamelin' 205
  The Ring and the Book 199, 208,
    210–20, 229–38; and *Old Yellow
    Book* 218–20, 232–3
  'The Statue and the Bust' 216
  'Two in the Campagna' 160–1, 201,
    203–4, 212
Budgen, Frank 58
Buol-Schauenstein, Karl Ferdinand 223
Byron, George 202

Capello, Bianca 175
Caponsacchi, Giuseppe 208, 211–12,
  214–16, 217, 218, 231–5
career 84
care, technical and ethical 54;
  technique as a form of 86

Carlyle, Thomas 215, 218, 220, 226,
  227
Carne-Ross, Donald 167 n.
Carpenter, Humphrey 30, 31, 32 n.,
  38, 42 n., 188 n., 190–1
Catullus 175
cautionary instruction 19
Cavalcanti, Guido 174, 175, 176–84,
  190–3
  (?)'Ballata II' 182–3
  'Donna mi prega' 178–82, 190–3
Cavour, Camillo 222–3, 225
Char, René 151–2
  Feuillets d'Hypnos 138 151–2
Chaucer, Geoffrey 147 n.
Chesterton, G. K. 213, 220–1
Churchill, Winston S. 51, 54 n., 190
circumstances 1, 8, 19, 20, 42, 84, 91,
  110, 129, 150, 163, 233; and
  contingent impurities of luck 87;
  and truth 45; of moral awareness
  90; of moral problems and values
  103; political 189; rebuked by
  64; sponsoring 237; of utterance
  127
Clarendon, George William Fredrick
  Villiers 223
Clark, Kenneth 176, 177
Clifton, Talbot 39, 43
Clifton, Violet 39
Cohen, J. M. 83 n., 168–71
Coleridge, Samuel Taylor 10, 13,
  16–17, 19–20, 119, 128, 139,
  148–9, 171
  'Dejection: An Ode' 119, 139, 148
  'A Letter to—.' 148–9
  'To William Wordsworth . . .' 149
Colette 4
colloquial language 120–2, 124, 132,
  138; pacified 124
colloquy 75
collusion 130
Comparini, Francesca, *see* Pompilia
Comparini, Violante 234
complacency 199–200
complicity 117, 196
comradeship 36, 40, 43
conflicting allegiances 39
contemporary political events 42
context 23, 85, 109–12, 114, 115,
  131, 134, 136, 150, 186, 190,
  216, 235; and decontextualizing
  169, 195; and definition of

context (*cont.*):
'success' 87, 94; in domestic
politics 34; loss of 184–5; and
meanings of words 48, 109–10,
194; political and historical 30,
43, 124; quotation out of 132,
135; and the reception of literature
139; technical 195; and
translation 156–7; in wartime
47–57
Contini, Gianfranco 155, 179 n., 181,
182 n.
Cooper, Philip 89 n., 95 n.
Corbière, Tristan 156 n.
Cornell, Julian 188 n.
Corrigan, Beatrice 219 n., 233 n.
crime 105; verbal 118
culpability 117
culpable innocence 186
cultures: and mediation 184–6;
understanding between 174–6
Cumaen Sybil 134

Dale, Peter 157, 169–70
Daniel, Arnaut 174
dates 30, 67
Davie, Donald 24 n., 49, 55, 58 n., 59,
62, 71, 72–3, 75, 76, 77, 79, 80,
107–8, 109, 112, 126, 133,
167 n., 181 n.
'Mandelstam's Hope for the Best'
112 n.
Davies, Earle 187 n.
Deese, Helen 103 n.
degli Uberti, Anna 162–4
dependence 26
de Rachewiltz, Mary 192 n.
De Vane, William Clyde 221 n., 222 n.
de Vega, Lope 170–1
'¿Que tengo yo que mi amistad
procuras?' 170–1
Diaghilev, Sergei 41
dialogue 75, 77, 107, 170
diction 20, 22, 78
Dick, Anne 89
Dido 75–6
difficulty 106, 108–9, 112–13
Donne, John 68, 113, 117 n., 122
'Hymn to God my God, in my
sicknesse' 122
'A Valediction Forbidding Mourning'
113
Drummond, John 188

Dryden, John 75–6
The Aeneid of Virgil 75–6

Eastman, Barbara 191 n.
Eden, Anthony 153, 190
Edwards, Michael 171 n.
Eliot, T. S. 21, 22, 24, 45–57, 61, 86,
100, 106, 109–10, 117 n., 125,
126, 136, 144 n., 153, 174, 182,
183, 195–7, 223–4, 237
After Strange Gods 117 n., 195
Ash-Wednesday 144n.
Collected Poems 1909–1962 48 n.,
50 n., 52 n., 117 n., 144 n., 152 n.
'East Coker' 48
'For Lancelot Andrewes' 117 n.
Four Quartets 47, 49, 50, 52
'Little Gidding' 117 n.
On Poetry and Poets 48 n., 50 n.,
56 n., 110 n.
'Reflections on *Vers Libre*' 24 n.
'Rudyard Kipling' 48 n., 50 n.,
51 n., 52 n., 53 n., 56 n., 57 n.
Selected Essays 106 n., 117 n.
'The Dry Salvages' 45–57, 152
'The Metaphysical Poets' 106 n.
'The Music of Poetry' 48 n., 110 n.
The Sacred Wood 61 n., 86 n.,
100 n., 174 n.
*The Use of Poetry and the Use of
Criticism* 22 n., 106 n.
The Waste Land 50, 195
To Criticize the Critic 24 n.
'Tradition and the Individual Talent'
61, 100, 174
Empson, William 71–2, 86, 87, 107 n.,
119, 172, 196
'Aubade' 86–7
'Let It Go' 119
encounter 11, 138, 151
endurance 10, 13, 54, 93; and
achievement 72; 'Endurance of
Poets' 113–14; of the irreparable
103; and rhyme and rhythm 129;
and verse writing 55–6
envy 143–7, 155, 158, 171, 172; in a
critic 148; envious attacks 167;
envious damage 157; escape from
147; and gratitude 152, 158;
idealization and 148–9; and
jealousy 144–5, 147, 158; and a
translator 149–50, 152; and
untranslatability 156, 158

equaiity 36, 44
Erlich, Victor 120
erotic atmosphere 40
errors 116, 118–19, 131, 184
ethical distances 101–2
Everett, Barbara 45, 164
exculpation 74
exemplary 123; sufferings 118

facts 218; and fancy 236; knowing
    the 219–20; and poetic
    imagination 232–3
failure 93, 200, 218; apparent
    216–18, 222–4, 235
faith 46
familiar style 107–9
family 87, 105, 209–10
Farquhar, George 2
fascism 155, 175–6, 184–94;
    antifascismo 153; middle-class
    antifascists 154; the word
    'fascism' 189–90
fatalism 65
fate 65
faux pas 116
Fawley, Arabella 69
Fawley, Jude 69
Feinstein, Elaine 151 n.
Fenollosa, Ernest 126
Fenwick, Isabella 11–12, 13
Ford, Ford Madox 70, 88
forgiveness 116
Forster, E. M. 108
Fortini, Franco 153
fortune 63, 147
Fox, Charles James 21, 22, 23
Franceschini, Guido 208, 211, 214,
    220, 229, 231–2
Franco Bahamonde, Francisco 153
Freud, Sigmund 3–4
friends 70, 86, 105–9, 112–14, 117 n.,
    119, 139–41, 162, 182, 200–1
Frobenius, Leo 174–5

Gandhi, Mohandas Karamchand 184
Gardner, Helen 47
Garnett, Richard 70
Gauguin, Paul 88, 90–2, 93, 94
George V 154
Gest, J. M. 218–20, 232–3
Gibbon, Edward 67–71, 75, 78
Gide, André 126, 153
Gifford, Emma Lavinia 58, 62, 64,
    65–6, 67, 69–70, 71, 75, 77, 79,
    80–1
Gifford, Gordon 70
Gifford, Henry 112 n.
Giotto di Bordone 224, 227
Gittings, Robert 69–70, 80
Gladstone, William Ewart 223
Glover, Jon 123
Gongora, Luis de 168–70
    'De la brevedad engañosa de la vida'
        168–70
Goodman, Alice 9–10
Gortschakoff, Alexandr Mikhailovich
    223
Gosse, Edmund 62, 200
grasp 198–238
Green, T. H. 122, 182 n.
Griffiths, Eric 20 n., 137, 161 n.,
    177 n., 182 n.
Guarnieri, Silvio 154
guilt 44, 45, 196, 213, 215; empirical
    98, 120; historical 7; and privilege
    45
gusto 203, 206–8, 210

Hall Griffin, W. 220–1
Hamilton, Ian 9 n., 101 n.
Hampshire, Stuart 100 n.
hands 209–16, 219
Hanold, Norbert 3
Hardwick, Elizabeth 85, 87, 91
Hardy, Florence Emily 60
Hardy, Thomas 58–82, 164, 166, 200
    'A Broken Appointment' 68
    'After a Journey' 59, 75–80
    'Afterwards' 62
    'A January Night (1879)' 164
    'A Man was Drawing Near to Me'
        65, 66
    A Pair of Blue Eyes 58
    'A Thunderstorm in Town' 61
    'Beany Cliff' 80, 81
    Jude the Obscure 62, 69, 70
    'Lausanne in Gibbon's Old Garden:
        11–12 p.m.' 66–71
    ' "My Spirit will not Haunt the
        Mound" ' 68
    'On the Departure Platform' 164
    'Overlooking the River Stour' 62
    'Places' 80–1
    'Poems of 1912–13' 72, 75, 79
    'Self-Unconscious' 63, 67
    The Collected Letters 62n, 67 n.

Hardy, Thomas (*cont.*):
  'The Convergence of the Twain' 66
  'The Darkling Thrush' 164
  'The Going' 72–4
  'The Haunter' 75–9
  'The Phantom Horsewoman' 80–1
  'The Self-Unseeing' 62–3, 67
  'The Voice' 75–7
  'The Voice from the Thorn' 66
  'The Voice of Things' 66
  'The Wind Blew Words' 66
  'The Wind's Prophecy' 64–5, 66
  Variorum Edition of the Collected Poems 61 n.
  'When I Set Out for Lyonnesse' 64
  'Your Last Drive' 72, 74–5
Hazlitt, William 145, 146, 148, 203, 206, 207, 210
Heaney, Seamus 9 n., 86, 88, 95, 112 n., 121 n., 133
Heath, Edward 135, 136
Hill, Geoffrey 23, 98–9, 105–41, 149, 157–8, 168, 170–1, 182 n.
  'An Apology for the Revival of Christian Architecture in England' 118, 131–2, 134
  'Annunciations' 108, 109, 117
  Collected Poems 106 n., 115 n., 119 n.
  For the Unfallen 109, 115 n.
  'Four Poems Regarding the Endurance of Poets' 113–14
  'Funeral Music' 140
  'Homage to Henry James' 117–18
  'In Memory of Jane Fraser' 115–16
  'Interview' (with John Haffenden) 118, 123–4, 134, 140
  King Log 108, 115
  'Lachrimae' 120, 170–1
  Mercian Hymns 123–5, 132–7, 140
  'Our Word Is Our Bond' 112, 133
  'Poetry as "Menace" and "Atonement"' 98, 105, 116
  'Redeeming the Time' 125
  'Robert Lowell: Contrasts and Repetitions' 124, 157
  Tenebrae 170
  '"The Conscious Mind's Intelligible Structure": A Debate' 138 n.
  'The Living Poet' (radio programme) 115, 118
  The Lords of Limit 23, 98 n., 99 n., 105 n., 106 n., 110–12, 119 n.,
122, 128, 131 n., 138 n., 149 n., 182 n.
  'The Lowlands of Holland' 130
  The Mystery of the Charity of Charles Péguy 116, 128–31
  'The Poetry of Allen Tate' 116, 130
  'The Songbook of Sebastian Arrurruz' 117–20, 138–9
  'The World's Proportion' 110 n.
  'Tristia: 1891–1938' 112–13
  'What Devil Has Got Into John Ransom?' 99, 105
Hitler, Adolf 32, 33, 153, 175
Holmes, Sherlock 116
Home, Daniel 209–10
Hopkins, Gerard Manley 125, 128
Horace 142
Horne, P. 107 n.
Hoyland, Geoffrey 30
human imperfection 60, 63
Hunt, Leigh 213
Hutchinson, Mary 19 n., 148–9
Hutchinson, Sara 18, 19 n., 139, 149

imaginative: appropriation 18; 'as if' 237–8
inattention 116
intercession 103, 208
interlocutors 85, 86, 106–8, 110, 134, 136, 137, 139, 140, 147
intuition 228–30, 237
irreparability 75
irreparable: events 234; finality 73
Italian unity 221–6, 238

Jack, Ian 201–2, 213, 217, 235
James, Henry 230
Jarrell, Randall 104
  'The Woman at the Washington Zoo' 104
Jędrzejewicz, W. 33 n.
Jensen, Wilhelm 3
Jesus Christ 56, 121–3
Johnson, Lyndon B. 8–9 n.
Johnson, Samuel 89, 92, 157
  'On the Death of Dr Robert Levet' 89
Jonson, Ben 114, 128
  'Inviting a friend to supper' 114
Joyce, James 58, 122, 184
judgement 116
Juliet 127

justifications 94
juxtaposed voices 76

Karenina, Anna 96, 97
Karlin, Daniel 144 n., 199, 210
Kay, George 165, 167
Keats, John 114, 131, 137 n., 138, 139
    'Ode to a Nightingale' 131
    'Sleep and Poetry' 114, 139
    'To Autumn' 137
Kermode, Frank 28 n., 40 n.
Killham, John 213, 217, 229–30, 237
Kipling, Rudyard 47, 50, 52, 56, 57
    'Danny Deever' 56
Kirkup, James 143 n.
Kitasono, Katue 51 n., 173
Kjär, Ruth 4–5
Klein, Melanie 2–5, 7, 145, 147–8
Kodama, S. 143 n.
Kokoschka, Oskar 36 n.
Korbel, Jósef 33

Langbaum, Robert 212–13
Lawrence, D. H. 24–5
Legouis, Émile 18 n.
Leone, Alfonso 161, 162
Levet, Robert 89
Lewis, Alun 150
    'To Rilke' 150
Lewis, Percy Wyndham 173–4, 182,
    184, 193
Lincoln, Abraham 49–50
Lipski, Jozef 33 n.
Lothian, Philip Henry Kerr 51
love 38–40, 176–82; and Agape
    39–41, 44, 45; and altruism 40,
    41 n., 43; and brotherly 41;
    constancy in 201–2; and Eros
    39–41, 45; and homosexual erotic
    41 n.; and neighbourly 40; secular
    and divine 202, 207; and sexual
    satisfaction 176–7; and universal
    41
loved ones 199
loved ones' words 83
lovers 201, 211–12, 214–15, 218
Lowell, Commander 88–9
Lowell, Harriet 83
Lowell, Robert 8–9, 83–104, 142–3,
    156–8, 164, 165–70
    Collected Prose 8 n., 87 n., 88 n.,
        89 n., 91 n.
    Day by Day 98 n., 103 n.

'Dolphin' 90
'Doubt' 101
'Epilogue' 103
'Exorcism' 85, 102
'Fall 1961' 83
For Harriet and Lizzie 88 n.
For the Union Dead 83 n., 85 n.
History 157
'Home After Three Months Away'
    90
Imitations 156–8
'In Memory of Arthur Winslow' 84
'It Did (Elizabeth)' 87, 91
'Jean Stafford, a Letter' 98 n.
Life Studies 86–7
Near the Ocean 168
'Near the Unbalanced Aquarium'
    88–9
'Night Sweat' 85
Notebook 85 n., 88 n., 89 n., 102
'Robert Lowell' (television
    programme) 83
Selected Poems 8 n., 83 n., 85 n.,
    88 n., 89 n., 95 n.
Selected Poems (ed. J. Raban) 90 n.
'Summer Between Terms' 99
'The Coastguard House' 157,
    165–8, 169
The Dolphin 84, 85 n., 100, 102,
    103
'The Lesson' 83
'The Old Flame' 95–6, 98
'The Ruins of Time' 168–70
'Waking Early Sunday' 8–9
Lucie-Smith, Edward 130
luck 55, 88, 91, 93, 99; bad 18;
    constitutive, extrinsic, intrinsic 92,
    97, 104; good 84; moral 100;
    moral bad 7, 8; 'Moral Luck'
    83–104
Luff, Mr 18 n.

Mack Smith, Denis 194
MacNeice, Louis 4, 29
Mairet, Philip 47, 52
Mandelstam, Nadezhda 112, 118
Mandelstam, Osip 106, 110, 112–14,
    118, 121, 124, 132, 138, 142 n.
    '[Stalin Epigram]' 113
    'Tristia' 113
Mann, Erika 32
Manning, Fredric 195, 196

marriage 25, 65, 73, 76–8, 201, 202, 212

Marriott, J. A. R. 222–3

Marx, Karl 184

Mazzini, Giuseppe 221

Mazzolini, Serafino 189

megalomania 8, 157, 169–70

Melchiori, Barbara 216

Meltzer, Donald 7–8

Merwin, W. S. 113 n.

metre 14–15, 19, 20, 21, 22, 129, 302

Metternich-Winneburg, Clemens 221, 225

Mezzasoma, Fernando 194

milieux 110

Mill, John Stuart 219, 226

Miller, Betty 209–10

Miller, Karl 104 n.

Millgate, Michael 64 n., 69 n., 70 n.

Milton, John 68–71, 147, 171–2
  Paradise Lost 171–2

misprints 116

mistakes 46, 89, 103, 174

moment in history 45

money 120, 123–5; and debasement 120–1

Montale, Eugenio 142 n., 152–6, 157, 158–68, 217
  'Ah!' 162 n.
  'Annetta' 162, 164
  'Arsenio' 167 n.
  'Due nel crepuscolo' 160 n.
  'Eastbourne' 152–6
  'I limoni' 160
  'Il tu' 163
  'Intenzioni (intervista immaginaria)' 153, 160
  'La casa dei doganieri' 142 n., 157, 160–8
  Le occasioni 152, 158, 162–3
  L'opera in versi 152 n., 162 n., 164 n., 217 n.
  Selected Essays 153 n., 164 n.
  Sulla poesia 153 n., 159 n., 164 n.
  The Second Life of Art 153 n., 159 n.

Montesperelli, Francesca 159 n.

Moore, Marianne 83

moral: absolutes 228; aesthetic 60, 227; action 23; agent, artist as 92; colouring 229–30; failures 19; landscape 101–3; problems 103; reflection 88; values 87, 97, 103

Morgan, Edwin 142 n.

mother 9; 'destroying her creativeness' 147; and maternal loss 10, 13, 15, 19

music 21; and meaning 47

Mussolini, Benito 25, 153, 154, 175–6, 185–6, 187–8, 194–5

Nabokov, Vladimir 142 n.

Nagel, Thomas 7, 18, 90

Napoleon III 225

Nero 123

Nijinsky, Waclaw 41

Nussbaum, Martha C. 235 n.

Oastler, Richard 111

occasion 17, 30, 31, 50, 63, 110, 114, 139, 150, 151, 152–6, 158, 160, 162–4, 166, 171; imaginary character of 161

Offa (King of Mercia) 123, 124, 132, 134, 140

omnipotent fantasy 4, 8, 26

opportunism 121, 163

Orwell, George 28 n.

Osgood, James R. 67

other beings 9, 207

otherness 143; of foreign poetry 142

other people 97, 106, 174, 197; and autobiography 100; 'Hell for the *other people*' 117 n., 195

others: responsible connections with 90; risk to 92

others' agony 54–6, 152; and rhythm 55

others' lives 86, 204

others' sufferings 94; community and isolation of 152; 'other people's sorrows' 86; unfounded intimacy with 114

others' words 12, 23, 58, 66, 81–2, 83–4, 86; absorption or individuation in poems 84; colouring and authority of 71

others' writings 83

Ovid 113

Owen, Wilfred 37–8
  'Strange Meeting' 37–8

own voice 67; and punctuation 67; and the speech of another 68

own words 17

Oxford English Dictionary, the 1–2, 70, 76 n., 108, 115, 127, 145, 200, 203, 206 n.
Oxford, Robert Harley 108

Pasolini, Pier Paolo 187–8
Pasternak, Boris 142
Patmore, Coventry 171
patriotic: enthusiasm 17; pride 17–18; shame 7; sigh 153–4
patriotism 130–1, 191–3, 221–2
Paulin, Tom 62, 68, 73, 75
Pavolini, Alessandro 194
Pearlman, Daniel 195
Pearson, Gabriel 84, 87, 143
Péguy, Charles 116, 127–9, 140
Penelope (Molly Bloom) 58
Perse, St-John 126–7
Peter (Apostle) 122
Petrarch, Francesco 177
Pharisees 134
physical reserve 62
place names 13–14, 31–3, 153
places 49–50
Plath, Sylvia 86
'Daddy' 86
Plato 25, 198
Poe, Edgar Allan 150
poetic: absolutes 235; ambitions 37; ear 45; knowledge, scepticism about 226–8; imagination 230, 233, 236; medium 25; speech 121, 134; wisdom 46
'poetry makes nothing happen' 28–9
polemic in poetry 53, 57
political events 53, 153
politicians 25, 51, 134–8, 153; and poets 25, 137, 185–7, 190, 194–5, 222–5
politics 105
Polonsky, Antony 33 n.
Pompilia (Francesca Comparini) 208, 211–12, 214–15, 218, 229, 231–5
Pontius Pilate 134
Pope Innocent XII 215, 220, 229, 231, 235
Pope Pius IX 225
position 105–41
Pound, Ezra 25, 51 n., 88, 117 n., 125–7, 133, 134, 142–3 n., 157, 160, 162, 173–97, 202, 203
  Addendum for Canto C 196
  'A Retrospect' 125 n.

Cantos XIV–XV ('Hell Cantos') 117 n., 195–6
Canto XXX 196
Canto XXXVI 175, 180–2
Canto XLI 185–6, 188
Canto LXXII 190
Canto LXXIII 190–3, 196
Canto LXXIV 174–5
Canto LXXX 194–5
Canto LXXXI 196, 197
Canto LXXXIV 194
'Cavalcanti' 176–7
Collected Shorter Poems 133 n.
'Donna mi prega' (Pound's text and trans.) 177–82
Ezra Pound and Japan 51 n., 173 n.
Homage to Sextus Propertius 133, 134, 157
Jefferson and/or Mussolini 25 n., 173, 185, 187, 203 n.
Make it New 125
'Mesmerism' 202
Pound/Joyce 184 n.
Pound/Lewis 182 n., 184 n.
'Pound's Interrogation at Genoa' 189 n., 194 n.
Rime (ed. Pound) 183–4
Selected Letters 188 n.
Selected Poems (ed. T. S. Eliot) 183
Sonnets and Ballate of Guido Cavalcanti 182–3
The Cantos of Ezra Pound 175 n., 185, 217
Their Letters (Pound and D. Shakespear) 182 n., 195 n.
The Literary Essays of Ezra Pound 88 n., 125 n., 176 n., 177 n., 181 n.
The Pisan Cantos 174–5, 194–6, 197
'The River-Merchant's Wife: A Letter' 142–3 n.
The Spirit of Romance 194
The Translations of Ezra Pound 178 n., 190 n.
Umbra 183
Powell, Enoch 134–7
power: men of 108; omnipotent 125
Pozzi, Antonia 192
'La vita sognata' 192
Praz, Mario 184
preconceived 59
predestined 58, 65

presidents (of the USA) 8 n., 51, 190
process 177; 'by which our knowledge
    is developed' 184, 188, 196;
    'within the process' 189
project 84, 94, 100
Propertius, Sextus 174
prophetic 224–7
protagonists 86
Proust, Marcel 101
public and private 108
Purkis, John 117

Raban, Jonathan 90
Radetzky von Radetz, Joseph 222
Ransom, John Crowe 99, 108, 110,
    111, 120, 126, 234, 236–7
rape 190–3, 207
Ravel, Maurice 4
Read, Herbert 184
readers 70, 86, 110; authorial
    responsibility to 125–6
rebuke 70
reciprocity of words 75
reconciliation 50, 52
reconstruction 38
recovery, act of 95
rectitude 101
redemption 122, 125, 128, 139; and
    suffering 129; and time 132
Reed, Jeremy 142 n.
regret 1, 6, 97, 172; agent-regret 97,
    104
Reid, Richard 191 n.
relatives 86
Rembrandt van Rijn 177, 206
remorse 89, 98–9; impure motive 117
reparation 1–9, 10, 11, 12, 19, 20, 22,
    52, 89, 95, 143, 149; actual 99;
    aggressive and reparative impulses
    116; 'An Attempted Reparation'
    115; and the creative medium
    3–4; and creativeness 148; and
    envy 146; and 'the great
    irremediable things' 9;
    idealization opposing 148; and
    irremediable wrong 6; and
    irreparability 1, 5, 11, 12, 19, 20,
    22, 96; and personal or public
    history 5; and reiteration 104;
    and renewal 194; and 'repairing
    the whole world' 8; and
    reparative emblem 21, 29, 99
reproach 94

resignation 96
responsibility 7, 9, 16, 24, 38, 88, 97,
    196; poetry a form of responsible
    behaviour 136; for the truth 42;
    and words as an ideal currency
    131; of a writer for his words 128
restore 120
reviewers 70
revision 11, 25–8, 29, 31, 33, 35–6,
    42–3, 45, 54, 74, 76, 78, 88, 96,
    100, 143, 158; 'An automatism of
    constant repair' 104; compulsive
    99; and context 24–46; and
    cunning 71; and finishing 26, 47,
    51; and luck 99; and
    instrumentality of art 29; 'as a
    matter of principle' 43; and
    meanings in relations 26; and
    regret 99; and reparation 99; and
    respect for others 27; and
    synonyms 43; and terrorism
    194–5; and tinkerings 43; and
    violence 27
rhyme 204–5
rhythm 58, 78, 79, 203; and
    inevitability 204–5; regular 63;
    thematic function of 80–1, 202
Ricasoli, Bettino 225
Riccioni, Damaso 189
Richards, I. A. 50–1, 102–3
Ricks, Christopher 8–9 n., 130, 144 n.
Rilke, Rainer Maria 104, 150, 156,
    158
    'Archäischer Torso Apollos' 104
Rimbaud, Arthur 142 n., 156, 158,
    167 n.
Rizzardi, Alfredo 167 n.
Roberts, David 98 n.
Rochester, John Wilmot 111
Roosevelt, Franklin D. 8 n., 51, 52,
    190
Rossetti, Dante Gabriel 182–3
Rubens, Peter Paul 177
Rudman, Mark 167 n.
Ruskin, John 60, 201, 227–8
Rymer, Miss 209

sacrifices 93
Salingar, Leo 216–17, 235
scholarly: error 119; passion 118;
    taste 119; temptation 118
Scott, Walter 146, 148

Scovell, E. J. 103 n.
Segal, Hanna 8
Seidel, Fredrick 156
self-consciousness 61–2
self-delusion 131
self denial 216
self-inculpation 19
self-justification 103
self-knowledge 158, 174
self-maiming 67
self-rebuke 72
Sereni, Vittorio 149–52, 158–9,
    162–3
sexuality 43
sexual well-being 40
Shakespear, Dorothy 195
Shakespeare, William 28, 101, 111,
    127, 144, 146–7, 148
  'Sonnet 29' 144–7, 148
shame 88, 120, 196, 214
Shaw, J. E. 179 n., 180 n., 181
Shelley, Mary 107 n.
Shelley, Percy Bysshe 107, 108, 198,
    225–6
  'Ode to Naples' 225
Sidgwick, Henry 122
Sidney, Philip 69, 78, 218
  'With how sad steps, ô Moone . . .'
    69
sin 120, 215
situation 38, 91, 110–12, 128, 133,
    139, 165, 201
Smalley, Donald 219
Smith, Stan 32, 35–6, 37, 42–3
Snodgrass, Iris 30, 39
solecism 114–18, 131; mock-solecisms
    117
Solmi, Sergio 149–50, 151, 158
Sophocles 174
Southwell, Robert 111, 122
Spenser, Edmund 147 n.
spiritualism 208–10
sprezzatura 202–6
Stafford, Jean 95–6
Stalin, Josef 113, 114
Stein, Leo 10
Stevens, Wallace 10
Stock, Noel 189
Stokes, Adrian 7, 24, 145 n., 176
success 84, 87, 92, 93; and career 93;
    and decisions made by artists 91;
    others' 147; as a poet 87; and
    retrospective justification 91–2

suicide 87
suspicion 109
Swaab, Peter Alexander 14, 15–16, 18
Swift, Jonathan 108, 110–11, 122,
    137, 138
Swinburne, A. C. 125 n., 136

Tansill, Charles Callan 51 n.
Tate, Allen 91, 99, 106 n., 130
Tennyson, Alfred 31–2, 44–6, 119
  In Memoriam VII 119
  'The Palace of Art' 44–5
'tinkering with fact' 86
Titian 206
Tolstoy, Alexei 112
Tomlinson, Charles 143, 151 n.,
    157 n., 179 n.
Tommasei, Nicolò 238
topical allusion 14, 47, 52
transfiguration 121–2, 124, 128, 139
translation 127, 142–72; and betrayal
    173–97; envy, gratitude, and
    142–72; ethics and psychology of
    156; and illusory literalism
    167 n.; morality and aesthetic
    value 167 n.; and overcoming
    isolation 151
Trevelyan, G. M. 221, 224
Trotter, David 187 n.
trust 109; between writer and reader
    128; and fiduciary symbols 127
truth 231; disclaimers of access to
    229–30; historical and imaginative
    217–20; -telling 236
Tsvetayeva, Marina 112, 151 n.
tyrants 27

unforeseen 58, 59, 77, 79; in contrast
    to the preformed 61; and death
    73; excellence 82; irregularities
    60; little of 67; occurrences 64;
    and resistance to 61; thwarting
    the truly 75
Updike, John 148

Vaihinger, H. 238
Valéry, Paul 43
Vallon, Annette 18–19 n.
value 218, 228, 230, 236; of coins and
    words 125; exchange 123; and
    experience 233–4
Vasari, Giorgio 227

Vendler, Helen 142, 143, 165, 169
Vermeer, Johannes 103
Villari, Luigi 186, 188
Virgil, 75–6, 134, 135
visible self-revision 88
Vittorio Emmanuele III 154, 175
vocation 84
Vronsky, Alexis 96, 97

Wainwright, Jeffrey 120
Ward Jouve, Nicole 181 n.
Wat (ghost) 209
weakness 45
Wedgwood, Julia 215–16, 236
Weil, Simone 116, 118
Wheeler, Burton K. 52
Whitman, Walt 49–50
  'When Lilacs Last in the Dooryard
    Bloom'd' 49–50
wife 62, 67, 70, 85, 95, 201, 209–11,
    234–5, 238; an artist deciding to
    leave his 87; curious rebuke to
    73; and death 66; and destiny 65;
    and irreparable fact 72; as victim
    98
Williams, Bernard 1, 2, 5, 87, 88,
    91–4, 96–8, 99–100, 101–2, 104
Williams, William Carlos 167 n.
Williamson, Alan 9 n.
Winters, Yvor 64 n., 76, 133–4
Wittgenstein, Ludwig 237–8

Wollheim, Richard 2, 5–6, 10–11, 21,
    24 n., 148
words: another's 58–82; debasement
    and redemption of 122, 131;
    quoted or spoken 58, 66, 73,
    74–5; and rebuke 75
Wordsworth, Dorothy 18–19 n., 148
Wordsworth, Richard 19 n.
Wordsworth, William 1, 6, 8–23, 111,
    119 n., 122, 129, 131, 138–9,
    148–9
  'Immortality' Ode 122
  'Michael' 10
  'Old Man Travelling' 14
  Poems, in Two Volumes 11 n., 17 n.
  'Preface to *Lyrical Ballads*' 20, 129,
    139
  'Resolution and Independence' 138
  'The Female Vagrant' 23, 139
  'The Idiot Boy' 22
  'The Leech-Gatherer' 18
  *The Letters of William and Dorothy
    Wordsworth* 18 n., 21 n.
  The Poems 20 n., 119 n.
  The Prelude (1805) 139
  'The Sailor's Mother' 6, 10, 11–23
  'The Singing Bird' 12, 14, 18 n.
world's events 32

Yeats, W. B. 9, 28, 29

Zapponi, Niccolò 186, 187